FODOR'S TRAVEL PUBLICATIONS

are compiled, researched, and edited by an international team of travel writers, field correspondents, and editors. The series, which now almost covers the globe, was founded by Eugene Fodor in 1936.

OFFICES
New York & London

Fodor's Great Travel Values: Japan

Editor: Deborah Jurkowitz
Area Editor: Helen Brower, Peter Popham, Hollistar Ferretti
Maps: C. W. Bacon

FODOR'S

GREAT TRAVEL VALUES™

JAPAN

FODOR'S TRAVEL PUBLICATIONS, INC.
New York & London

915 .2

Z 283412

MANUFACTURED IN THE UNITED STATES OF AMERICA
10 9 8 7 6 5 4 3 2 1

CONTENTS

FOREWORD

While every care has been taken to ensure the accuracy of the information contained in this guide, the publishers cannot accept responsibility for any errors that may appear.

All prices quoted in this guide are based on those available to us at the time of writing. In a world of rapid change, however, the possibility of inaccurate or out-of-date information can never be totally eliminated. We trust, therefore, that you will take prices quoted as indicators only, and will double-check to be sure of the latest figure.

Similarly, be sure to check all opening times of museums and galleries. We have found that such times are liable to change without notice, and you could easily make a trip only to find a locked door.

When a hotel closes or a restaurant produces a disappointing meal, let us know, and we will investigate the establishment and the complaint. We are always ready to revise our entries for the following year's edition should the facts warrant it.

Send your letters to the editors of Fodor's Travel Publications, 201 E. 50th Street, New York, NY 10022. European readers may prefer to write to Fodor's Travel Guides, 9-10 Market Place, London W1N 7AG, England.

GREAT
TRAVEL
VALUES
TM

JAPAN

INTRODUCTION

◆

By Helen Brower

*Helen Brower is a New York–based freelance writer who
has traveled widely in the Far East.*

Despite Japan's image as an expensive travel
destination, value-conscious travelers who take the time to
plan ahead will find that they can do virtually everything
the well-heeled visitor does, but at a much lower cost.

You don't have to skimp on creature comforts or elimi-
nate all but the bare essentials to travel in Japan on a
moderate budget. Regardless of how much you've set aside
for your trip, you can be assured of a quality travel
experience. Part of this is due, of course, to the superb
facilities Japan offers in all price ranges, but also to
centuries'-old attitudes regarding hospitality. Gracious
service and attention to the needs of visitors is an in-
grained part of Japanese tradition. Here, tipping is the
exception rather than the rule. No matter what price
category lodgings you select, chances are that soon after
you arrive, a steaming hot cup of tea and a tray of sweets
will be delivered to you—on the house, of course.

The buses, trains, and taxis you'll use to get around will
all be impeccably clean and in mint condition. When you
ask directions even of a non-English-speaking Japanese, he
probably won't leave you until he's satisfied you've under-
stood his instructions. And don't be surprised if he accom-
panies you for a few blocks, even though it's out of his way,
just to make sure you get to your destination. In case
there's no one around to help, the Japanese almost always

1

post signs in English, as well as in Japanese—in trains, restaurants, stores and other public places.

In a world where time-honored customs and ancient landmarks are constantly threatened by the encroaching demands of the modern age, one of the bonuses of a visit to Japan is its enviable ability to uphold tradition and, at the same time, move with confidence into the future. The Japanese respect for their history and cultural heritage is passed from one generation to the next. Wherever you go in Japan, you will see well-mannered groups of uniformed schoolchildren on field trips to shrines and other ancient monuments.

Similarly, there are few people with as great an awe of nature as the Japanese. It's not uncommon to see senior citizens—as well as members of the younger generation—making an arduous climb up a hillside, to spend an hour or so wordlessly admiring a lake or mountain landscape. Many of the things the Japanese themselves do in their free time, and that may appeal to you as well, cost nothing or next to nothing.

A good way to experience the real Japan, and at the same time, conserve funds, is to explore outside the major cities. Though moderately priced accommodations and dining are available in the large cities, the smaller towns afford even greater opportunities for keeping a lid on expenses.

Each region of Japan has its own special arts and handicrafts traditions, its own local cuisine and colorful festivals. A trip to these off-the-beaten-path towns and villages will cost less than a comparable stay in a major city, and will provide you with memories to last a lifetime.

The Japan Alps, for instance, are strung with lovely old castle towns like Kanazawa, admired for its performances of traditional Noh drama, its superb Kutani ceramicware, and one of Japan's three most beautiful landscaped gardens, Kenrokuen Park, built by the once-powerful Maeda clan.

In Central Honshu, the town of Gifu is famous for a long tradition of creating exquisite paper lanterns and parasols, and for an age-old method of fishing for the local river smelt by using trained cormorants.

Takayama is a little jewel of a city that is referred to as "Little Kyoto." Its impeccably preserved houses and shops offer glimpses of 17th-century Japan. In spring and fall, the city is the setting for a dazzling pageant and processions of brilliantly decorated floats.

On Japan's Inland Sea is Miyajima Island. The Itsukushima Shrine here stretches out over the water, so that every day at high tide the whole structure gives the illusion that it is rising up out of the sea.

A good way to get to know the country and the people in relaxed surroundings is to take advantage of the Japan National Tourist Organization's "Japan Home Visit System," available in about 15 cities. Your hosts might be young professionals who live in a Western-style house, or a family who will greet you garbed in the traditional kimono, and usher you into a living room with tatami mats and sliding shoji screens.

Every time of year is festival season in Japan. Before leaving home, contact a branch of the Japanese National Tourist Organization (JNTO) for a schedule of the year's festivals, then make sure to plan your itinerary around one or more of these colorful events.

New Year's in Japan is celebrated at shrines throughout the country, but few are more popular on this occasion than the Shinshoji Temple, conveniently—for the visitor—located in the village of Narita, near New Tokyo International Airport. If you have a long layover, a trip into the town of Narita to see the temple is highly recommended.

For about five days in February, Japan's premier winter sports resort, Sapporo, on the island of Hokkaido, plays host to an exciting Snow Festival, with a spectacular exhibition of snow and ice sculptures displayed on the promenade.

In mid-May, during the Aoi Matsuri, or Hollyhock Festival, at the Shimogamo and Kamigamo Shrines in Kyoto, the opulence of Japan's ancient imperial processions is reproduced with dazzling pageantry.

The year's most romantic festival is the Tanabata. Held in early July, it is celebrated throughout the country and marks the once-a-year meeting of the separated lovers, the stars Vega and Altair, on their journey through the Milky Way.

Brilliantly colored floats are the main attraction during Kyoto's Gion Matsuri, the city's biggest annual festival.

Held in July, it traces its origins back to a period in the 9th century when the citizenry sought the protection of the gods against a plague.

In early August, during the Kanto Matsuri, a hardy band of daredevils in Akita perform hair-raising balancing acts on bamboo poles hung with lighted lanterns.

The Okunchi Festival in early October traces its roots to ancient China, and features a dragon dance and floats at the Suwa Shrine in Nagasaki.

Shichi-go-san, in mid-November, is the day children aged three, five, and seven, wearing their best kimonos, visit their local shrines to thank the gods who have given them good health and fortune.

In mid-December, the Hagoita-ichi, one of Tokyo's best open-air flea markets, at the Asakusa Kannon Temple, is the ideal place to stock up on the New Year's decorations for which this market is famous.

The Japanese are some of the world's most enthusiastic fans of both spectator and participatory sports—from baseball to golf, Thoroughbred racing to marathons. No athletic event is more popular or more closely associated with Japan, however, than sumo wrestling. Historians say the first sumo match was performed before the emperor in A.D. 200, and with the gradual rise of a military class, the rules governing this highly ritualized martial art became more refined. Westerners who view the Japanese as a subdued people who always keep their emotions in check will change their perceptions radically once they find themselves in the midst of a wildly cheering, shouting throng during a championship sumo match. Tournaments are held six times a year—in January, May, and September in Tokyo; in March in Osaka; in July in Nagoya; and in November in Fukuoka. Tickets bought on the same day can cost you as little as ¥600 or ¥700.

Another Japanese tradition, Kabuki theater, started in the 17th century under the Tokugawa shogunate. Originally performed by women, Kabuki, which is characterized by magnificent costumes and subtle gestures, eventually evolved into a theatrical form where male actors now play all the characters. Many of these actors have, in fact, become matinee idols among loyal female fans.

Tokyo's National Theatre and the Kabukiza—considered

the best Kabuki theater—stage plays most of the year. The Tourist Information Center in Tokyo will provide visitors with 10 percent discount coupons for first-class tickets (usually ¥6,800) at the National Theatre. One-act plays at the Kabukiza normally cost about ¥600 to ¥800. Seats in the National Theatre's upper gallery cost around ¥1,200 to ¥1,500.

The first-time visitor to Japan might wish to consider some of the following practical tips before planning an itinerary.

After arriving at Tokyo's Narita Airport, instead of taking the limousine from the airport—still quite a distance from many Tokyo hotels—choose one of the low-cost buses that goes directly to the hotels. Costs vary according to routing but average about ¥2,500 to ¥3,000 from Narita to downtown Tokyo.

The names of the hotels served by each bus route are clearly posted, but if your hotel is not listed among them, check your map for a stop close to your lodgings or ask for information at the JNTO Information Desk at Narita Airport. Similarly, if you land at Osaka International Airport, you can take an airport limousine directly to downtown Osaka, Kobe, downtown Kyoto and selected hotels. To downtown Osaka hotels, the trip is about 30 minutes and costs approximately ¥400. To Kobe, the ride is about 40 minutes and costs around ¥650. To downtown Kyoto, the airport limousine takes approximately an hour and costs about ¥800.

You can save approximately 40 percent on your train travel around Japan by purchasing a Japan Rail Pass, but you must buy it before you leave home. The Pass is sold in the U.S. at Japan Air Lines offices (for those flying JAL), and at several travel companies, including Japan Travel Bureau International, Nippon Travel Agency, Kinki Nippon Tourist, and Tokyu (Note: it's "u," not "o") Corp. You will be given an Exchange Order and instructions for obtaining the actual Japan Rail Pass once you've arrived in Japan. You have a choice of traveling ordinary or Green class and of purchasing a pass valid for seven, 14, or 21 days. There are also special children's fares.

Basically, what the pass includes is unlimited travel in

most categories of Japan Railways' trains. Seat reservations can be made at no extra cost with the pass. As an example of how much you can save, a seven-day pass in ordinary class that will cost you ¥27,000 would cost ¥48,000 if you paid the regular fares and surcharges.

Once in Japan, local transportation passes will allow you to take unlimited rides on most subway lines in Tokyo and bus lines in Kyoto and Osaka at special reduced rates.

Japan offers an excellent system of long-distance buses operating between major and some secondary cities. For those whose schedules permit and who choose not to buy a Japan Rail Pass, bus fares are considerably less than regular fares on express and "bullet" trains.

Japan is one of the world's most economically and technologically advanced nations. For the traveler, that means it isn't necessary to stay at a top hotel to be assured of satisfactory accommodations. Japan's less expensive hotels and inns frequently offer a level of service and facilities that in most countries would be available only at top-ranking hotels.

You can take advantage of one of several discount hotel-coupon plans that can be purchased in the United States or in Japan. These include the JTB (Japan Travel Bureau) Sunrise Super Saver, the NTA (Nippon Travel Agency) Hotel Pass, the Kintetsu Hotel Coupons "Stay 'n Save," the Tokyu Top Hotel Coupons, and the JAL Room & Rail.

If you decide on JTB's coupon offer, for instance, you will receive discount coupons valid at 78 hotels in 49 Japanese cities. Using the coupon, you will pay only ¥60,000 (or ¥6,000 per person, per night) for five nights' accommodations in a double room.

You can travel as the Japanese do, and save money at the same time, by staying at a ryokan or a minshuku, both traditional-style Japanese inns, where you'll sleep snuggled in a billowy quilt on a *futon* (mattress), in a tatami-matted room, unwind in a Japanese bath, and dine on excellent seasonal and regional culinary specialties.

Be sure, however, that you don't book into one of the country's many luxury ryokan, but at an economical one, like the members of the Japanese Inn Group (JIG) head office address: c/o Hiraiwa Ryokan, 314, Hayao-cho, Kaminoguchi-agaru, Ninomiya-cho-dori, Shimogyo-ku, Kyoto 600; tel. (075) 351–6748. Tokyo Liaison Office: c/o Sawanoya Ryokan, 2-3-11, Yanaka, Taito-ku, Tokyo 110; tel. (03) 822–2251. JIG is well represented throughout the country. Rates for its affiliated ryokan average about ¥3,500 to ¥5,000 for singles, and approximately ¥6,800 to ¥8,000 for doubles.

Minshuku, which usually include two meals in their prices (ryokan rates generally do not include any meals), are favored by Japanese students and other budget-conscious travelers seeking clean, comfortable, family-style accommodations. Rates average about ¥5,000 or ¥6,000 per person, per night. You can write directly to the minshuku to reserve accommodations in advance. JNTO offices will provide visitors with lists of the country's minshuku network.

Japan has one of the world's most extensive and best-run youth-hostel networks, and a comparatively new type of no-frills lodging facility called the business hotel, which offers clean and functional accommodations. There are also hundreds of small, European-style pensions where you can start the day with a typical American breakfast and finish with a superb French dinner.

Since Japan is a mountainous country with very little grazing land, beef is a luxury, and is usually priced accordingly. Consequently, the Japanese are fish-eating people. If you are watching your pocketbook, you would be well advised to follow their example.

The most common and most popular fish dishes are sushi and sashimi, but if your palate rebels at the thought of raw fish, try *tempura*—deliciously prepared shrimp and other seasonal fish deep-fried with vegetables—or *kaiseki* cooking, another typically Japanese method for combining fish, vegetables, mushrooms, and seaweed in a tasty sauce.

For a hearty and inexpensive repast, do as Japanese workers all over the country do and lunch at a neighborhood noodle restaurant. *Soba,* made of buckwheat flour, and *udon,* made of wheat flour, are the two most popular kinds of noodles. They are served in a thick broth, usually with fish or chicken, and vegetables in clean, simple, friendly surroundings.

Other good dining values are offered by the dining rooms of large department stores and the tiny sushi eateries and lunchrooms located in the underground shopping malls of most cities. A good way to avoid surprises when the bill arrives at the end of a meal is to dine at restaurants that display in their windows plastic replicas of the dishes served, along with their prices. This method also avoids language problems—all you have to do is point to what you want.

If American-style fast food is what you're after, Japan's major cities now boast such establishments as McDonald's, Wendy's, Pizza Hut, and Kentucky Fried Chicken. Inexpensive fast-food-type Japanese lunches can be purchased also at establishments usually located near rail stations. A typical lunch box contains *gyudon-ya*—egg, rice, pickles, *miso* (soybean) soup, and green tea.

Supermarkets and the food sections of department stores now also sell take-out fast foods. Reasonably priced, they include selections of Japanese or Western foods.

If you're in the mood for after-dinner socializing, head for one of the beer halls frequented by Japanese workers and students. In the summertime, many office buildings and department stores transform their rooftops into beer gardens. This is an inexpensive way to spend the evening, and a perfectly respectable and accepted method of getting to meet the locals on their home turf.

You might also try a *karaoke* pub. Karaoke is the Japanese version of sing-along, which is exactly what the patrons are expected to do in these cheerful, relaxed night spots.

The discotheques and cabarets that cater to young people who are not on expense accounts are also good, modestly priced choices for an evening's entertainment.

Shopping is an integral part of most people's trips. A good money-saving rule of thumb is to shop for Japanese-made goods like cameras, transistor radios, pearls, woodblock prints, and lacquerware, as they will usually cost less than imported articles.

If you're looking for inexpensive, attractive souvenirs to take back home to friends and family members, good suggestions include stationery and other paper products, colorfully illustrated paper bookmarks, rice bowls, alarm "card" clocks, and *yukatas*—informal cotton kimonos.

Many stores offer tax-free shopping to foreigners who present a special form called a Record of Purchase of Commodities Tax-Exempt for Export. The forms are available at the stores, and must be filled out and attached to your passport. You can save anywhere from 5 to 40 percent by shopping at these stores, which display a "Tax-Free" sign at the entrance. These tax-free shops are generally found in hotels, shopping centers, and in special sections of major department stores. Some of the best tax-free establishments are the International Arcade and Japan Tax-Free Center in Tokyo, and the Kyoto Handicraft Center.

Japanese department stores are another good place to shop because they offer such an enormous variety of items. Also, there are usually a few salespeople who speak some English. Department stores in Japan also offer a mind-boggling array of entertainment and services. There are supervised play activities for children while their parents shop, international dining rooms and gourmet fresh foods, and even sports and cultural events.

In some of the major cities, there are neighborhoods that specialize in certain categories of merchandise. In Tokyo, for instance, the shops in the Akihabara district offer substantial discounts on electric appliances, and a good selection of computer equipment. For camera and audio equipment, the place to go is Tokyo's Shinjuku or Ikebukuro district. For one-stop shopping, try the Oriental Bazaar in Tokyo and the Kyoto Handicraft Center. Both offer a large selection of items at reasonable prices.

In order to help visitors save time, as well as money, the Japan National Tourist Organization operates a Good-Will Guide service. All of the volunteer goodwill guides display a special ID notebook or a Good-Will Guide card and badge.

There are about 25 Tourist Information Centers around the country, where multilingual staffers dispense information and brochures. Also available is the Japan Travel-Phone nationwide telephone service operated by JNTO for English-speaking travelers who need assistance. Outside of Tokyo or Kyoto, calls are toll-free. All you do is dial

0120–222–800 for information in eastern Japan, and 0120–444–800 in western Japan.

If you are calling from Tokyo or Kyoto city limits, make a local call to the Tokyo TIC at 502–1461 or the Kyoto TIC at 371–5649. The cost is only ¥10 for three minutes and is available daily throughout the year from 9 A.M. to 5 P.M.

An English-language taped update on special events in the Tokyo and Kyoto areas is available by calling the JNTO's Teletourist Service at 503–2911 in Tokyo and (075) 361–2911 in Kyoto.

Touring on a budget has its challenges but also its rewards. By traveling, dining, and sightseeing as the Japanese themselves do, you begin to see the country through Japanese eyes, an enriching experience that no amount of money can buy.

PLANNING YOUR TRIP

by Peter Popham

Peter Popham is a freelance writer who has lived in Japan for over eight years. His work appears in the Sunday Times and other leading papers and magazines around the world. He writes on cultural topics for Tokyo's Mainichi Daily News and recently published his second book, Tokyo: The City at the End of the World.

Before You Go

NATIONAL TOURIST OFFICES. *The Japan National Tourist Organization* supplies free information and advice. Its addresses are as follows:

Tokyo Kotsu Building, 10th floor, 2-10-1 Yuraku-cho, Chiyoda-ku, Tokyo

630 Fifth Avenue, New York, NY 10111

333 North Michigan Avenue, Chicago, IL 60601

1519 Main Street, Dallas, TX 75201

360 Post Street, San Francisco, CA 94108

624 South Grand Avenue, Los Angeles, CA 90017

165 University Avenue, Toronto M5H 3B8, Ontario, Canada

167 Regent Street, London W.1., England

115 Pitt Street, Sydney, NSW, Australia

2 Exchange Square, 8 Connaught Place, Central, Hong Kong

56 Suriwong Road, Bangkok, Thailand

The organization runs three invaluable *Tourist Information Centers* (TICs) in Japan, which provide the sort of detailed information a tourist needs on the spot. Addresses are:

Tokyo: 1-6-6 Yuraku-cho, Chiyoda-ku; Tel. (03) 502–1461.

New Tokyo International Airport (Narita): Airport Terminal Building; Tel. (0476) 32–8711.

Kyoto: Kyoto Tower Bldg., Higashi-Shiokojicho, Shimogyo-ku; Tel. (075) 371–5649.

All three offices are open 9 A.M.–5 P.M. on weekdays, 9 A.M.–noon on Sat., closed Sun. and holidays.

ENTRY REQUIREMENTS. In addition to needing a passport, Americans must obtain a visa from a Japanese consulate. Tourist visas are generally granted for 90 days and valid for five years.

11

Tourists with permission to stay longer than 90 days must register with their local ward office within 90 days of first entry. They are then issued an Alien Registration Card, which they are expected to carry at all times.

Citizens of Canada and several other countries do not need visas as long as they do no work while in Japan and do not stay longer than the period stamped on the passport by immigration officials upon entry. This period may be as long as six months or as short as two; check with the Japanese Embassy in your country.

Cholera immunizations are no longer required unless you come from an infected area.

HEALTH AND INSURANCE. The *International Association for Medical Assistance to Travelers* is a worldwide association of physicians whose training meets British and American standards, who are fluent in English, and whose purpose is to help travelers. Write to IAMAT, 736 Center Street, Lewiston, NY 14092. In Japan IAMAT has member hospitals or clinics in Tokyo, Kobe, Yokohama, Osaka, Kyoto, Hiroshima, and Okinawa.

The water in Japan is as safe as anywhere in the world. Occasional cases of food poisoning, more often than not from packed lunches *(bento)*, are reported, but they are rare. Mosquitoes and cockroaches are a problem in summer, though the mosquitoes do not carry malaria.

BUDGET PACKAGE TOURS. A wide range of economical package tours to Japan is offered by the *Japan Travel Bureau, Fujita Travel Service, Hankyu Express, Tobu Travel Company, Japan Gray Line,* and *Domestic Creative Tours*.

Of particular interest is JTB's *Sunrise Super-Saver* package, intended to be used in tandem with the Japan Rail Pass. This is a time and money saving way to design your own tour. The program covers 75 hotels in 48 cities. JTB makes the first hotel reservation and you do the rest. Upon arrival at the first hotel, travelers pick up hotel coupons to cover the trip. A five-night coupon costs ¥35,000 for a single room accommodation. For ¥60,000, two people can spend five nights at a mix of hotels and ryokan.

Regular tours organized by JTB include morning and afternoon tours of Tokyo, ¥4,500 each; a one-day tour of Hakone and Kamakura for ¥17,500, which includes return travel by Shinkansen "bullet" train, and a one-day round trip to Nikko and Mashiko for the same price.

Other Sunshine Tours go to Kyoto, Osaka, Kyushu, and various points in between. Eight- and nine-day tours that include cruises through the famous Inland Sea and disband in Osaka make departure convenient from Osaka International Airport. Two alternative routes in Kyushu are 13 days each. None of these tours is specifically oriented to the budget traveler but they save a great deal of time and trouble for the traveler daunted by the idea of touring the country on one's own.

The Fujita Travel Service calls itself Japan's largest bus tour operator. The Fujita Group owns several modern hotels along the routes of its tours; naturally, its tourists stay in them. Fujita's itineraries are similar to those of JTB. Its one-day Nikko Country Tour costs ¥15,000, including lunch. Fujita also offers Superexpress Tours from Tokyo to Kyoto, eastbound tours from Kyoto and Osaka, and Inland Sea and Kyushu Tours.

A new type of tour is offered by *Domestic Creative Tours Ltd*. Oriented to foreigners living in Japan, it offers economical access to a broad range of places and activities not covered by the traditional operators. Examples are ski tours in Hokkaido, the Sapporo Snow Festival, hot-sand bathing near Kagoshima, Kyushu, and swimming and marine sports in Okinawa. Further details can be obtained from *P and B International*, Heights Akasaka 406, 7-6-52 Akasaka, Minato-ku, Tokyo 107; Tel. (03) 589–3299.

WHEN TO GO. Japan is worth visiting at any time of the year. The most popular seasons, however, are spring and autumn. Spring is the time for the beloved cherry blossoms, while autumn holds the brilliance of fall foliage and the most reliably comfortable weather.

Climate. Spring is showery and cool until April; from June on, the humidity rises with the temperature, becoming the rainy season from mid-June to mid-July; and August is hot and very close. From September to November Japan enjoys balmy weather with long, dry, clear spells, disrupted by typhoons from time to time. Japan is narrow and long, geographically comparable to a region extending from the latitude of Maine in the north to Georgia in the south. Accordingly, regional weather variations are great. Hokkaido gets lots of snow (it has the best skiing in Asia) and has no rainy season; Okinawa in the far south, by contrast, is subtropical much of the year.

Average temperatures, in centigrade

	January	April	July	October	Annual Average
Kanazawa	2.6	11.5	24.8	15.8	13.7
Kyoto	3.5	13.1	26.1	16.7	14.8
Nagasaki	6.2	15.0	26.4	18.8	16.6
Naha	16.0	20.8	28.2	24.1	22.3
Sapporo	-5.1	6.1	20.2	10.4	7.8
Tokyo	4.1	13.5	25.2	16.9	15.0

Average rainfall (in milliliters) and humidity percentage (in parentheses)

	Spring	Summer	Autumn	Winter	Annual Average
Kyoto	56(67)	145(76)	239(74)	122(72)	1,638(73)
Naha	122(79)	142(82)	174(74)	149(70)	2,118(78)
Sapporo	118(68)	64(80)	90(74)	104(75)	1,141(74)
Tokyo	49(66)	122(79)	140(74)	203(57)	1,503(69)

SPECIAL EVENTS. January. *1st:* New Year's Day (national holiday). Japan's answer to Christmas. Millions visit shrines to pray for a prosperous year while families have huge feasts. *15th:* Adults' Day. People who attain the age of 20 during the year put on gorgeous kimonos to visit shrines.

February. *3d or 4th:* On *setsubun,* the last day of winter by the lunar calendar, devils are exorcised at temples by throwing beans and chanting the words, "Fortune In, Devils Out!" *11th:* National Foundation Day, a national holiday.

March. *3d: Hinamatsuri* or "Dolls' Festival." In traditionally minded families, little girls unpack fragile dolls symbolic of emperor and courtiers, and arrange them on cloth-covered shelves. *20th or 21st:* Vernal Equinox, a national holiday. Known as *higan* in Japanese, on this day services for the souls of the dead are held at Buddhist temples throughout the country.

April. *8th:* Buddha's Birthday, commonly known as *Hana Matsuri,* or "Flower Festival." *29th:* Emperor's Birthday, a national holiday.

May. *3d:* Constitution Memorial Day, a national holiday. *5th:* Children's Day, formerly Boy's Day. Marked by colorful carp-shaped streamers flying from high poles in gardens, symbolizing masculine courage. The period circumscribed by the holidays on April *29th* and May *3d* and *5th* is known as "Golden Week," when millions of Japanese go on trips.

June. No fixed nationwide festivals in this month.

July. *7th: Tanabata* or Star Festival. The day of the annual meeting of the stars Vega and Altair on their journey through the Milky Way is celebrated with gaudy streamer festivals in various parts of the country.

August. Early August: *O-Bon,* Buddhist All-Souls festival, when many Japanese return to their birthplaces and welcome the spirits of dead relatives back to their homes.

September. *15th:* Respect-for-the-Aged Day, a national holiday. *23d or 24th:* Autumnal Equinox, a national holiday.

October. *10th:* Health-Sports Day, a national holiday.

November. *3d:* Culture Day, a national holiday. *Bunka-sai,* culture festivals, are held at schools and on university campuses throughout the country. *15th: Shichi-go-san* festival. *Shichi-go-san* means "7-5-3," and these are the ages of children who are dressed in elaborate kimonos and taken to shrines to be blessed. The activity takes place both before and after this date, too. *23d:* Labor Thanksgiving Day, a national holiday.

December. *25th:* Christmas for Japan's small minority of Christians. Not a national holiday.

In addition to these events, many local festivals are held throughout the year in different parts of the country. Details are given in the regional chapters below.

WHAT TO PACK. Japan's four distinct seasons of fairly predictable weather make this less of a problem than in some countries. Bring winter clothes for December to February; spring clothes, including rainwear and folding umbrella, for March to May; summer clothes, including swimsuits and some light rainwear (an umbrella that doubles as a parasol) for June to August; and autumn clothes and rainwear for September to November.

Synthetic materials are good if they are of the wash-and-wear variety. Dress conservatively—loud colors and flashy accessories will make you stand out and may offend local traditions and taste. Paths leading to temples can be rough, so good walking shoes are in order for sightseeing. It may be wise to bring your favorite toilet articles; if they are available in Japan they are likely to be costly. Facial tissues, American brands of toothpaste, etc., can be obtained but at a higher price. Pack toilet paper since public lavatories frequently lack it.

Other useful items: picnic set, can opener, bottle opener, corkscrew; instant coffee, (you can always get hot water); alarm clock; flashlight, for interiors of temples and some museums where interesting details may be high, remote, and in shadow; passport photos, in case you need extra documents; sunglasses (the light in Japan is bright); small gifts such as little purses, handkerchiefs, and perfume sachets to give instead of tips.

LANGUAGE. Japan may be the most solidly monolingual country in Asia, which is bad news for the traveler. Only a small minority of Japanese can speak English with any skill, though all study it for years in school. The situation is arguably better in Tokyo than elsewhere.

More and more foreigners study Japanese these days, due to the country's increasing economic prominence, and the shelves of English-language bookshops are filled with study aids. One of the most useful is *Japanese for Busy People,* produced by the Association for Japanese Language Teaching and published by Kodansha International. The books cost ¥3,000 and accompanying tapes, ¥7,500.

TRAVEL FOR THE DISABLED. The Language Service Volunteers of the Japanese Red Cross have published an English-language book entitled *Accessible Tokyo,* intended to make life easier for handicapped foreign visitors. For a copy write to Japan Red Cross Headquarters, 1-1-3 Shiba-Daimon, Minato-ku, Tokyo. Volunteers are also available to answer queries at (03) 438–1311, extension 503, after 2 P.M. on Saturdays.

STUDENT TRAVEL. Foreign student cards are not normally recognized in Japan. There is no cheap rail pass for students like those found in Europe, but Japan Railways operates a discount ticket system aimed at teenagers (though there is no age limitation). This is called *Seishun Juhachi Kippu: for* ¥11,000, five coupons are presented, each allowing one day's unlimited travel on nonexpress trains and ferries within the Japan Railways system. To take Shinkansen "bullet" trains or other express trains you must pay extra. A leaflet describing the system in detail is obtainable at Tourist Information Centers.

The serious backpacker will find hitchhiking in Japan gratifyingly easy. There are only two problems: it's hard getting out of the enormous cities; and drivers are sometimes embarrassingly helpful.

The TIC has a useful leaflet called *Reasonable Accommodations in Japan* that contains details of 250 hotels and ryokan in two price categories: ¥4,000–¥7,000, and under ¥4,000, in 40 cities around the country.

Getting to Japan

HOW TO GET THERE. Japan is reachable by air and by sea. The two major international airports are the New Tokyo International at Narita, which is actually in the neighboring prefecture of Chiba and at least an hour's journey, by road, from the Tokyo City Air Terminal; and Osaka (Itami) International Airport. The Tokyo Airport at Haneda mostly caters to domestic flights, with the notable exceptions of certain flights from Taiwan, and of carriers bringing V.I.P.s.

Other airports handling international flights are at Sapporo on Hokkaido, Nagoya, Niigata, and Komatsu on Honshu, Fukuoka, Kagoshima, Nagasaki, and Kumamoto on Kyushu, and Naha on Okinawa.

International seaports are at Yokohama, Nagoya, and Kobe on Honshu, and at Nagasaki and Kagoshima on Kyushu.

Travel Agents. A reliable travel agent is necessary to your well-being. She or he can tell you what is and what isn't available, and what the current travel bargains are. (These change all the time.) The agent can handle your individual requirements or attach you to a group.

By Air

Flight time from Honolulu to Tokyo is seven hours, from Los Angeles to Tokyo is 9½ hours. New direct flights from London to Tokyo take 11½ hours, Paris to Tokyo a little longer. Via Moscow, the London to Tokyo flight time is 14½ hours. Sydney to Tokyo takes 9½ hours.

First-class, executive-class, and economy-class cabins are available on many major carriers. If you are an independent traveler paying full fare (not in a group or using any kind of discount ticket), you may change your carrier for different sectors of your trip. Some trans-Pacific airlines have arrangements with steamship companies to fly passengers across, join a cruise ship for part of the itinerary (among the islands of Indonesia perhaps, or into Korea or Mainland China), then return by plane.

Group rates for package and charter tours remain the most economical. It is always worth inquiring into "excursions," "APEX," and any other special fares. Even typical economy fares between Los Angeles and Tokyo, for example, can vary by several hundred dollars depending on how long in advance the reservation is made (and paid for), how long a stay is involved, whether any land arrangements are tied in, how many stopovers are included, and other factors.

Some charter tour packagers simply block-book seats on major airlines at reduced prices. Some major airlines offer special charterlike prices in order to boost travel on certain routes during certain periods. Regardless of formal status, all flights must meet the same U.S. federal government standards of aircraft maintenance and safety, crew qualifications, and reliability.

Given the distance and cost involved in any trip to Japan, many travelers try to maximize the time and money spent by taking in other locales in the area. Korea is only a short, separate trip away from Japan. A popular sweep through Southeast Asia would include Taiwan, Hong Kong, Bangkok, and Singapore. Between Bangkok and Singapore, a stop may be made at Kuala Lumpur, capital of Malaysia.

If you are so ambitious as to decide upon a visit to the South Seas, from Japan you may fly to Manila, Bali, then go on to Sydney, Australia, and Auckland, New Zealand. As well as all the hinterland of these countries opening up for you, you are also placing yourself well for advancing into the islands of Micronesia and Melanesia.

Luggage. Regulations for air travelers from the United States base baggage allowances on size. Economy-class passengers may each take two pieces of baggage provided that the sum of their dimensions is not over 2 m. 70 cm., or 106 inches (neither piece being more than 1 m. 58 cm., or 62 inches, combined height, width, and length). First-class allowance is two pieces up to 1 m. 58 cm., or 62 inches, overall dimensions each, total 3 m. 16 cm., or 124 inches. There is also a 32-kilogram (70-pound) limit for each piece of luggage. Penalties for regulation contravention are severe.

To and from Britain. If you're traveling to Japan on a scheduled airline ticket, you'll realize the return fare is equal to a round-the-world fare, as Tokyo is halfway around the globe from London. You may wish, therefore, to take advantage of a wide number of stopovers allowed on such a ticket. These, on the Southern route, represent nearly every major tourist destination in the northern hemisphere. You can pop in to the Middle East, India, Singapore, Bangkok, Hong Kong, Taiwan. From Tokyo, you can return the same way to stop at different cities, or continue around the world to Hawaii and North America, before crossing the Atlantic to home.

By Sea

An increasing number of passenger ships as well as freighters having limited accommodation for passengers are calling at ports in the Far East. Since schedules are extremely variable, it is advisable to plan well in advance.

Among the American travel agencies handling travel by sea are: *Air and Marine Travel Service,* 501 Madison Avenue, New York, NY 10022; *Pearl's Freighter Tips,* 175 Great Neck Road, Great Neck, NY 11021; *Freighter Travel Service,* 201 E. 77th Street, New York, NY 10021.

The following list gives some of the possibilities of travel by sea:

Pearl Cruises of Scandinavia, with an office under this name in San Francisco, regularly schedules cruises to China aboard this company's flagship, the one-class M/S *Pearl* of Scandinavia. The *Pearl,* 12,456 tons, cruises from Hong Kong to China, Korea, Kobe in Japan, and back to Hong Kong. Tours are sold in both the U.S. and Europe for 12 two-way cruises on the route annually.

Royal Viking Sea, of the Royal Viking Line, 1 Embarcadero Center, San Francisco, CA 94111, sails from California to the South Pacific, Indonesia, Singapore, Hong Kong, Japan, and Hawaii.

The Cunard Line's *Queen Elizabeth II* calls at 30 ports from New York, on round-the-world cruises.

P. & O. Cruises have *The Princess Diana,* the world's latest luxury liner, going into round-the-world service. *The Princess Diana,* 40,000 tons, is claimed to be the most technically advanced deep-sea passenger ship ever built.

Hapeg-Lloyd's new cruise ship, M/V *Europa,* sails east from Genoa, taking 115 days to go around the world, calling at Kobe, Nagoya, and Yokohama in Japan.

The *Pacific Princess,* 20,636 tons, takes 70 days to travel around the world. The ship, which calls at Kobe and Yokohama in Japan; is celebrated as television's "Love Boat," filmed in Far Eastern locations.

Knutsen Line of Norway, has three vessels that ply between Western Australia and Japan, calling at Nagoya, Yokohama, Osaka, and Moji. They are the M/S *Lloyd Bakke,* the M/S *Anna Bakke,* and the M/S *Ragna Bakke.*

Once a month, a Soviet passenger ship sails from England via the Atlantic and Pacific to Yokohama, where time permits visits to Kamakura and Hakone. The *Mikhail Lermontov,* 20,000 tons, one of five "writer class" passenger ships named after famous Soviet writers, takes 96 days to sail around the world.

Getting Around Japan

By Air. The three major airlines are Japan Air Lines (*Nihon Koku* in Japanese), All Nippon Airways (*Zennikku*), and Toa Domestic Airlines (*Toa Koku*). JAL serves only major cities; the others serve less-traveled destinations as well. The airlines have a strong advantage over rail transportation for destinations in Kyushu and Hokkaido, where the Shinkansen does not run—though, inevitably, they are more expensive.

By Train. Japan's *Shinkansen* "bullet" trains are rightly regarded as among the world's fastest, safest, and most punctual. Special features of the *Hikari* super-expresses include compartments for wheelchair passengers, and observation cars. The trains do not have baggage cars, and have only limited overhead space, so travel light.

The Hikari covers the 556 kilometers between Tokyo and Osaka in approximately three hours, stopping only twice en route. From Tokyo it reaches Okayama, 733 kilometers away, in something over five hours. The *Kodama* stops at more stations and takes an hour longer. Fares are the same.

The original Shinkansen line goes from Tokyo to Hakata, at the northern tip of Kyushu. More recent services connect the capital (from Ueno Station, a few stops north of Tokyo Station) with Morioka in the northeast of the main island (this is the *Tohoku* line) and Niigata on the Japan Sea coast (the *Joetsu* line). The faster trains on the Tohoku lines are called *Yamabiko* and the slower ones *Aoba;* on the Joetsu line the faster are called *Asahi,* the slower, *Toki*.

There are frequent and super-punctual departures on all these lines. Here are some sample fares, including the express charge that must be paid to travel on any Shinkansen train: Tokyo-Kyoto, ¥12,600; Tokyo-Hakata, ¥20,000; Ueno-Morioka, ¥12,600; Ueno-Niigata, ¥9,200.

Telephone calls can be made to and from Shinkansen trains. From most areas you imply dial 107, though to call Tohoku trains from outside Tokyo or Sendai, dial 0252-107. For Joetsu trains, dial 0250-107 when outside Tokyo or Niigata. Three-minute calls from the trains cost ¥300 for short distances and ¥600 for long distances. Calling to the trains costs the usual charge plus a ¥100 handling fee.

Japan Railways operates good value long-distance coach services between four major cities. Tokyo to Nagoya takes 6 hrs. 40 mins. and costs ¥6,000 for a reserved seat; Tokyo to Kyoto, 8 hrs. 40 mins., ¥7,800; Tokyo to Osaka, 9 hrs. 20 mins., ¥8,200.

Cheaper and more leisurely rail trips can be made on the older lines, which provide a creditable cover of the archipelago. A large number of special ticket deals are offered by JR (Japan Railways), giving unlimited travel within stipulated lines over seven days, 10 days, or longer for bargain rates. Unfortunately, details are not available in English, and there is not enough space to describe them in detail here. *Furii-kippu* and *mini-shuyu-ken* are the words to use when you ask your Japanese friends to tell you details of these services.

Japan's numerous private railways are a strikingly better value than Japan Railways. Most operate in the capital and Kyoto and Osaka regions and go back and forth between city centers, bedroom suburbs, and resort areas. Two popular private lines in Tokyo are the *Tobu* line to Nikko and the *Odakyu* line to the Hakone resort area, near Mt. Fuji. Both use air-conditioned special express "Romance" cars, twice the price of the regular service but faster, genuinely luxurious, and still of good value compared to JR services. The special express fare on the Odakyu line from Shinjuku to Hakone-Yumoto, for example, is ¥1,280; the Shinkansen fare from Tokyo station to Odawara, near Hakone, is ¥3,480, well over twice as much.

In the Kansai region, the *Kinki Nippon Railway* provides double-decker "vista dome" cars between Osaka and Nagoya and through the scenic Kii Peninsula, and operates a good air-conditioned service between Osaka and Nara.

Japan Rail Passes, fashioned after the Eurailpass system, are available for foreign visitors and can be purchased at the overseas offices of JAL, JTB, and Nippon Ryoko. *It is important to remember that these passes cannot be purchased in Japan*. The pass is valid for travel on JR trains to anywhere in Japan for one, two, or three weeks. For travel in regular coaches, passes cost ¥27,000 (seven days), ¥43,000 (14 days), and ¥55,000 (21 days). "Green class" (first-class car) passes cost ¥37,000, ¥60,000 and ¥78,000 for the same periods.

By Car. Foreign visitors can drive in Japan with international drivers' licenses obtainable through automobile associations in their own countries. In Japan, drivers keep to the left of the road. The Japan Automobile Federation has an English language "Manual for Drivers and Pedestrians." Road maps using the Roman alphabet are available at large bookstores.

A good but expensive toll freeway service now links Aomori in northern Honshu with Kumamoto in central Kyushu. The cost of freeway travel rivals or exceeds that of air travel when the cost of gas and tolls are taken into account.

Rent-a-car agencies are found in the cities; *Toyota Rent-a-Car* and *Nissan Rent-a-Car* are the largest chains. The costs are about ¥5,000 and up per day.

By Subway. The subway is the fastest and most economical way of getting around within cities. Trains are clean and safe, services frequent and punctual. The biggest and most infamous problem is the crowding at rush hour. Subways are greatly preferable to city bus services, which usually take longer and have route details written in Japanese only.

By Taxi. Taxis are numerous and usually easy to find (though late at night it is hard to get them to stop), but they are by no means cheap. Minimum charge for the first two kilometers in a compact taxi is ¥430, and ¥470 for a full-size one. The fare rises ¥80 per 405 meters after that, and there is a time charge when it is held up in traffic. Taxi drivers can be relied on to find only the most well-known destinations. If possible, remember to board with the phone number of your destination, so the driver can call ahead for directions if necessary.

By Sea. All parts of the archipelago are linked by ferry and steamer services. Popular routes for sea travel are through the island-studded Inland Sea and between Kagoshima in southern Kyushu and the islands of Okinawa.

By Bike. Bicycles can be rented by the hour for a few hundred yen in many resort areas. They are generally allowed on both the road and the sidewalk.

Staying in Japan

CUSTOMS. Firearms, pornography, counterfeit currencies, and drugs other than alcohol and tobacco are always forbidden. Certain fresh fruits, vegetables, plants, and animals are also barred. Liquor, tobacco, watches, radios, tape recorders, cameras, film, appliances, etc., are limited to "reasonable amount for personal use."

CURRENCY. Japanese money comes in ¥10,000, ¥5,000 and

¥1,000 notes, and ¥500, ¥100, ¥50, ¥10, ¥5 and ¥1 coins. On arrival, stock up with a good supply of ¥50 and ¥100 coins for the ubiquitous vending machines.

CHANGING MONEY. Only the greenback and major European currencies may be converted to yen in Japan; if in doubt, travel with traveler's checks, or convert into yen before you leave home. Checks and cash are best changed at banks, which are open 9 A.M.–3 P.M. Mon.–Fri., and 9A.M.–noon on Sat. (but are closed on the second and third Saturdays of each month). To get the best value for your own currency, keep a keen eye on the exchange rates, which fluctuate wildly.

TIPPING AND TAXES. The practice of tipping is contrary to Japanese custom and sense of delicacy. When a Japanese rewards another with money, he does it discreetly, usually enclosing the money in an envelope and leaving it on a tray. In most day-to-day dealings, tipping is not customary.

On the other hand, little gifts are never wrong as expressions of your appreciation for special services performed for you. And never forget that in this land of ceremony and politeness, a simple "thank you" is worth a great deal.

While tipping is almost unknown in restaurants, a service charge is sometimes included in the bill, especially in restaurants oriented to foreign customers. In addition, if the bill per person is above ¥2,500, a tax of 10 percent is levied by the government.

ELECTRICITY. Electric current in Japan is all 100 to 110 volts, AC, but the cycles vary, depending on where you are. The eastern half of the country is on a 50-cycle basis, the western half on 60 cycles, the dividing line being approximately halfway between Tokyo and Nagoya, near the city of Shizuoka.

METRIC CONVERSION. In Japan, you will constantly be faced with the kilometer, meter, and centimeter. Temperature is measured in centigrade (Celsius), weight is calculated in grams and kilograms, and liquid measures in liters.

WHERE TO STAY. Accommodations in Japan can be organized broadly into Western-style and Japanese-style lodgings. The former provides the foreign visitor with something similar to what he would expect to find at home—the usual sort of bed, bath, decor and so on, though dimensions are often smaller and quarters extraordinarily cramped. The latter, best exemplified by the *ryokan*, provides traditional Japanese accommodations, with tatami floors, little furniture, and Japanese food.

Hotels. Japanese hotels are of two varieties, tourist and business. In tourist hotels you may expect to find the same sort of accommodations and service you would expect in a business or downtown-type hotel in a large American or European city. Japan business hotels *(bijinesu hoteru)* are the salvation of the traveler on a budget, being reasonably priced and equipped with most of the conveniences of more expensive hotels, except space. "Shoebox" is the word commonly used to describe business-hotel rooms, but they are usually very clean and convenient. Rates average ¥6,000 per person per night.

Another category of an inexpensive hotel that may tempt the curious is the *avec* or "love hotel." Couples rent rooms by the hour or overnight and do not have to give their names. No meals are provided, and charges run from about ¥5,000 up per night. These hotels are always found in the entertainment sections of cities, and are readily recognized by their garish and comical architecture.

Ryokan. *Ryokan,* Japanese-style inns, are rarely cheaper than their Western-style equivalents, and can often be more expensive. Usually, however, breakfast and dinner are included in the overnight rates. Some of the higher priced ryokan have private bathrooms attached to each room, but many have two large and elaborate communal baths, instead, to accommodate men and women.

Staying at a ryokan is one of the true delights of a visit to Japan. While fully modernized in terms of plumbing, electricity and so on, the best of these inns are virtually unchanged in atmosphere since the time of the samurai. In a truly traditional inn you are surrounded by the exquisite simplicity of Japanese design: translucent paper windows, sliding doors, tatami mat floors, alcoves for exhibiting flowers and pictures, corridors of polished natural wood, and delicate gardens. Everything is immaculate.

In a ryokan the way of living is as traditional as the decor. Shoes are removed at the *genkan,* the hallway, and stored there until you need to go out again; inside the building you wear slippers, though when you enter a tatami room these, too, are removed. There are separate slippers in the lavatory, which are meant to be worn only there.

The Japanese traditionally bathe in the evening, and so should you—though in some ryokan you may enjoy a bath at any time. Soap outside the bath, never in, rinse thoroughly, and then climb in. The water may be too hot, but there will be a cold tap to provide relief. Enthusiasts, which is to say almost the entire population of the archipelago, stay for ages, getting in and out dozens of times.

An inn will provide you with a light, cotton, kimonolike robe, a *yukata*. In winter there is also a thick *dotera*, which should be worn over the yukata. Sometimes a small jacketlike garment will also be provided, for when you venture outside. A truly traditional place will also provide raised wooden clogs and paper parasols, so that you can look and feel like something out of *Shogun*.

One of the chief delights of the ryokan is the elaborate meals, which should be sampled by all but the congenitally timid. Tell the maid you wish to eat *washoku*, Japanese food, and you will get the same huge spread of inscrutable tidbits as the Japanese guests. If you prefer to stick with more familiar items ask for *yoshoku*, Western food.

After your bath and meal the maid will lay out your bed, consisting usually of two futons, one of foam rubber and one of cotton. The small white object she places on the bed last of all, which seems to be filled with walnut shells, is your pillow. Be grateful: in the old days they slept on wooden ones.

Minshuku. A less expensive and very attractive alternative to the ryokan is the *minshuku*, the Japanese equivalent of a bed and breakfast or pension accommodation in the West. As in the ryokan, the ambience is traditional and two meals are provided for those that want them, but the accommodations are simpler and service sparer. For example, guests are expected to lay out and clear away their own futon, and meals are served in a common dining room instead of in the individual guest rooms, as in ryokan. You should also bring your own towels, though yukata are provided. The Japanese are much more easygoing about sharing sleeping quarters with strangers than is the case in the West, and if you are traveling alone in a busy season you will be expected to share your minshuku room with one or more other people.

The Japan National Tourist Organization has produced an invaluable guide to minshukus that are safe, inexpensive, clean, and receptive to foreign guests. Call JNTO at (03) 216–1903, or write them at Tokyo Kotsu Kaikan Bldg., 2-10-1 Yurakucho, Chiyoda-ku, Tokyo 100, Japan, and ask for "Minshukus in Japan." The minshukus recommended charge around ¥5,000 per night, including two meals.

Kokumin Shukusha. These are public lodgings that provide simple, hotel-style accommodations in scenic places or national park areas known for their natural beauty. More than 300 are operated by the Ministry of Health and Welfare, while another 130 privately operated lodgings are authorized by the National Park Association. Lodging is about ¥5,000 per day including two meals, plus a 10-percent service charge. Advanced reservations should be made through the Japan Travel Bureau. The Kokumin Shukushas are somewhat impersonal and bureaucratic in atmosphere compared to ryokan and minshuku.

Kokumin Kyuka Mura. Also operated by the government, these are vacation villages established in more than 30 locations around Japan. They offer a wide range of recreational possibilities, from skiing and mountain climbing to tennis and theater, and are reasonably priced at about ¥6,000 per day, including two meals. Accommodations should be reserved in advance through the Japan Travel Bureau.

Pensions. A new alternative for the visitor to Japan is to stay in a Japanese country pension, pronounced as in English, not French. These are really modern, Western-style equivalents of the minshuku, often with cute, chalet-style architecture and names like "Broken Egg," "Mind Games," or "Nutty Inn." The cost for a one-night stay with breakfast is ¥4,500–¥6,000, depending on the season and the quality of room. Many pensions have tennis courts attached and are located in pretty spots. They offer a good chance to have a firsthand look at the way up-to-date young Japanese prefer to spend their leisure time. A company called *Abita, Inc.* publishes a pamphlet detailing pensions in 15 popular holiday spots around the country, and it has just enough English to be useful. Call Abita, Inc. at (03) 407–2333 or write 6-3-9 Minami-Aoyama, Minato-ku, Tokyo, and ask for the pamphlet "Japan Pension and Country Inn."

Youth Hostels. Japan has the most extensive network of youth hostels outside Europe. Visitors from other countries who are members of their own youth hostel associations, affiliated with the International Youth Hostel Federation, will be accepted at all hostels in Japan. Visitors without cards may apply for international guest cards at the national office of *Japan Youth Hostels* at Hoken Kaikan, 1-1 Sadohara-cho, Ichigaya, Shinjuku-ku, Tokyo 162.

In Japan there are no age restrictions for people wanting to stay at youth hostels. Advance booking is indicated, and travelers should arrange to arrive at hostels before 9 P.M. Married couples may stay in the same room, and all are permitted to stay at any one hostel for up to three consecutive nights. The standard overnight charge is around ¥2,700, with sheet rental, baths, supper, and breakfast costing extra.

WHERE TO EAT. The best tip for saving money on food in Japan is to go native. Restaurants serving inexpensive and wholesome Japanese dishes of all descriptions are found in abundance in every part of the country. If you can happily dine on such meals as sushi, *soba, udon,* or *ramen* noodles, Japanese-style pork cutlet *(tonkatsu),* and grilled fish, you will be able to eat well at very modest expense wherever you go.

Any restaurant with a window filled with vinyl models of available dishes is certain to be relatively inexpensive. Good sushi is always expensive, but acceptable sushi is available for as little as ¥100 per two-piece portion at so-called *kai-ten sushi-ya,* shops in which the sushi travels round on a little conveyor belt until a customer snaps it up. *Onigiri,* rice balls with a filling of grilled salmon or other fish, are inexpensive and popular for picnics.

For those with no stomach for Japanese food, American fast food and Japanese imitations are available everywhere. McDonald's Japan, the market leader, has more than 570 branches in the country, and the product is close to indistinguishable from the American one—some even maintain the Japanese is better.

Restaurants often have set lunches that are much cheaper and more creatively served than both à la carte dishes and dinners. Several of the best hotels, too, feature all-you-can-eat buffet breakfasts and lunches that are of excellent value and will keep you going all day.

SHOPPING. It has been many years since Japan was a Mecca for bargain hunters, and the recent rise of the yen against the dollar has made it even less so. Even *Akihabara,* the famous cut-rate electronics section of Tokyo, struggles to compete with equivalent bargain centers abroad—although for some products it may still have the edge.

The numerous department stores are the best places to look for out-of-the-way items, and the basement food halls are a fascinating banquet for the senses. Incidentally, the Japanese have been growing larger during the past few years; and therefore looking for larger sizes in clothing is no longer the torment that it used to be, though large sizes in shoes are still a problem.

When shopping for souvenirs remember that most parts of the country have one or more craft products of which they are particularly proud, whether it's a special type of pottery or an unusual style of doll. Such items make good presents.

For the best concentration of traditional kites, yukata, swords, pots, lacquerware, etc., sections of the city with a long-term orientation to the foreign tourist, such as Harajuku in Tokyo, are the best bet. The single best shop we know of for such items is *Oriental Bazaar,* on Harajuku's Omotesando Street.

Foreign visitors may avoid paying tax on a wide range of articles including jewelry, furs, and electronic equipment by shopping at authorized tax free stores, which include those in hotel arcades and the Japan Taxfree Center. Take your passport with you and be prepared to show the items you have bought to customs officers when you leave the country. Typically, savings are between 10 and 15 percent.

OPENING AND CLOSING TIMES. Banks are open 9 A.M.–3 P.M., Mon.–Fri., and 9 A.M.– noon on Sat., but are closed on the second and third Sat. of each month. Business and government offices are open from 9 A.M.–5 P.M., Mon.–Fri., and until noon on Sat. An increasing number of businesses work a five-day week. The post office, following the lead of the banks, does not handle money or insurance business on the second and third Saturdays of each month. Department stores are open from 10 A.M. to about 6 P.M. (sometimes later), and usually take a weekday holiday instead of Sunday. Local shops often stay open till 8 or 9 P.M., and some do not take regular holidays.

MAIL AND TELEPHONES. Japanese public telephones come in wonderful profusion and numerous colors. They are simple to use and are usually in good working order. Some (pink, red, blue) accept only ¥10 pieces, some (yellow, red) accept ¥10 and ¥100 pieces, others (small green ones) accept only telephone cards (available from tobacconists and other shops, and handy for those who have many calls to make). The big green phones, which are becoming more and more common, take ¥10, and ¥100 pieces, and cards as well.

To make a call, lift the receiver and insert coin or card. Insert another coin before the time is up to keep going. Dial 104 for directory inquiries (in Japanese). A local call costs ¥10 for three minutes.

To make **overseas calls** through the operator, dial 0051 from anywhere in Japan. Some of the green card-accepting phones mentioned above can also be used for making overseas calls by direct dial. Insert your card, dial 001, wait for the beeps, and then dial country, city, and subscriber number, remembering to omit the initial zero from the city number. Have fresh cards handy if you want to keep the conversation going. Direct dialing is substantially cheaper than going through the operator.

For foreign tourists in difficulties of any sort, one call to the Travel-Phone service should help to solve them. Available from 9 A.M. –5 P.M. throughout the year, the service is toll-free outside Tokyo and Kyoto and costs the same as a regular phone call within these cities. Dial 0120–222–800 in eastern Japan, and 0120–444–800 in western Japan to connect. If you call from a public phone, insert a ¥10 coin before dialing and it will be returned when the call is over. If in Kyoto, dial 371–5649 for the same service; in Tokyo dial 502–1461.

For foreign tourists, taped information on current events in Tokyo is available on 503–2911 in English, 503–2926 in French.

Mail rates vary according to destination. These are:

	Asia, Australia	Canada, USA	Europe
Airmail letter			
up to 10 gm	¥110	¥130	¥150
for each extra 10 gm	¥ 70	¥ 90	¥110
Airmail postcard	¥ 80	¥ 90	¥100
Aerogram	¥110	¥120	¥110

Ordinary **cablegrams** are ¥118 per word to the United States, and close to ¥200 per word to most of Europe. Seven words is the minimum. Urgent telegrams may be sent at double the ordinary rate. Letter telegrams, somewhat slower, are about half the ordinary rate, and the minimum is 22 words.

TOKYO

◆

By Hollistar Ferretti

Tokyo has its roots as a castle town and that influence can still be seen. Known as Edo before the Meiji Restoration, the first castle was built in 1457 by Ota Dokan, a warrior of repute who recognized Edo's strategic potential for commanding the water and land transportation routes of central and northeastern Japan. To secure his position, he rerouted the Hirakawa River, the first of many engineering feats that has changed the geographical face of today's Tokyo. Ota's tenure was short-lived, as his own jealous feudal lord had him murdered. Edo fell into oblivion until 1590 when the warlord Hideyoshi Toyotomi defeated the Hojo clan and gave their extensive territory to his powerful ally and potential adversary, Tokugawa Ieyasu, in exchange for Ieyasu's important holdings on the eastern sea route.

Ieyasu's followers thought he had the worst of the deal. Edo, his chosen site for his fortress, was mostly marshland between hills and the sea and seemingly offered little possibility for expansion. Ieyasu, however, turned those disadvantages to a strength. He built his castle on the same site Ota had chosen and fortified it with a series of concentric moats and massive stone walls. The word concentric may give an orderly impression. Actually, Ieyasu's moats were more on the order of a sinuous web of waterways. The marshlands were drained to create moats, and rivers were pressed into service to effect a formidable defense framework. It also made Edo a healthier place to live and provided a transportation system within the city. When Ieyasu became Shogun in 1603, he established his base of government at Edo. He planned his fortress city well. Edo castle was the largest in the world. It was never attacked.

In 1868, political power reverted from the Shogun to the Emperor. The era (1868–1912) was named Meiji to indicate "enlightened rule" and "Restoration" was added to suggest the return to imperial rule after an eight-century hiatus. The Emperor, taking advantage of the already established government infrastructure, moved his capital from Kyoto to Edo and renamed it Tokyo, Eastern Capital.

If you place a map of Ieyasu's Edo over a map of the present-day Tokyo, you'll see much has remained true to his original plan. The tourist may well wish he'd opted for a convenient grid-type system rather than the radial pattern, but look at it as one of the charms of this exciting city. The narrow, winding streets between main arteries, planned to impede an invading army, could provide an unexpected adventure.

Consider Tokyo as a collection of towns. You'll hear names such as Roppongi, Ginza, Akasaka, Shibuya, and Shinjuku. They are all sections of Tokyo, each a complete neighborhood with shops, offices, houses, apartments, etc., with distinctive characteristics. Learn to identify the place you're looking for by area and then zero in on the address. Some helpful terms are *ku* (ward), *cho* (district), and *chome* (section). In the past few years the main arteries have been named and the street signs are in Romaji (Roman alphabet).

The Western facade of Tokyo puts the traveler at ease. Beware—it's an illusion. Western ideas have indeed been adopted, but in the process the Japanese have adapted them to suit their own lifestyle. This is Asia; enjoy the difference. The service alone makes for an unforgettable experience. Tokyo may be the second-largest city in the world, but it's safe. If you are looking for directions, don't hesitate to ask a passerby. Not everyone speaks English, but a great percentage will give it a try. If the first person you approach ignores your request it's the language barrier; try another. The Japanese are very kind to foreigners, treating them as guests in their country.

Before striking out on your Tokyo adventure, pick up maps of the city and of the subway and train systems.

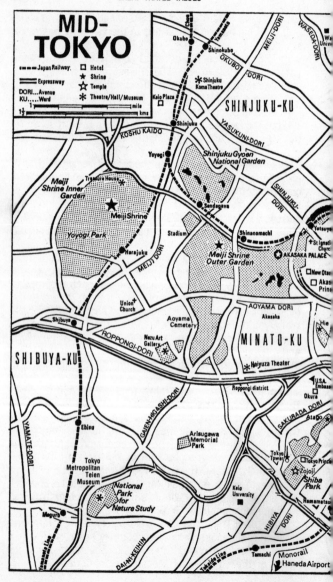

MID-TOKYO

Japan Railway   □ Hotel
Expressway   ★ Shrine
DORI...Avenue   ☆ Temple
KU.....Ward   ✳ Theatre/Hall/Museum

1 1½   mile
                        kms

Chuo
Okubo
Shinokubo
OKUBO-DORI
✳ Shinjuku Koma Theatre
Keio Plaza
SHINJUKU-KU
Yamanote
MEIJI-DORI
WASEDA-DORI
Wa
Univer

KOSHU KAIDO
Shinjuku
YASUKUNI-DORI

Yoyogi
Shinjuku Gyoen National Garden

Treasure House
Meiji Shrine Inner Garden
★ Meiji Shrine
Yoyogi Park
Sendagaya
SHINJUKU-DORI

Shinanomachi
Yotsuya
St Ignatiu Churc

Stadium
★
Meiji Shrine Outer Garden
AKASAKA PALACE

Harajuku
MEIJI-DORI

New Otan
Akasa
Prince

Union Church
AOYAMA DORI
Akasaka

Aoyama Cemetery

Shibuya
ROPPONGI-DORI
Nezu Art Gallery
MINATO-KU
Hie

SHIBUYA-KU
✳ Haiyuza Theater

GAIEN-HIGASHI-DORI
Roppongi district
U.S.A. Embass
Okura

Ebisu
SAKURADA DORI
Atago

YAMATE-DORI
Arisugawa Memorial Park
Tokyo Tower
Tokyo Prince

Tokyo Metropolitan Teien Museum
☆ Zojoji
Shiba Park

✳ National Park for Nature Study
Keio University

Meguro
HIBIYA DORI
Hamamatsu

Yamanote Line
DAI-NI-KEIHIN
Tokaido Line
Tamachi
Monorail
Haneda Airport

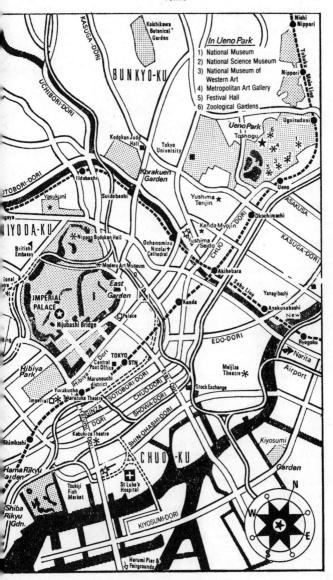

In Ueno Park
1) National Museum
2) National Science Museum
3) National Museum of Western Art
4) Metropolitan Art Gallery
5) Festival Hall
6) Zoological Gardens

Hotels often have them for the asking or you can find them at the Tourist Information Center (TIC) at 1-6-6 Yurakucho. If neither source is readily available, stop at a bookstore and buy a "Detailed Map of Central Tokyo for Sightseeing and Business," published in English by Nippon Kokuseisha. A taxi may take you directly to your destination, but consider the mass transportation system. Subways and trains are clean, efficient, reasonably priced, and make better time than street transport. Station signs are clearly marked in English, but don't be afraid to ask your way of fellow passengers. We'd suggest you not try the bus system on your own unless you are riding to the end of the line.

Since the city was built around the castle, it seems a good place to start the adventure of exploring Tokyo. The Shogun's majestic castle is now gone. In its place is the more modest Imperial Palace. The moat surrounding the palace grounds was the inner defensive perimeter of the Edo castle. Today the sidewalk skirting it is a popular jogging route and at noontime it's crowded with health-conscious office workers. Entry to the Eastern Garden of the palace grounds is possible through the Ote, Hirakawa, or Kita Hanebashi gates. There is no charge, but you'll be given a plastic token at the entrance to be returned on your departure. Open from 9 A.M. to 4 P.M., with no admission after 3 P.M., it's closed Mondays and Fridays and on special state occasions.

As the Shogun's castle, it contained four fortresses in a maze of moats and massive stone walls. Each maru (fortress) enclosed a number of buildings. The *Hon Maru,* located in the center on the highest ground, was the residence of the Shogun and contained halls for conducting affairs of state. Nearby was the *Ni no Maru,* residence for the retired Shogun when he made way for his successor. The present Imperial Palace is on the site of the one-time *Nishi no Maru,* formerly the site of the heir apparent's residence. The *Kita no Maru,* the fourth bastion, is today a public park of the same name outside the moat. Unfortunately, the buildings of the old regime have either fallen victim to fire or have been destroyed. You'll need some imagination to furnish the site. The water labyrinth has been filled in, but some vestiges of its old grandeur remain in the sweep of spacious lawns. You can still see the remnants of a garden designed by the master Kobori Enshu, and of some scattered buildings. Here was the monumental center of the largest city in the world, and at one time the most beautiful.

Tokyo's modern financial and government center, Marunouchi, meaning "within the castle walls," had been within the outer castle fortification. With the end of the shogunate, the feudal lords no longer had to maintain residence in the capital city. Their land holdings became a military drill and parade ground and the site for ministry buildings. When it was evident that the emperor was safe from attack, many of the moats were filled in and walls torn down. Marunouchi became the showcase for Western-style buildings, including the Tokyo Station. The 1945 air raids lopped off the domes and the top two floors of the station, but it still stands. Plans are now to move the Tokyo metropolitan government offices from Marunouchi to Shinjuku. Once more the face of Marunouchi will change, although it seems likely it will remain an important financial center.

Close by is Hibiya Park, the first Western-style park in Japan. One of the military exercise grounds was landscaped into a strolling park and opened to the public. The Hibiya Public Hall and the Metropolitan Public Library are on the premises. There's no entry fee and it's open 24 hours a day.

With all of Japan under his jurisdiction, Ieyasu introduced common coinage. The Ginza area was the location of the first mint in unified Japan. Ginza is the name of the silver guild. Even though the mint was later moved, the name remains. The area became a theatrical and entertainment center before it was renovated to a modern shopping center during the Meiji era. Existing structures were torn down to make way for broad streets and brick buildings. It looked very British, but brick was an unfortunate choice, for in this humid climate the merchandise was soon prey to mildew and mold and it proved an unhealthy place to live and work. Once this problem was resolved, Ginza won the reputation as the fashion center of the country. It was Japan's stage for Western innovations, including the first Western drugstore, stores featuring Western fashions, and a restaurant serving Western food. The buildings had show windows, something new for Japan; sidewalks were built and gaslights installed. For many Japanese, the Ginza still retains much of that glamour. Several of the leading department stores are here, as are restaurants of every ethnic origin, and numerous bars and bistros. At night you can still see geisha in their rickshaw on their way to an exclusive party. The visitor is warned to be cautious about casually dropping into bars. Check whether or not there is a minimum or cover charge and if they employ hostesses. That friendly girl who so thoughtfully pours your drinks and chats with you may well work for the establishment and you'll be charged for her time. Japanese businessmen entertain their clients here on their expense accounts.

Ginza may not hold the same charm for the Westerner as it does the Japanese, but it is still worth the visit and not just for the shops. A performance of *Kabuki* should be on the visitor's list. It's worth a splurge. The colorful spectacle is a masterpiece of staging and costuming and has changed little over the centuries. English language tapes are available for rent so the storyline is easily followed. The building itself is an interesting structure in the opulent style of a Momoyama period palace constructed with modern materials.

Nearby Shimbashi has an atmosphere of its own. The first railroad in Japan ran between Yokohama and Shimbashi. The port of Yokohama was the gateway to Japan for the foreign tourist of yesterday and the Shimbashi station was their entry to Tokyo. A number of small eateries and bars made use of the space under the tracks, and they remain today, patronized by the salaryman with no expense account. They're good fun if you speak Japanese.

Tsukiji has its origins in the 17th century when the overcrowded city was extended into reclaimed land in the bay. Under shogunal rule it was the site of a navigational school for mariners, although it was strictly forbidden to sail outside the country. During the Meiji Restoration it was the site of a navy training center. When foreigners were allowed to live in Tokyo, a section of Tsukiji was set aside for their housing, a school was established, and an elegant hotel was constructed. Somehow it failed to attract many foreigners; they seemed comfortably ensconced in Yokohama. The hotel was destroyed by fire and never rebuilt and with the repeal of extraterritorial rights for foreigners in 1899, restrictions were lifted on where they could reside. Few opted to remain in Tsukiji.

In 1900 St. Luke's Hospital was built here, one of the city's most prestigious hospitals with facilities for foreigners.

Today Tsukiji is famous for its wholesale fish market. About 90 percent of Tokyo's fish comes through here. From 5 to 6 A.M. wholesalers bid in lively auction and then their purchases are brought to their individual stalls. Restaurateurs and fishmongers shop the stalls for their daily supplies. When they've finished their buying, it's carted off to a loading bay to be delivered. The fish market scene is greatly appreciated by tourists, but be warned: Dress for it, keep out of the way, and watch your step. By 9 A.M. the action's over. You might want to cap the experience with a sushi breakfast—there's plenty of fresh fish available.

Near the Tsukiji market is Hamarikyu Koen, a large public park, with wide paths winding through large sweeps of lawn and wooded areas and over a large tidal pool, beautiful in every season. On reclaimed land, it has an interesting history. Originally the villa of a feudal lord (Matsudaira of Koshu Province), it became the shogun's detached palace in 1709 when Ienobu succeeded to the title. From the description, it was a beautiful place before fire claimed the buildings, and the gardens succumbed to neglect. With the Meiji Restoration, the land was turned over to the Imperial Household. The gardens were reestablished; a large brick residence, pavilions, and teahouses were built. It was used largely for entertaining on a royal scale. Ulysses S. Grant, former American President, and his wife were housed here on their visit to Japan in 1879. In 1945 it was given to the municipal government and turned into a public park. The buildings are gone and a section that includes two of the lakes has been fenced off as a nature preserve, but the garden grounds are well worth a visit. Open from 9 A.M.–4:30 P.M., closed Monday; admission fee ¥200.

At the far end of the garden, diagonally across from the entrance, is Hinode pier, where boats ply the Sumida River from Hamarikyu to Azuma Bridge in Asakusa. The boats leave from either direction at 40-minute intervals and cost ¥560 for adults, ¥280 for children. You'll have to close your eyes and imagine the shoreline of the Sumida River lined with willow trees and geisha houses. Today you'll see only the backs of warehouses and factories. The Kuramae Kokugikan Sumo Arena will be on your left after the Kuramae Bridge. They have three 15-day tournaments a year in Tokyo, during the months of January, May, and September. If you are in town at that time, be sure to go. Japan's national sport is colorful pageantry, a carryover from the past.

Asakusa is best known to the tourist as the location of Sensoji, more popularly known as the Asakusa Kannon Temple, one of the two oldest temples in the city. Legend has it that on the 18th day of the third month of 628, two brothers on a routine fishing expedition caught a golden statue of Kannon, the goddess of mercy. They created quite a sensation when they returned with the statue and presented it to their lord Haji no Nakatomo, who enshrined it in his house. Sometime later Sensoji was built with a hall to hold the Kannon. Time after time it was rebuilt, and the legend of the Kannon has persisted. During the Great Kanto Earthquake, the Temple remained unscathed, although other buildings in the neighborhood were flattened. However the luck didn't last through the second World War when it was hit by bombs. Interestingly enough, during the rebuilding, tiles and other evidence were found dating back to the latter half of the seventh century, giving credence to the legend.

Entry to Sensoji is through the red Kaminarimon (Thunder Gate). The god of the winds is on the right and the god of thunder on the left. The long avenue leading to the temple, Naka Mise dori, is lined with shops, many of which have been handed down from father to son for hundreds of years. The old stalls were torn down to be replaced with more functional brick. Recently Tokyoites are recognizing the charm of preserving many of the traditional ways, and the neighborhood has voted to redesign Naka Mise in the old style.

The atmosphere around Asakusa is a bit different from other sections of the city, being more informal, earthier.

With a number of Kabuki theaters in its confines, it became known as an amusement center, and in later years musical theater and movies flourished here. It remains a comfortable, fun section of the city.

Nearby is Asakusabashi, a wholesale district for restaurants, but quite willing to sell to anyone interested. If this does not particularly appeal to you, take a double-decker bus to Ueno, the site of a shrine dedicated to the spirit of Ieyasu. It is ironic that it is also the site of a decisive battle between the Emperor's forces and those loyal to the Shogun in 1868. Today it's a public park housing a number of buildings, among them the Tokyo National Museum, Tokyo Metropolitan Art Museum, Tokyo University of Arts Exhibition Hall, National Museum of Western Art, concert halls at Bunka Kaikan, Ueno Zoo, and the Shitamachi Museum. You can easily spend a day here.

Ueno station offers easy access to Ueno Park and its many attractions. If you walk along the small street next to the tracks going toward Okachimachi Station, you'll be on Ameyoko, the bargain basement of the city that had its beginnings after World War II as an outlet for black market goods. Today it's a lively melange of more mundane, cheaper merchandise.

If you've walked to Okachimachi Station, take the train, either the Yamanote line or the Keihin Tohoku to the next station, Akihabara. If you haven't left Ueno, board either train at that station and it's two stops. Akihabara is Japan's biggest wholesale district for electronics and electrical appliances, over 600 shops in all. You may not be able to bargain in other districts, but try your hand at it in Akihabara. They're eager for sales, and savings can be up to 35 percent. It's quality merchandise they're selling—in fact, many manufacturers test run their new products in Akihabara.

For another kind of experience, visit Roppongi (on the Hibiya subway line), a favorite night spot for foreigners. Every night is Saturday night in this section of town where discos and eateries abound. For the most part you don't have to worry about being overcharged. Akasaka, on the Chiyoda subway line, is another interesting entertainment center, but not as popular with foreigners.

Back on the JR Yamanote line, Shibuya has a wealth of

young, trendy shops and a vast movie theater complex. Buildings with one boutique after another make comparative shopping easy. Many are outlets for internationally known designers. In the past few years the do-it-yourself movement has caught the fancy of the Japanese and an institution called Tokyo Hands was born in Shibuya. The Tobacco and Salt Museum, despite its name, often has excellent exhibits of woodblock prints. The NHK complex, home of Japan's public broadcasting corporation with its excellent performing arts hall, is also in Shibuya and is well worth the visit if you're interested in the behind-the-scenes activities of broadcasting. One stop from Shibuya on the Inokashira line is Komabatodaimae, the Japan Folk Crafts Museum (Nihon Mingeikan).

Again on the JR Yamanote line, the next stop, Harajuku, is another fashionable center catering to the young and the young-at-heart. Hanae Mori has a building housing her accessories and haute couture. There's a coffee shop on the ground floor and a branch of the elegant French restaurant, L'Orangerie, on the fifth. Sunday brunch at L'Orangerie is a pleasant experience and the ¥3,500 per person buffet includes tax and service charge, an elegant splurge for a small outlay. Kansai Yamamoto is another top designer in the area. He claims to have led the way for the multitude of trendy boutiques. The Oriental Bazaar is wonderful for browsing for a great variety of Japanese merchandise and we'll wager you won't leave empty-handed.

Harajuku and nearby Yoyogi underwent drastic changes for the 1964 Olympic Games held in Tokyo. Houses were cleared to make way for the broad avenue, Omote Sando. Occupation forces, using a former Japanese army drilling ground as quarters for their personnel, were asked to vacate and return the land to the Japanese government to accommodate the Olympic participants. Today that land is Yoyogi Park, where the Meiji Shrine is located. The main entrance is near Harajuku Station. Pass through the giant torii and stroll along a drive that winds through a heavily wooded section. You'll pass a garden famed for its irises in May and June, but always a well-tended pleasure. If you don't pass it, it's a ¥300 diversion on the way to the shrine. Amid this natural grandeur, the shrine was built to honor the Meiji Emperor and his consort, the Empress Shoken. The Homotsuden, the Treasure Museum containing furniture, clothing, and other articles belonging to the imperial couple is also on the grounds, beyond the shrine buildings. The shrine is self-supporting, not state-owned, and there's a small entry fee.

On the west side of the Shinjuku Station, there's a cluster of skyscrapers that include a number of hotels. On both sides of the station you'll find several discount camera shops offering the best buys in cameras in town. The east side of the station has several department stores, countless bars, discos, and eating places. It also has a seamy side and it's best to stay clear of small dark streets. Ni chome has a plethora of gay bars, many of which no longer admit foreigners, whom the Japanese believe to be responsible for bringing AIDS into the country. The beautiful Shinjuku Gyoen is a wonderful park with broad expanses of lawn—a rare commodity in crowded Tokyo. Besides that blessed green, which is part of the Western-style garden, they also have a traditional Japanese garden. Famed for its cherry blossoms, Shinjuku Gyoen is the scene of the Prime Minister's annual spring garden party.

Ikebukero has a whole city of shops and restaurants underground and, by way of contrast, the Sunshine 60 Building, the tallest building in Asia, has 60 floors of shops and restaurants above ground. Ikebukero's Seibu Department Store is reputedly the largest department store in the world.

Although we've only touched upon several of Tokyo's many districts, not half by far, we hope we've given you an idea of all that the city has to offer. Each section has a distinct character of its own making a visit to Tokyo a rich and varied experience. Enjoy!

PRACTICAL INFORMATION FOR TOKYO

Prices have not gone up all that much within Japan. However, as foreign currency has weakened against the yen, dollars simply do not go as far. The Japanese are well aware of this dilemma and are taking steps to alleviate some of the financial strain for tourists.

The Transport Ministry has announced the establishment of the

International Tourism Development Research Center as of September 1987, with initial funds of ¥200 million. Basically it is a nonprofit organization to help Third-World countries develop tourist spots, but domestically they are issuing transport and hotel discount cards to foreigners to encourage travel within Japan. The government is also urging local tourism agencies to issue discount cards to foreign visitors for museums, shrines, temples, etc. For information and the availability of such cards, contact the Japan National Tourist Organization (JNTO), 10th floor of the Tokyo Katsu Kaikan near the JR Yurakucho Station, telephone 212–2403. Open Mon. through Fri. from 9:20 A.M.–5:30 P.M. Closes at 12:30 P.M. on Sat. closed Sun.

If you are in Japan for a week or more and plan to travel outside the Tokyo area, it would pay to purchase a Japan Rail Pass good for travel on any of the JR trains, buses, or ferry boats. These passes are *not* sold in Japan, but may be purchased from any authorized travel agent outside Japan. For one week the cost is ¥27,000, for two weeks ¥43,000, and for three weeks ¥55,000. Prices quoted are for ordinary train seats. First-class ticket prices are ¥37,000, ¥60,000, and ¥78,000.

If you are a summer traveler, discount train tickets are available to beach and mountain areas. This offer is primarily directed to the Japanese, so all information at the various stations is in Japanese. Check with JNTO on what's available and ask for a note to the station master where you buy the ticket. Perhaps the front desk at your hotel will oblige.

A free ticket in Tokyo is not free of charge but it does give you access to any JR train in the city. The cost is ¥700 and it can be purchased at the ticket office of any JR station, at all Japan Travel Bureau offices, or at travel agencies. For another ¥400 you can also use the subway and bus systems that day. Figure out how much public transportation you will need in one day; it might add up to a worthwhile savings.

How to Get There

From The Airport. The most convenient way to get from Narita to Tokyo is by taxi, but the 66-km run to central Tokyo costs about ¥20,000 or more if the expressway is crowded. The airport limousine bus runs frequently between Narita and the Tokyo City Air Terminal (TCAT) and the 70-minute ride costs ¥2,500. From TCAT you can taxi to your hotel. If you have already booked your hotel room, check the timetable for the airport express that goes directly to downtown hotels in the Akasaka, Ginza, Tokyo Central, Shiba, and Shinagawa areas. These buses do not run as often as the airport limousine so you'll have to decide if it's worth the wait. The charge is ¥2,600 or ¥2,700, depending on the area. The ticket booth is almost directly across the hall from the customs exit, a bit to the right.

If you are traveling light, you may opt for a short shuttle bus ride and the train. The six-minute bus ride from the terminal to Narita Airport Station is ¥190. Once there, you can transfer to the Keisei Skyliner train; the fare is ¥1,510 for a one-hour ride to Ueno Station, with one stop at Nippori Station for passengers transferring to the JR line. The limited express on this line is ¥810 and takes 75 minutes; the express is also ¥810 and takes 90 minutes. An alternative is to take the Asakusa subway line. From the Narita Airport Station, the subway fare is calculated by distance. For example, it costs ¥920 to Higashi Ginza, a 98-minute ride.

If you have arrived on China Airlines you will land in Haneda Airport. China Airlines is the only international carrier with landing rights here. From Haneda a taxi costs about ¥3,000–¥4,000, depending on where your hotel is located. The monorail is a convenience here. Signs in English will guide you. The fare to Hamamatsucho Station is ¥290. From here you can board either the JR Yamanote line or the JR Keihin Tohoku.

Useful Addresses and Information

TOURIST INFORMATION. Call 503–2911 (or 503–2926 in French) between 7 A.M. and midnight for a 90-second rundown on special events in Tokyo and the surrounding area for that particular week. For more specific information, they'll refer you to the *Tourist Information Center* (TIC); Tel. 502–1461, 6-6 Yurakucho, 1-chome, on the ground floor of the Kotani Bldg. TIC also has an office at the New Tokyo International Airport at Narita; Tel. (0476) 32–8711. If you're outside of Tokyo, you can call toll-free any day from 9 A.M.–6 P.M. Use either a yellow or blue phone. Dial 106 and say, "Collect call TIC." Your ¥10 coin will be returned to you.

Another convenience for tourists is *Travel-Phone* at 0120–222–800. It is a toll-free number outside of Tokyo (your ¥10 will be returned) and regular phone fare within the city. They'll assist in finding hotels or restaurants.

Tour Companion, a weekly giveaway, lists weekly events,

entertainment possibilities, and restaurants. Geared to the tourist, it can be picked up at most hotels.

CURRENCY EXCHANGE. Banking facilities are available at Narita for changing your currency into yen. A currency-exchange counter is located near the exit after you leave customs. Japanese currency is issued in ¥10,000, ¥5,000, and ¥1,000 notes. The denomination of the coins is ¥500, ¥100, and ¥50 in silver; copper ¥10; brass ¥5; and aluminum ¥1. In Tokyo, most banks have a foreign currency window, but hotels also change money or traveler's checks, as do many shops.

The Bank of Japan has put an automatic currency exchanger at their Shibuya branch. It automatically converts yen into an equivalent amount of U.S. dollars calculated from the day's yen-dollar exchange rate—a real time saver. Changing yen back to dollars before you leave the country is no problem. Major banks in the city will do so. Narita Airport has an exchange center set up just before you enter the departure area.

Banks are open weekdays from 9 A.M. to 3 P.M. (with cash card windows open until 6 P.M.), and from 9 A.M. to noon on Sat. Closed every Sun., national holidays, and the second and third Sat. of each month.

Most hotels and restaurants accept major credit cards including American Express, Diners Club, MasterCard, and Visa. Some but not all shops honor them.

EMBASSIES AND CONSULATES. U.S.A. **Embassy and Consulate,** 1-10-5 Akasaka, Minato-ku; Tel. 583–7141. Consular hours, Passport and Citizenship branch, 8 A.M.–4 P.M. Mon.–Fri. Closed holidays.

Australian Embassy and Consulate, 2-1-14 Mita; Tel. 453–0521. Consular hours 9 A.M.–noon, 2–4 P.M. Mon.–Fri. Closed holidays.

British Embassy and Consulate, 1 Ichiban-cho; Tel. 265–5511. Consular hours 9 A.M.–noon, 2–4 P.M. Mon.–Fri. Closed holidays.

Canadian Embassy, 7-3-38 Akasaka; Tel. 408–2101. Consular hours 9 A.M.–12:30 P.M., 2:30–4:30 P.M. Mon.–Fri. Closed holidays.

New Zealand Embassy, 20 Kamiyamacho; Tel. 467–2271. Consular hours 9 A.M.–12:30 P.M., 2–5 P.M. Mon.–Fri. Closed holidays.

EMERGENCIES. In using these numbers, speak slowly and clearly. The Japanese answering these phones do not always have a good command of the English language. If you can't communicate, call TELL, the Tokyo English Life Line at 264–4347, explain the situation, and they will place the call for you.

Fire and ambulance, dial 119. **Police,** dial 110. **Hill Pharmacy,** 4-1-6 Roppongi; Tel. 583–5044. Open 8 A.M.–7 P.M. Mon.–Sat., but will open shop for emergencies outside stated hours. Near Roppongi Station on the Hibiya subway line.

Tokyo Community Counseling Service (TCCS), Tel. 950–4665, for emergency counseling. Normal hours 9 A.M. to noon, Mon.–Fri. at 434–4992. In some cases, it's useful to call your embassy.

LOST AND FOUND. In every instance, speak slowly and distinctly when calling. It may be necessary to have the hotel clerk or a Japanese friend call for you. If calling at a lost and found office, ask the hotel clerk to write a note for you.

Lost and Found Department Metropolitan Police Department, Keishicho Ishitsubutsu, 1-9-11 Koraku; Tel. 814–4151. Open 8:30 A.M.–noon and 1–4 P.M. Mon.–Fri., 8:30–11:30 A.M. Sat., closed Sun. It is customary to give the finder 10 percent of the value of the item.

For items lost in taxis, contact the **Tokyo Kindai-Ka Center,** Shinsekai Bldg., 33 Shinanomachi; Tel. 355–0300. Open 24 hours daily.

For items lost on subway lines: if on private lines, check at the Ueno Station of the Hibiya line; Tel. 834–5573. For the Metropolitan Toei lines, Kotsu Kaikan, 1st fl., 2-10-1 Yurakucho; Tel. 216–2953. Open 9 A.M.–5 P.M. Mon.–Fri., closes at noon Sat., closed Sun.

For items lost on Japan Railway (JR): in the Tokyo Station; Tel. 231–1880. Open daily 6 A.M.–11 P.M.

For items lost on Metropolitan Buses: same as Toei, Kotsu Kaikan, 1st fl., 2-10-1 Yurakucho; Tel. 216–2953. Open 9 A.M.–5 P.M. Mon.–Fri., 9 A.M.–noon Sat., closed Sun.

MEDICAL SERVICES. When in need of medical attention, communication is of prime importance. The hospitals and clinics listed here have English-speaking doctors and staff. Not all hospitals accept emergency cases. Check with the ku (ward) for a nearby hospital that will. If language is a problem, call the Tokyo English Life Line at 264–4347. Someone there will help you.

CLINICS. International Clinic, 1-5-9 Azabudai; Tel. 582–2646 or 583–7831. General practice and surgery. Accepts emergencies.

Tokyo Medical and Surgical Clinic, No. 32 Mori Bldg. 2d floor, 3-4-30 Shibakoen; Tel. 436–3028. Comprehensive medical service, X ray, minor surgery, pharmacy, laboratory. Hospital transfer is necessary. Accepts emergencies.

HOSPITALS. St. Luke's International Hospital (Sei Luka Byoin), 1-10 Akashi-cho; Tel. 541–5151. No emergencies accepted. Application for entry 8:45–11 A.M. No applications accepted on Sun. or holidays.

St. Mary's International Catholic Hospital (Seibo Byoin), 2-5-1 Naka Ochiai; Tel. 951–1111. No emergencies accepted. Application for entry 8:30–11 A.M. No applications accepted on Sun. or holidays.

CHURCHES, SYNAGOGUES AND TEMPLES. Services for the following are in English, except for Jewish and Muslim houses of worship.

Anglican-Episcopal: **St. Alban's Church,** 3-6-25 Shiba Koen. Holy Communion services Sun. at 8 A.M. and 10 A.M. Sunday School 10 A.M. Evening prayers 5 P.M.

Tokyo Holy Trinity Church, 2-10-11 Daizawa. Holy Communion service Sun. at 12:45 P.M.

Baha'i: **Tokyo Baha'i Center,** 7-2-13 Shinjuku. Meetings on Sat. in English and Japanese.

Baptist: **Tokyo Baptist Church,** 9-2 Hachiyamacho. Sun. services 11 A.M. and 6 P.M. Church School 9:45 A.M. Wed. service 7 P.M.

Buddhist: Lectures in English at the **Tsukiji Honganji Temple** near Tsukiji subway stop on the Hibiya line. Sun. 10:30 A.M.

Catholic: **Franciscan Chapel Center,** 4-2-37 Roppongi. Masses Sat. 6 P.M., Sun. 8 A.M., 10 A.M., noon, and 6 P.M. Weekdays, 8 A.M. Confessions anytime.

St. Anselm's Benedictine Church, 4-26-22 Kamiosaki. Sun. Mass 11:45 A.M.

Eastern Orthodox: **Nicolai-do Cathedral,** 4-1 Kanda Surugadai. As the building itself is something special, built in 1884 by Josiah Conder, it's open from 1–4 P.M. daily. Divine Liturgy at 10 A.M. Confessions are heard after the Sat. 6 P.M. service. Youth meeting at 1:30 P.M. Services are trilingual—Japanese, Russian, and English.

Interdenominational: **International Christian Assembly** meets on the 4th floor of the Tokyo American Club, 2-1-2 Azabudai. Sun. service 10 A.M.–noon.

International Christian University Church, 3-10-2 Osawa. Bilingual service Sun. 10:30 A.M.

Tokyo Union Church, 5-7-7 Jingumae. Sun. services 8:40 A.M. and 11 A.M.

Jewish: **Jewish Community Center,** 3-8-8 Hiroo. Sabbath services Fri. at 6:30 P.M. and Sat. at 9:30 A.M.

Muslim: **Ahmadiyya Muslim Center,** 404-7-25-13 Umeda; Tel. 849–7899. Prayers every Fri. 1:15 P.M. For information call 849–7899 from 8–10 P.M.

Zen Meditation: **Eiheiji Tokyo Temple,** 2-31-34 Nishi Azabu. Mon. 7 P.M.–9 P.M. Fee ¥100. No appointment necessary, but beginners should arrive by 6:30 for basic instruction.

Rinsenji Temple, 4-7-2 Kohinata. Wed. at 7 P.M. Fee ¥500. Make your reservation by calling 943–0605.

Ryogenji Temple, 5-9-23 Mita. The first Mon. of every month at 1:30 P.M. Fee Y200.

Sennoji Temple, 4-5-12 Mita. The second Sun. of every month, except July, 6:30 P.M. Foreigners must understand Japanese. Fee ¥100.

Tokaiji Temple, 3-11-9 Kita Shinagawa. The second and fourth Sun. of the month at 6:30 P.M. Beginners should be there at 6 P.M.

PUBLICATIONS. You'll find plenty of English-language reading material in Japan. The weekly tabloid-sized *Tour Companion* is directed to the tourist and has a wealth of information on what is happening in Tokyo during any given week, complete with directions and maps. This publication is available at no cost in hotel lobbies, clubs, supermarkets, military bases, airports, and travel agencies. Another free weekly publication is the *Weekender*. Geared to the foreign resident, it has a section on the week's happenings in Tokyo. A relative newcomer in this category, *City News,* is also basically for the foreign resident, but it is filled with interesting reading for the tourist. *Newsweek* and *Time* are both published in Japan.

Many of the hotel bookshops have an excellent selection of American and British magazines, and in some cases, newspapers. Five English-language daily newspapers are printed in Japan. Morning papers are the *Japan Times, Mainichi Daily News, Shipping and Trade News,* and the *Yomiuri.* The *Asahi Evening News* is the single evening paper. The U.S. Military in Japan publishes the *Pacific Stars and Stripes,* a daily. Also available in many hotels and newsstands in foreign residential areas are the *International Herald Tribune, Wall Street Journal, USA Today,* and many other familiar newspapers.

Among the periodicals available in Tokyo are *The East,* a magazine devoted to Japanese history as well as timely topics; *The Economist; Forecasts,* a semimonthly music/theater arts calendar; *The Magazine; Tokyo Business Today;* and *Tokyo Journal,* with a City Scope section as a monthly guide.

MAIL, TELEPHONE AND TELEGRAPH. Post offices are open 8 A.M.–5 P.M. weekdays and until noon on Sat. except for some small stations that may not be open Sat. **The Central Post Office** near Tokyo Station is open 9 A.M.–7 P.M. Mon.–Fri., Sat. 9 A.M.–3 P.M., and Sun. and holidays 9 A.M.–12:30 P.M. Also, it is open for express mail 24 hours a day.

The Kokusai Denshin Denwa (KDD) Telegraph Office 1-8-1 Otemachi; Tel. 211–5588. Open 24 hours a day. Other KDD offices are in Nihonbashi, 270–5886; Shinbashi, 501–8281; Shibuya, 407–4321; Kyobashi, 561–7855; Marunouchi, 201–1331; Yaesuguchi, 212–1302; Chiyoda, 211–4867; TCAT (Tokyo City Air Terminal) 665–7366; World Trade Center Bldg., 435–5471 and Shinjuku, 347–5000. Telegrams or a telex can also be sent from hotels.

Telephones come in many colors in Tokyo. The small red phones in front of shops are for local calls, as are the blue phones in booths. Local calls are ¥10 for three minutes. Larger red phones are for long distance calls and will take up to ¥60 at a time. The yellow phones for long distance will take ¥100 coins. The green phone takes telephone cards. For the correct area code, dial 100. It is possible to call a passenger aboard the Shinkansen if you know the train number and time of departure; Tel. 248–9311.

For overseas calls anywhere in the world, dial 0051 for the overseas operator. Collect call service is available between Japan and U.S.A., Canada, European countries, Republic of Korea, Hong Kong, Taiwan, and Australia. Check with your hotel— chances are they'll be registered with KDD for International Subscriber Dialing and you can dial direct. The advantage is that direct dialing is invoiced for every six seconds, while a call placed through the operator includes the basic charge for the initial three minutes plus a charge for every additional minute. The savings are considerable. Calls made between 8 P.M. and 8 A.M. and on Sat., Sun., and national holidays are at a lower rate.

Getting Around

You can still see rickshaws in Tokyo, but they're only to transport geisha. Considering that Tokyo consists of 23 wards, 26 satellite cities, five towns and one village, it may be just as well. However, a superb network of trains and subways efficiently brings this conglomerate together. They are all color-coded for easy identification. Most hotels have free public transportation maps that are also available at all stations.

By Train. Train fare is calculated by distance, though the minimum fare on the JR lines is ¥140. Both train and subway tickets are purchased from machines.

The JR green *Yamanote* line circles the center part of the city, one going clockwise, the other counterclockwise with such major stations as Tokyo, Shimbashi, Hamamatsucho, Shinagawa, Shibuya, Shinjuku, Ikebukuro, Ueno, and Akihabara. The orange *Chuo* line originates at Tokyo Station and cuts across the Yamanote circle on to the western outskirts of the city with stops at Kanda, Ochanomizu, Yotsuya, Shinjuku, Nakano, Ogikubo, Mitaka, Tachikawa, and Hachioji. The blue JR *Keihin Tohoku* line runs from Omiya through Yokohama to Ofuna. In Tokyo it runs parallel to the Yamanote line between Shinagawa and Tabata. The yellow *Sobu* line runs parallel to the Chuo line between Mitaka and Ochanomizu and continues on toward Chiba.

Other lines outside the JR group branch out to the suburbs. Fares start at ¥70. The *Tokoyo* and *Inokashira* lines originate from Shibuya, the *Seibu* and *Tobu* lines from Ikebukuro, and the *Keisei* line from Ueno.

The superexpress *Shinkansen,* or ''bullet'' trains, leave Tokyo for western Japan from Tokyo Station. Those going to the north, Niigata or Morioka leave from Ueno Station. The cost is by mileage and by class. From Tokyo to Kyoto, the fare is ¥12,600 plus ¥5,400 for first class. Cars 1 to 5 are nonreserved, 11 and 12 are first class or green car, 8 is the dining car, 9 is buffet and the balance are reserved seats, ¥200 extra. From Tokyo to Niigata costs ¥9,600 + ¥4,200 for first class; to Morioka, costs ¥13,000 + ¥5,000 for first class.

By Subway. Tokyo has 10 subway lines, seven private and three municipally operated lines. Fares are for distance traveled and start at ¥120 for the private and ¥150 for the municipal.

The private subway lines are: *Chiyoda* (Yoyogi Uehara to

Ayase), *Ginza* (Shibuya to Asakusa), *Hanzomon* (Shibuya to Hanzomon), *Hibiya* (Naka Meguro to Kita Senju), *Marunouchi* (Ogikubo to Ikebukuro), *Tozai* (Mitaka to Nishi Funabashi), and *Yurakucho* (Ikebukuro to Shintomicho). The three municipal Toei lines are: *Asakusa* (Nishi Magome to Oshiage), *Mita* (Mita to Takashimadaira), and *Shinjuku* (Shinjuku to Funabori).

By Monorail. The monorail originates from the Hamamatsucho Station of either the green Yamanote line or the blue Keihin Tohoku line and goes to the Haneda Airport. Most of the domestic flights leave from Haneda if you're traveling to other parts of Japan. Be sure you get off at the end of the line for the airport. The fare is ¥290 one way.

By Bus. Buses crisscross the city for a set fare of ¥160. Unless you speak Japanese or are familiar with the stops on a particular run, or are simply riding from one end to the other, you'd be better off on the subway or train.

By Taxi. Taxis are the most convenient and the most expensive method of transportation. The basic fare for a regular taxi is ¥470 for the first 2 kms (1.2 miles) and another ¥80 for each additional 370 meters (.2 mile). There is a time charge of ¥80 for every 2 ½ minutes if traveling under 10 kms an hour due to slow traffic. Taxis may be hailed from the street or can be found at major hotels, railroad stations, and taxi stands.

Where to Stay

Note: The Japanese are proud of the service they offer and do not expect tips. You need not tip the restaurant waiter or waitress, taxi drivers, hotel porter, room maid, or anyone else who gives you service. Of course, if you ask for some special service, you would. When staying in an expensive ryokan, a traditional Japanese inn, it is customary to tip the room maid at least ¥1,000 at the beginning of the stay. Redcap porter service at Tokyo or Ueno Station is ¥300 per bag or suitcase.

APARTMENT HOTELS. These hotels supply cooking equipment and tableware. The arrangement not only saves money if you are planning to stay in Tokyo for at least a week, but you'll have the added comfort of being able to fix meals on your own. They are not all that popular in Japan, but we've located a couple in Tokyo. A deposit is necessary and the quoted price doesn't include the utility bill.

Residence INN Meguro, 3-13-21 Nishigotanda; Tel. 492–0505. Single: ¥36,400 weekly, ¥138,000 monthly. Double: ¥43,400 weekly, ¥168,000 monthly. Twin: ¥51,800 weekly, ¥210,000 monthly.

Residence INN Sangenjaya, 1-34-19 Kamiuma; Tel. 422–0501. Single: ¥43,400 weekly, ¥168,000 monthly. Double: ¥46,200 weekly, ¥177,000 monthly. Twin: ¥59,500 weekly, ¥231,000 monthly.

HOTELS. The following hotels are all priced moderately or inexpensively (exact prices are given). Also included are business hotels, which are geared to the businessman, featuring a number of clean, compact rooms near convenient, public transportation and offering a minimum of service. They are often without restaurant facilities, but vending machines will be in the hall. Many have added a few conveniences and no longer classify themselves as business hotels, largely because the novelty of the name has worn off. All of the hotels listed will have some English-speaking staff on duty. Unless specifically stated, you can expect a 10 percent tax and a 10 percent service charge to be added to your bill. The hotels are organized according to location. ◗ = Highly Recommended.

Minato-Ku

Akasaka Shanpia Hotel, 7-6-13 Akasaka; Tel. 583–1001. Single A, ¥7,200. Single B ¥7,600. Twin ¥13,400. Near Akasakamitsuke Station. In the midst of the nighttime amusement center.

Aoyama Shanpia Hotel, 2-14-15 Shibuya; Tel. 407–8866. Single A, ¥8,400. Single B, ¥8,800. Double, ¥13,000. Twin, ¥13,400. Near Shibuya Station. Famous for its restaurant featuring southern European dishes.

Asia Center of Japan, 8-10-32 Akasaka; Tel. 402–6111. Single without bath, ¥3,960. Single with bath, ¥4,840. Twin, ¥8,140. Tax and service charge included. Near Aoyama 1-chome subway station. Popular with students.

Atagoyama Tokyu Inn, 1-6-16 Atago; Tel. 421–0109. Single, ¥9,500. Twin, ¥12,000. Double ¥13,000. Near JR Hamamatsucho Station, Kamiyacho on the Hibibya subway line, or Onarimon on the Mita subway line. Convenient location and quiet.

Hotel Ibis, 7-14-4 Roppongi; Tel. 403–4411. Single, ¥9,000.

Twin, ¥15,000. Double, ¥14,000. Near Roppongi Station on the Hibiya subway line. Right in the center of the most popular area for foreigners.

Hotel Tokyo, 2-17-18 Takanawa; Tel. 447–5771. Single, ¥12,147. Twin, ¥14,680. Double, ¥19,740. Tax and service charge included. Near Sengakuji Station on the Asakusa subway line. Unique mixture of Japanese and European. They have a first-class Japanese restaurant.

Hotel Yoko Akasaka, 6-14-12 Akasaka; Tel. 586–4050. Single, ¥6,950. Twin, ¥11,000. Tax and service charge included. Near Akasaka subway station. Convenient to the business area.

Keihin, 4-10-2 Takanawa; Tel. 449–5711. Single, ¥6,800. Twin, ¥1,200. Across from JR Shinagawa Station. Convenient location. Popular with businessmen, tourists and students studying for examinations.

MaRRoad Inn, 6-15-17 Akasaka; Tel. 585–7611. Single, ¥6,500. Twin, ¥11,000. Tax and service charge included. Near Akasaka subway station. A quiet hotel surrounded by greenery in the center of the city. Has a good Chinese restaurant called the Marroad.

The President Hotel, 2-2-3 Minami Aoyama; Tel. 497–0111. Single from ¥9,000. Twin from ¥11,000. Double from ¥13,000. One minute from Aoyama 1-chome subway station. A little more luxurious but still economical.

Rainbow Hotel, 4-15-6 Shinbashi; Tel. 434–1641. Single, ¥5,200. Twin/double, ¥10,000. Tax and service charge included. Near the Karasumori exit of the JR Shinbashi Station. Convenient to businesses, stores, theaters, and other amusements.

Shiba Park Hotel, 1-5-10 Shiba Koen; Tel. 433–4141. Single, ¥9,500. Twin, ¥16,000. Double, ¥18,000. Near Zojoji Temple. Popular with foreign tourists.

Shiba Yayoi Kaikan, 1-10-27 Kaigan; Tel. 434–6841. Single, ¥5,500. Twin, ¥8,800. Tax and service charge included. Near JR Hamamatsu cho station. Newly built, nicely appointed.

Shinagawa Prince, 4-10-30 Takanawa; Tel. 440–1111. Single, ¥7,300. Twin, double, ¥12,000. Across the street from JR Shinagawa Station. Has great sport facilities: ice skating rink, bowling alleys, tennis courts, and an indoor swimming pool. There's also a supermarket on the premises.

Shinbashi Daiichi Hotel, 1-2-6 Shinbashi; Tel. 501–4411. Single, ¥9,500. Twin, ¥15,500. Double, ¥14,500. Near JR

Shinbashi Station. Started as a business hotel, but has expanded and enlarged its facilities. Comfortable.

Takanawa, 2-1-17 Takanawa; Tel. 443–9251. Single, ¥8,500. Twin, ¥14,000. Tax and service charge included. In a residential area near Sengakuji subway station. Quiet, yet conveniently located.

Takanawa Tobu Hotel, 4-7-6 Takanawa; Tel. 447–0111. Single, ¥7,800. Twin, ¥12,800. Triple, ¥15,300. Near Shinagawa Station. Reputable, warm atmosphere; good French restaurant.

Tokyo Grand Hotel, 2-5-3 Shiba; Tel. 454–0311. Single, ¥10,000, Twin, ¥15,000. Double ¥17,000. Near Shiba Koen Station on the Mita subway line. Calm atmosphere. Try the tea ceremony here.

Chiyoda-Ku

Central Hotel, 3-17-9 Uchikanda; Tel. 256–6251. Single, ¥5,400–¥6,500. Twin, ¥8,200. Tax and service charge included. Near Kanda Station. Rooms can double as an office from 10 A.M.–4 P.M.

Diamond, 25 Ichibancho; Tel. 263–2211. Single, ¥7,300. Twin, ¥13,000. Near Kojimachi subway station. Near the British Embassy and the Palace. Offers a good buffet.

Fairmont Hotel, 2-1-17 Kudan Minami; Tel. 262–1151. Single, ¥7,500. Twin, ¥16,000. Seven minutes from Kudanshita subway station. Faces Chidorigafuchi; guests can look across the moat to the Palace grounds.

Hotel Kayu Kaikan, 8-1 Sanbancho; Tel. 230–1111. Single, ¥9,700. Twin, ¥16,500. Near the British Embassy. Quiet. Management under the prestigious Okura Hotel.

New Central Hotel, 2-7-2 Kanda Ta-machi; Tel. 256–2171. Single, ¥5,700. Twin, ¥8,800. Double, ¥9,000. Tax and service charges included. Near Kanda Station. Single rooms can be also used as an office. Has a sauna.

Tokyo Green Hotel Suidobashi, 1-1-16 Misaki cho; Tel. 295–4161. Single, ¥6,300. Twin, ¥10,600. Double, ¥10,500. Tax and service charge included. Near Suidobashi train or subway station. Cozy, comfortable atmosphere, convenient location.

Tokyo Station Hotel, 1-9-1 Marunouchi; Tel. 271–2511. Single, ¥7,000. Twin, ¥14,500. Double, ¥15,000. Right at Tokyo Station, but still quiet. Convenient to Marunouchi financial district.

Toshi Centre Hotel, 2-4-1 Hirakawacho; Tel. 265–2811.

Single, ¥5,600. Twin, ¥10,600. Near the business section, but green and quiet.

Washington Akihabara, 1-8-3 Kanda Sakuma cho; Tel. 255–3311. Single, ¥6,000. Twin, ¥11,500. Near Akihabara Station. Part of the excellent chain of Washington Hotels geared for the businessman but with added luxuries. Located in the center of the electronic discount center.

Chuo-Ku

Ginza Capital Hotel, 2-1 Tsukiji; Tel. 543–8211. Main Bldg.: Single, ¥6,950; Twin, ¥11,980. Annex (new bldg.): Single, ¥7,550; Twin, ¥12,700. Triple, ¥14,850. Tax and service charge included. Near Tsukiji subway station. Ten-minute walk to Ginza. Good for business and shopping.

Ginza Daiei, 3-12-2 Ginza; Tel. 541–2684. Single, ¥8,750. Twin/double, ¥13,000. Tax and service charge included. Near Ginza subway station. Popular with foreigners.

Ginza Daiichi Hotel, 8-13-1 Ginza; Tel. 542–5311. Single, ¥11,800. Twin, ¥16,500. Near JR Shimbashi Station. Good location for Ginza shopping or business.

Ginza Marunouchi, 4-1-12 Tsukuji; Tel. 543–5931. Single, ¥9,000. Twin, ¥17,500. Double, ¥17,000. Near Higashi Ginza subway station. Quiet with well-furnished rooms.

Ginza Nikko Hotel, 8-4-21 Ginza; Tel. 571–4911. Single, ¥9,500. Twin, ¥17,000. Double, ¥14,500. Near Ginza subway station or JR Shimbashi Station, in the Ginza nightlife area. Owned and operated by Japan Airlines. Flight reservations can be made from the front desk.

Grand Central Hotel, 2-2 Kanda Tsukasacho; Tel. 256–3211. Single, ¥7,000–¥8,000. Twin, ¥11,500. Tax and service charge included. Near Kanda Station. Nicely furnished. Comfortable.

Hotel Den Harumi, 3-8-1 Harumi; Tel. 533–7111. Twin, ¥14,500. Double, ¥14,500. Triple, ¥16,500. Tax and service charge included. An individual can use a twin room for a single fee of ¥10,550. Furnished in a northern European style.

Hotel Gimmond, 1-6 Ohdenma-cho, Nihonbashi; Tel. 666–4111. Single from ¥6,500. Twin from ¥11,500. Near Nihonbashi Station. Good location. Has a multipurpose hall, good for exhibitions.

Hotel Heimat, 1-9-1 ¥aesu; Tel. 273–9411. Single, ¥5,000. Twin, ¥11,000. Double, ¥7,800. Tax and service charge included. Across the street from JR Tokyo Station, Yaesu exit. Good location.

Hotel Universe, 2-13-5 Kayabacho; Tel. 668–7711. Single, ¥6,400–¥7,000. Double, ¥9,500–¥10,000. Twin, ¥10,500–¥12,000. Near Kayabacho Station. A 15-minute train ride to Disneyland.

Hotel Urashima, 2-5-23 Harumi; Tel. 533–3111. Single, ¥6,000. Twin, ¥11,000. Double, ¥12,000. Tax and service charge included. Good for businessmen, sightseers, and families.

Kayabacho Pearl Hotel, 1-2-5 Shinkawa; Tel. 553–2211. Single, ¥5,800–¥6,500. Twin, ¥9,800–¥10,400. Triple, ¥13,000. Tax and service charge included. Near Kayabacho Station, just a few minutes walk from the Tokyo City Air Terminal. Also convenient to the stock exchange and the security business area.

Shibuya Ku

Hotel Sun Route, 2-3-1 Yoyogi; Tel. 375–3211. Single, ¥8,500. Twin, ¥16,000. Two minutes from JR Shinjuku Station. Part of the Sun Route chain geared for businessmen. Rooms are small, but well appointed and comfortable. Features several good restaurants.

Shibuya Business Hotel, 1-12-5 Shibuya; Tel. 409–9300. Single, ¥6,200. Twin, ¥9,200. Double, ¥9,500. Near Shibuya JR Station. Quiet.

Shibuya Tobu Hotel, 3-1 Udagawacho; Tel. 476–0111. Single, ¥9,800. Twin, ¥15,800. Double, ¥12,200. Near Shibuya JR Station. Convenient to the shopping and amusement areas.

Shibuya Tokyu Inn, 1-24-10 Shibuya; Tel. 498–0109. Single, ¥10,800. Twin/double, ¥15,800. Tax and service charge included. Two minutes from JR Shibuya Station. Simple but comfortable rooms.

Meguro Ku

Gajoen, 1-8-1 Shimo Meguro; Tel. 491–0111. Single, ¥7,000. Twin, ¥12,000. Family, ¥19,000. Near Meguro Station. In a quiet residential area. Old, but renovated in 1986; still keeps traditional atmosphere. Popular with the Japanese for wedding receptions.

New Meguro, 1-3-18 Chuo Cho; Tel. 719–8121. Single, ¥7,550. Twin, ¥11,000. Double, ¥13,900. Near Toyoko line Gakugeidaigaku Station. Small, but with good facilities.

Shinjuku

Hotel Sunlight, 5-15-84 Shinjuku; Tel. 536–0391. Single, ¥5,500. Twin, ¥8,800. Triple, ¥12,000. Near Shinjuku San-chome Station. Warm atmosphere.

Shinjuku New City Hotel, 4-31-1 Nishi Shinjuku; Tel. 375–6511. Single, ¥6,000. Twin, ¥10,800. Double, ¥13,000. Convenient and near Chuo Koen Park.

Taisho Central Hotel, 1-27-7 Takadonobaba; Tel. 232–1411. Single, ¥5,700 and up. Twin, ¥10,000 and up. Tax and service charge included. Near Takadonobaba Station. New.

Tokyo Business Hotel, 6-3-2 Shinjuku; Tel. 356–4605. Single, ¥3,800. Twin, ¥8,000. Tax and service charge included. Near Shinjuku San-chome subway station. Economical, quiet, and convenient for the businessman.

Washington Shinjuku, 3-3-15 Nishi Shinjuku; Tel. 343–3111. Single, ¥8,400. Twin, ¥14,500. Double, ¥10,500. A new high rise on the west side of Shinjuku Station. Economical, but nice facilities.

Shinagawa Ku

Hotel Hankyu, 1-50-5 Oi; Tel. 775–6121. Single, ¥4,300. Tax and service charge included. Near JR Oimachi Station. You can choose the floor you want to stay on.

Toko Hotel, 2-6-8 Nishi Gotanda; Tel. 494–1050. Single, ¥6,500. Twin, ¥13,000. Triple, ¥16,500. Tax and service charge included. Near Gotanda subway and train stations. Both comfortable and secure; a good hotel for women.

Sumida Ku

Pearl Hotel, 1-2-24 Yokutsuna; Tel. 626–3211. Single, ¥5,500. Twin, ¥9,400. Triple, ¥12,000. Tax and service charge included. Near Kokugikan, the arena for sumo wrestling bouts. About a 15-minute train ride to the business district.

Taito Ku

Hokke Club, 6-9-19 Ueno; Tel. 834–4131. Single, ¥4,800. Twin, ¥9,300. Double-deck beds, ¥6,200. Near Ueno Station. Convenient for sightseeing and shopping.

Ikenohata Bunka Center, 1-3-45 Ikenohata; Tel. 822–0151. Single, ¥4,950. Twin, ¥11,000. Tax and service charge included. Ten minutes from Ueno Station. Good facilities and service.

Takara Hotel, 2-16-5 Higashi Ueno; Tel. 821–0101. Single,

¥9,950. Twin, ¥14,500. Double, ¥16,300. Tax and service charge included. Near Ueno Station. They've upgraded their facilities to make this more than a business hotel.

Ueno Station Hotel, 2-14-23 Ueno; Tel. 833–5111. Single, ¥6,950. Twin, ¥12,700. Near Ueno Station and Ueno Park, in the heart of the Shitamachi area.

Bunkyo Ku

Hotel Satoh, 1-4-4 Hongo; Tel. 815–1133. Single, ¥5,900. Twin, ¥9,600. Tax and service charge included. Near Suidobashi JR Station. Features both Western and Japanese-style rooms. Good for groups.

Suidobashi Grand Hotel, 1-33-2 Hongo; Tel. 816–2102. Single, ¥5,900. Twin, ¥9,000. Triple, ¥12,000. Tax and service charge included. Near Suidobashi JR Station. They have special packages for watching sumo and/or pro baseball.

RYOKAN. A ryokan, or Japanese inn, provides a wonderful opportunity to experience the traditional Japanese way of living. When you enter the inn, you must remove your shoes and place them in a little cubbyhole in the *genkan* (hallway or entry). You will be given a pair of slippers which should be discarded when you enter your room. A *yukata*, cotton robe, will await you, and if the weather's cold, a *tanzen*, a heavier robe to be worn over the yukata. You may dine and sleep in your yukata.

The Japanese toilet, flush with the floor, is for squatting, not sitting, and you face the hood. You'll find plastic shoes just inside the door. These are used in the toilet only. The bath will be communal, though men separate from women. The same ritual is observed here as in a public bath. Wash and rinse first and then soak in the tub.

In low-budget ryokan, meals may be served in a communal room rather than in your own room. Some do not include two meals in the price and may charge extra for breakfast or dinner.

Bookings can be made at JTB or any travel agency. The information office in major train stations will have a listing of ryokan in the vicinity, but unless you understand Japanese this can be difficult. Check with the JNTO. You'll usually find some English-speaking staff, in the ryokan listed below.

The prices that follow are per person. However, each ryokan will have a long list of prices, depending on the room, how many will be sleeping in the room, and whether or not there are bath facilities.

Chuo-Ku

Yaesu Ryumeikan, 1-3-22 Yaesu; Tel. 271–0971. ¥12,000 per person with two meals. Close to Tokyo Station.

Minato-Ku

Okayasu, 1-7-11 Shibaura; Tel. 452–5091. All rooms are without baths. Western single, ¥3,600; Japanese single, ¥3,600–¥4,000. A 12-minute walk from either Hamamatsucho or Tamachi station. Quiet.

Taito Ku

Taito ku is the old Shitamachi area. It still retains much of the atmosphere of old Edo, where the people are friendly, down-to-earth, and will make you feel comfortable.

Katsutaro, 4-16-8 Ikenohata; Tel. 821–9808. Per person, ¥3,600–¥3,900 without bath; ¥4,400 with bath. Continental breakfast, ¥350. Air-conditioned rooms. Restaurant. A five-minute walk to the Ueno Zoo.

Kikuya Ryokan, 2-18-9 Nishi-Asakusa; Tel. 841–6404. Per person, ¥3,500 without bath; ¥3,800 with bath. Near Akasaka Temple. Continental breakfast, ¥300. Features comfortable rooms.

Mikawaya Bekkan, 1-31-11 Asakusa; Tel. 843–2345. Near Asakusa Temple. Per person, ¥4,500 without bath. Western breakfast, ¥350; Japanese breakfast, ¥500; Japanese dinner, ¥2,000. A five-minute walk from Asakusa Station on the Ginza subway line.

Sawanoya Ryokan, 2-3-11 Yanaka; Tel. 822–2251. Single room, ¥3,600 and up. Twin room, ¥6,000 and up. Triple room, ¥9,000 and up. Upon request, American breakfast, ¥300 or Japanese breakfast, ¥600. Near Ueno Park. Public bath, dining room, and restaurant on the premises. Air-conditioned rooms have refrigerators and TVs.

Suigetsu Hotel/Ohgaiso, 3-3-21 Ikenohata; Tel. 822–4611. Japanese-style, ¥3,500–¥4,800. Western-style, ¥5,300. American or Japanese breakfast, ¥800. Japanese dinner, ¥1,800 and up. Dining room, restaurant, laundromat. Air-conditioned rooms with refrigerators and TVs.

Sukeroku-no-yado, 2-20-1 Asakusa; Tel. 842–6431. Per person, ¥4,000–¥4,900. All rooms have private baths and toilets. Japanese-style structure preserves the traditional lifestyle. Air-conditioned. Try the dining room.

Bunkyo Ku

There's a cluster of ryokan in this residential area. It's not in the center of the city, but the subway brings you there quickly. Most of those listed below are near Tokyo University. All are clean and respectable; most have air-conditioning and TVs and many have Japanese gardens.

Chomeikan, 4-4-8 Hongo; Tel. 811–7205. Per person, ¥7,000 with two meals. Near Hongo San-chome subway station.

Fujikan, 4-36-1 Hongo; Tel. 813–4441. Per person, ¥6,500 with two meals. Near Hongo 3-chome subway station.

Hongo Kan, 1-28-10 Hongo; Tel. 811–6236. Per person, ¥8,000 with two meals. Near Hongo 3-chome subway station.

Koshinkan, 2-1-5 Mukogaoka; Tel. 812–5291. Per person, ¥5,500 with two meals. Near Kasugacho subway station.

Seifuso, 1-12-5 Fujimi; Tel. 263–0681. Per person, ¥6,000 without bath; ¥11,000 with bath. All rooms face a Japanese garden. Five-minute walk from Iidabashi Station.

Shimizu Gekkan, 1-30-29 Hongo; Tel. 812–6285. Per person, ¥9,500 with two meals. Near Hongo 3-chome subway station.

Tsutaya, 5-22-9 Hongo; Tel. 812–3231. Per person, ¥9,500 with two meals. Near Kasugacho subway station.

Shinjuku Ku

Inabaso Ryokan, 5-6-13 Shinjuku; Tel. 341–9581. Per person, ¥3,900 and up. Japanese breakfast, ¥600; American breakfast, ¥300. Phone for reservations. Near the famous Shinjuku Gyoen Park and the Shinjuku amusement center. Air-conditioned rooms with TVs and refrigerators. Laundromat available.

Kikaku, 1-11-2 Sendagaya; Tel. 403–4501. Per person, ¥12,000. Near Sendagaya JR Station, close to Tsuda Women's College.

Nagaragawa, 4-14 Yotsuya; Tel. 351–5892. Per person, ¥8,000. Near Yotsuya subway station.

Yashima, 1-15-5 Hyakunin cho; Tel. 364–2534. Per person, ¥3,000–¥3,500 without bath. Double, ¥7,000 with bath. Near Shinjuku Station and close to the Shinjuku amusement center.

Shinagawa Ku

Sansui So, 2-9-5 Higashi Gotanda; Tel. 441–7175. Per person, ¥3,800 without bath; ¥4,200 with bath. Breakfast, ¥800. Near Gotanda JR Station.

DORMITORIES. These simple lodgings offer little more than sleeping space but are worth considering if you want to economize.

Shinjuku Ku

Okubo House, 1-11-32 Hyakunin cho; Tel. 361–2348. Men only, ¥1,200. Men and women, two to a room, ¥2,400. Japanese rooms. Near Shinjuku Station.

Toshima Ku

English House, 2-23-8 Nishi Ikebukuro; Tel. 988–1743. Per person, ¥1,700–¥1,900. Long-stay arrangement, ¥3,000 for two. Near Ikebukero Station.

Kimi, 2-1034 Ikebukuro; Tel. 971–3766. Both Western and Japanese rooms. Single, ¥2,600–¥3,500. Twin, ¥5,000–¥5,500. Double, ¥4,500–¥5,000. Shared room, ¥2,000. Near Ikebukuro JR Station.

Nerima Ku

Yoshida House, 1-25-25 Kasuga cho; Tel. 978–3984. Per person, ¥1,300. Near Seibu line Nerima Station.

Nakano Ku

Shin Nakano Lodge, 6-1-1 Honcho; Tel. 381–4886. Per person, ¥2,700. Four to a room. Near Nakano Station.

YMCA/YWCA HOSTELS. This is undoubtedly the most economical lodging. Most youth hostels require a valid membership card. It is best to get one in your own country from a Youth Hostel Association belonging to the International Youth Hostel Federation. Hostels built with government funds do not require a membership card, only your passport. Hostels are usually built in scenic vacation spots, though YMCAs and YWCAs have several clean, comfortable and reasonable accommodations in Tokyo.

The rates for the following listings are ¥5,500 for one, and ¥10,000 for two without meals.

Chiyoda Ku

Japan YWCA Hostel, 4-8-8 Kudan Minami; Tel. 264–0661. Near Kudanshita subway station.

Tokyo YWCA Hostel, 1-8 Kanda Surugadai; Tel. 293–5921. Near Ochanomizu JR Station.

YMCA Asia Center, 2-5-5 Sarugaku; Tel. 233–0681. Near Suidobashi Station. .

Shinjuku Ku

Tokyo YWCA Sadohara Hostel, 3-1-1 Chigaya, Shadohara cho; Tel. 268–7313. Near Ichigaya Station.

MINSHUKU. Minshuku are rooms in private homes that sometimes include breakfast. Listings are available through the Minshuku Association. For information, write to Tokyo Kotsu Kaikan Bldg., 2-10-1 Yurakucho, Chiyoda-ku, Tokyo 100, or call 216–6556. You can be a member of a Japanese family for a night or two. Follow all the Japanese rules of etiquette and you'll be fine: shoes left in the *genkan,* no slippers on *tatami* mats, and plastic slippers in the toilet. No choice of food, you'll have family fare. Also remember there's no service. At night you'll be expected to spread your bedding on the tatami and in the morning fold it up and put it away.

Minshuku Chojuso, 4-15-19 Shinjuku; Tel. 378–3810. Per person, ¥3,300 without bath. Breakfast is included. Dinner, ¥800. Air-conditioned, laundry facilities, TVs.

Where to Eat

RESTAURANTS. In many restaurants, set lunches served mid-day are much less costly than à la carte dishes. This makes it possible to dine amid elegant surroundings, which would normally be outside the range of budget eating. In many moderately priced restaurants, vinyl models of the dishes offered are arranged in the window, with prices attached. You can indicate your choice by pointing.

For budget dining, check department store dining rooms, shopping center cafes, back street restaurants, and fast food franchises.

Price categories should be read as follows: *Moderate,* about ¥3,000 for lunch, ¥4,500 for dinner: *Inexpensive,* about ¥2,000 for lunch, ¥3,000 for dinner; and Low Budget, up to ¥2,000 for lunch or dinner. ● = Highly Recommended.

Remember: 10 percent tax is levied on bills of ¥2,000 and above. If your bill is ¥1,900 and your companion's ¥2,100, keep the two separate. If you put them together to make a total of ¥4,200, you wind up paying double the tax.

Credit cards: the most modest and the most extravagant and traditional Tokyo restaurants continue to spurn credit cards, but most of those in the *moderate* category below will accept payment by American Express, MasterCard and Visa, and sometimes others as well.

Reservations: Not required at these restaurants, though if you plan to go at a peak time—around 7 P.M., Tokyo dines early—it's worth calling to check how busy your restaurant of choice is. Nearly all Japanese in Tokyo take lunch at noon, so if you can delay your lunch until 1 P.M. you can be almost sure of a table and rapid service.

Japanese-Style

Moderate

● **5-Chome Tsubo-Han,** 3-9, Ginza 5-chome; Tel. (03) 571–3467. Elegant, antique-style restaurant serving everyday Japanese favorites such as *zosui*, rice and fish stew, *ochazuke*, and tea over rice.

Hassan, B1F., Denki Bldg., Roppongi; Tel. (03) 403–9112. Large portions of *shabu-shabu*, *sukiyaki*, *tempura*, tea ceremony cuisine, etc., at reasonable prices.

Inagiku, 4-5 Roppongi 4-chome; Tel. (03) 403–5507. This fine tempura operation's headquarters in Nihombashi is expensive, but this branch is decently priced and of good quality.

Noboritei, 12-6, Shimbashi 1-chome; Tel. (03) 571–0482. A fine place to sample delicious broiled eel.

Inexpensive

Musashino Sobadokoro, 55-11, Nakano 5-chome; Tel. (03) 389–4751. A small buckwheat *soba* (noodles) shop in this west Tokyo suburb, famous for its quality and purity.

● **Otako Honten,** 4-4 Ginza 3-chome; Tel. (03) 561–8246. A delicious place for *oden*—a tasty Japanese stew made of fried and stuffed tofu, vegetables, fish sausage, etc.

Yabu Soba, 10 Kanda Awaji-cho 2-chome; Tel. (03) 251–0287. An excellent, high-quality noodle shop close to the center of town.

Low Budget

Decent and inexpensive food is widely available in Tokyo. Ask around for specialty *tonkatsu-ya*, pork cutlet restaurants, and neighborhood *sushi-ya*, sushi shops, in particular.

British

Inexpensive

The Rising Sun, 9-3 Yotsuya 1-chome. Authentic British pub with Irish landlord that prepares fine shepherd's pie, bangers and mash, fish and chips.

Chinese

Chinese restaurants are plentiful in Tokyo and throughout Japan. The neighborhood ones are the cheapest, though somewhat Japanized. The ones listed below can be quite expensive, but need not be if you choose modest noodle or rice dishes.

Moderate

Fu-Ling, 8-4 Roppongi 4-chome; Tel. (03) 401–9769. A Cantonese restaurant open to 4 A.M.

South China, 35 Jingumae 6-chome, Shibuya-ku; Tel. (03) 400–0031. A large and established Cantonese restaurant with a good reputation.

Tokyo Daihanten, JC Bldg., 17-3 Shinjuku 5-chome; Tel. (03) 202–0121. Huge and splendid Szechuan-style restaurant.

French

On the whole, Tokyo's excellent French restaurants are the places to go for a splurge rather than a cheap meal. The places listed below permit a compromise.

A Tantot, Axis Bldg. 17-1, Roppongi 5-chome; Tel. (03) 586–4431. A stylish restaurant in Tokyo's center of modern design, offering outdoor lunch in fine weather, and at good value for ¥1,800.

●**Bistro 33,** Bell Bldg., 27-1 Nishi-Ikebukuro 3-chome; Tel. (03) 986–7487. Authentic bistro with set lunch priced under ¥1,000.

Chez Figaro, 4-1 Nishi-Azabu 4-chome; Tel. (03) 400–8718. Popular bistro in trendy part of town with lunch priced at about ¥2,000.

Ciao, Akasaka Pine Crest Bldg., 5-27 Akasaka 7-chome; Tel. (03) 586–6971. French cafe in central Tokyo with very reasonably priced spaghetti and other dishes.

German

Moderate

Alte Liebe, 29-8 Minami-Aoyama 2-chome; Tel. (03) 405–8312. German dishes accompanied by live music.

Bel Rudi, 11-45 Akasaka 1-chome; Tel. (03) 586–4572. Cheerful beer-hall atmosphere with live music.

EX German Snack Bar, 7-6 Roppongi 7-chome; Tel. (03) 408–5487. Superb sausages and German beer.

Lohmeyer's. Igami Bldg., 3-14 Ginza 5-chome; Tel. (03) 571–1142. Long-established restaurant near Ginza's Sony Building.

Indian

Moderate

Maharao, Hibiya Mitsui Bldg., 1-2 Yurakucho 1-chome; Tel. (03) 580–6423. Very popular, always crowded. Part of a successful chain.

●**Moti,** Roppongi Hama Bldg., 2-35 Roppongi 6-chome; Tel. (03) 479–1939. Some of the best Indian food in Japan. Two other branches in Akasaka.

Nair's, 10-7 Ginza 3-chome; Tel. (03) 541–8246. A little piece of India; friendly and informal.

Indonesian

Moderate

Bengawan Solo, 18-13 Roppongi 7-chome; Tel. (03) 408–5698. National dishes, strongly spiced.

Sederhana, 5-4, Kami-Osaki 3-chome; Shinagawa-ku; Tel. (03) 473–0354. A rarity in Japan, a true neighborhood ethnic restaurant.

Italian

Moderate

Borsalino, S.K. Heim Bldg., 8-2 Roppongi 6-chome; Tel. (03) 401–7751. Authentic dishes in relaxing atmosphere.

●**Nicola's,** Roppongi Plaza, 12-6 Roppongi 3-chome; Tel. (03) 401–6936. Famous for its 50 varieties of pizza.

Roma Sabatini, Center Bldg., 29-8 Dogenzaka 2-chome; Tel. (03) 461–0495. Copy of the original restaurant in Rome.

Natural Food Restaurants

Moderate

Manna, 16-5, Shinjuku 1-chome; Tel. (03) 344–6606. Established vegetarian restaurant run by Seventh Day Adventists. Brown rice set lunch.

Sasanoyuki, 15-10, Negishi 2-chome, Taito-ku; Tel. (03) 873–1145. Large, accessible restaurant with a vast array of *tofu* dishes.

●**Tenmi,** 10-6 Jinnan 1-chome, Shibuya-ku; Tel. (03) 496–9703. Tokyo's leading natural food restaurant.

Steak and Prime Ribs

Steak is expensive in Japan, but the following restaurants are more reasonable than most.

Moderate

Chaco Atago Ten, MY Bldg., 4-1 Nishi-Shinbashi 3-chome; Tel. (03) 432–4850. Western-style charbroiled steaks.

Colza, Clover Bldg., 15-10 Roppongi 7-chome; Tel. (03) 405–5631. Specializes in *teppanyaki* steak and seafood.

Suehiro, Kintetsu Bldg. 4-10 Ginza 4-chome; Tel. (03) 562–0591. A chain famous for its Kobe steak, with branches in Harajuku, Ikebukuro and Shinjuku.

OTHERS. American fast-food chains are very well established in Tokyo. *McDonald's* leads the field, but *Kentucky Fried Chicken, Wendy's Hamburgers, Arby's Beef Sandwiches, Mister Donut,* and *Baskin-Robbins* are all well represented. Local imitations have sprung up, *Morinaga* and *First Kitchen* among them.

Japanese chain restaurants that sell reasonable and inexpensive food include *Fujiya* and *Coq d'Or.* Most big buildings in central Tokyo have concentrations of cheaper restaurants in their basements. Other good bets are the city's numerous German-style beer halls, including *New Tokyo* at Sukiyabashi and *Lion Beer Hall* in Shinbashi. In locating these and other restaurants, the area maps printed in the monthly *Tokyo Journal* and *Tour Companion* (weekly, free), both available in the bookstores of major hotels, are invaluable.

For breakfast, many coffee shops offer "morning service" *(moningu sabisu).* This means that with morning orders of coffee or tea, something extra, such as a boiled egg and salad or a sandwich, is thrown in for free. Good value.

HOTEL DINING. Although top hotel dining rooms are expensive, their coffee shops fall within the moderate category. *Cycles* at the Imperial and *Humming* in the basement of the Palace are among the popular hotel coffee shops. The Capitol Tokyu, formerly the Tokyo Hilton, offers breakfast and lunch buffets in the cocktail and tea lounge, while the New Otani's Top of the Tower buffet breakfast provide the best view in town.

What to See and Do

Tokyo can well be classified as one of the most exciting cities in the world. It is Japan's capital and largest city. With the country's growing importance on the world scene, everyone and everything comes to Tokyo. That broad statement includes heads of state, top businessmen, the best of the performing artists, scientists, philosophers, and adventurers.

Despite foreign influences, the Japanese have not neglected their own heritage. They may be abreast of the latest technology and they may be leaders in international business or fashion, but somehow they've accepted the new while preserving the old. This is part and parcel of the charm of Tokyo. Even a modern office building housing one of the world's largest business firms will not neglect to have a small shrine on the rooftop.

One of the special joys of Tokyo is the *matsuri,* or neighborhood festival. Check the Teletourist Service at 503–2911 to find out if there is one on during your stay. Pick up the *Tour Companion* for details and location. These shrine festivals have an infectious air. The whole community joins in and they welcome visitors.

MUSEUMS AND GALLERIES. Public museums were unheard of in Japan until the Meiji era and yet the oldest extant museum in the world is in Nara. Shosoin, the treasure house of the Todaiji Temple, holds not only ritual objects once used in the temple, but also the personal possessions of Emperor Shomu (701–756). This collection is still not open to the public per se, but every autumn, when they air and check the contents, some of them are put on display in the **Nara National Museum.**

Japan's other national museum is in Ueno Park in Tokyo, the largest museum in the country. Open 9 A.M.–4:30 P.M. Closed Mon. Admission ¥250, but for some loan exhibits, higher. One unique feature of the **Tokyo National Museum** begs attention of history buffs. The Horiuji, a temple near Nara built by order of Prince Shotoku around 601, presented 319 precious objects from the temple to the Imperial Household in 1878. These have been entrusted to the museum and are housed in a special two-story building, the Horiuji Homotsukan, located just behind the Hyokeikan. This exhibit is open only on Thursdays and if it is rainy or hot and humid, they don't open since the exhibits are quite old and fragile.

Japan systematically grades and categorizes its art objects with ratings such as National Treasure, Important Cultural Properties, and Important Art Objects. This applies not only to museum pieces, but also to many objects found in temples, shrines, and private collections. A few years ago, the tally of the Tokyo

National Museum's works of art hovered near 90,000. Of these, some 84 have been designated National Treasures and 521 are Important Cultural Properties. Understandably, not all are on display at the same time. The museum is actually three buildings. *Hyokeikan* holds archaeological objects. The center building, *Honkan,* has Japanese art, and *Toyokan* is for art of countries outside of Japan.

National Museum of Science, 7-20 Ueno Koen. Open 9 A.M.–4:30 P.M. Closed Mon. and Dec. 28–Jan. 4. Sections on astronomy, botany, geology, zoology, science, and engineering.

National Museum of Western Art, 7-7 Ueno Koen. Open 9 A.M.–4:30 P.M. Closed Mon. Admission ¥250. The collection of Kojiro Matsukata with its Rodin sculptures and impressionistic paintings form the nucleus of the museum. Other important works have been added.

Tokyo Metropolitan Art Museum, 8-36 Ueno Koen. Open 9 A.M.–5 P.M. Closed Mon. Admission free. Displays of the museum's own art and they also rent out galleries for other collections. If they sponsor an exhibit from abroad there is an admission fee.

And that's only in Ueno Park! Japan may have had a late start in establishing museums, but they've made up for lost time. With some 1,560 museums to choose from, we'll offer a limited selection. For information on those not listed, contact TIC.

Asakura Sculpture Gallery, 7-18-10 Yanaka, Taito-ku. Open 10 A.M.–4 P.M. Sat., Sun., and Mon. Closed Tues.–Fri. Admission ¥250. After the death of the sculptor Fumio Asakura, his house and studio were turned into a museum.

Bridgestone Museum of Art, 1-10-1 Kyobashi. Open 10 A.M.–5:30 P.M., but from 11 A.M.–5:45 P.M. on Sat. Closed Mon., and closed Sun. during July and August. Admission ¥400. An excellent collection of Western painting and sculpture by well-known artists.

Eisei Bunko Foundation, 1-1-1 Meijirodai. Open 10 A.M.–4 P.M. Closed Sat., Sun., and holidays, and between exhibits. Admission ¥500 adults; ¥200 university or high-school students; younger students free when accompanied by an adult. The collection is from the Hosogawa family, who had been shogunal deputies. Features Chinese antiquities, Noh robes and masks, tea ceremony utensils, and Japanese paintings.

TEPCO Electric Energy Museum, about a five-minute walk from the Hachiko Plaza of the Shibuya JR or subway station. Open

10:30 A.M.–6:30 P.M. Closed Wed. Admission free. The seven-story building is in the shape of a robot's head. Built by Tokyo Electric Power Company, the exhibits are entertaining as well as educational for both children and adults.

Goto Art Museum, 3-9-25 Kaminoge. Open 9:30 A.M.–4:30 P.M. Closed Mon. Admission ¥550. This collection of Keita Goto, founder of the Tokyo Kyuko railroad company, consists of paintings, ceramics, calligraphy, tea ceremony utensils, etc. It contains four priceless illustrations from the 12th- century Tale of Genji scroll, put on display the first week in May.

Hatakeyama Museum, 2-20-12 Shiroganedai. Open 10 A.M.–5 P.M. spring and summer, and 10 A.M.–4 P.M. for the autumn and winter exhibitions. Closed Mon. and between exhibitions. Admission ¥550. Most exhibits are related to the tea ceremony, but there are also paintings and Noh robes.

Idemitsu Art Gallery, 3-1-1 Marunouchi. Open 10 A.M.–5 P.M. Closed Mon. Admission ¥550. Outstanding Chinese and Japanese ceramics, paintings, and prints.

Japan Folk Crafts Museum, 4-3-33 Komaba. Open 10 A.M.–5 P.M. Closed Mon. Admission ¥700. Here is one museum where the building itself is an expression of *mingei,* a word coined by Yanagi Soetsu meaning "arts of the people." Wonderful textiles, pottery, furniture, and all manner of beautiful, utilitarian folk craft.

Kurita Museum, 2-17-9 Nihombashi Hamacho. Open 10 A.M.–5 P.M. Closed Mon. Admission ¥500. A part of the Hideo Kurita collection of Imari and Nabeshima-ware of the 18th and early 19th centuries.

National Museum of Modern Art, 3 Kitanomaru Koen. Open 10 A.M.–5 P.M. Closed Mon. Admission ¥500. Regular exhibits of famous 20th-century Japanese artists plus frequent loan exhibits of famous Western and Japanese artists.

Crafts Gallery of the National Museum of Modern Art, 1-1 Kitanomaru Koen. Open 10 A.M.–5 P.M. Closed Mon. Admission ¥250 or ¥500 if you also buy your ticket to include the National Museum of Modern Art. They are within walking distance of each other. Fine collection of beautiful utilitarian articles for daily use, textiles, pottery, lacquerware, metal work, etc.

Nezu Institute of Fine Arts, 6-5 Minami Aoyama. Open 9:30 A.M.–4:30 P.M. Closed Mon., the day after a holiday, between exhibits, and the month of August. Admission ¥550. A private gallery with over 7,000 pieces of work representing the finest of Japanese art. In addition they have some Gandhara sculptures and Korean ceramics. The core of the collection is built around that of Kaichiro Nezu, founder of the Tobu Railroad Company. Garden and teahouses on the premises.

SHORT-TERM STUDY. The following classes are available to the casual tourist with time for just a few lessons in Japanese arts or crafts, cooking, etc.

Bonsai Meijuen. Tel. 401–0923. One-month courses in the art of dwarfing trees and plants to miniature size.

Akahori Cooking School. 3-1-40 Mejiro; Tel. 953–2251. Reservations necessary. Classes in either Japanese or Chinese cookery.

Sushi School. Yuuki Bldg. 4th fl.; 3-10-44 Minami Aoyama; tel. 479–1425/6. One-day lessons available. Classes on Thurs. evenings and Sat. mornings.

Ozawa Doll School. In Akasaka; Tel. 408–8232. Traditional doll-making.

Mataro Doll Craft Academy. 5-15-12 Ueno; Tel. 833–9661. Instruction in Kimikomi-type doll-making with themes of Imperial Court and Heian era.

Ikenobo Ikebana College. 2-3 Kanda, Surugadai, near Ochanomizu station; Tel. 292–3071. The oldest flower-arranging school in the area. Reservations required.

Ohara School of Ikebana. 5-7-17 Minami Aoyama; Tel. 499–1200. This school is the originator of *moribana* (flower arrangements in low containers). Reservations required two days in advance.

Sogetsu School. 7-2-21 Akasaka; Tel. 408–1126. Leader of the avant-garde movement in flower arrangements. Reservations must be made by the preceding Mon.

Eishin Kimono Institute. Ikedayama Heights, Rm. 602, 5-22-33 Higashi Gotanda; Tel. 443–8563. Learn how to wear a kimono. Ask for Mrs. Aiko Miura, who speaks English.

Pottery School of Japan. Nippon Togei Club, 1-5 Jingumae, c/o Togo Shrine; Tel. 402–3634. Special class given in English on Tues.

TRAVELING WITH CHILDREN. Children's play parks dot every neighborhood. **Hama Detached Palace Garden,** Hama Rikyu Teien, has large expanses of land for fun and games. Don't be put off by the name **Nature Education Park** (Shizen Kyoikuen), 5-21-5 Shiroganedai—it's not a school but 20 hectares of forest preserve. Paths take visitors through woods, reed plains, and swamps. Open 9 A.M.–3 P.M. Closed Mon. Admission ¥100. Note: Only 300 visitors are allowed at one time.

Akasaka Mitsuke Rowboat Rental, 4-Kioi-cho; Tel. 261–2176. Row around the moat from noon to sunset, or until 10 P.M., May through August. Closed Dec.–Feb. ¥500 per hour or pedal boats ¥600 per 20 minutes.

Himonya Park Row Boating, 6-9 Himonya; Tel. 714–8101. Open from 9 A.M.–4:30 P.M. ¥50 for 30 minutes. Gakugei-Daigaku Station on the Toyoko line.

Meiji Outer Garden Cycling Course, Meiji Jingu Gaien, Kasumigaoka-cho; Tel. 582–3311. Free bikes, no age limits. Open 8 A.M.–4 P.M.

National Children's Castle (Kodomo no Shiro), 5-53-1 Jingumae, Shibuya-ku; Tel. 797–5666. Japan's state-of-the-art tribute to children, commemorating the International Year of the Child, has 14 stories above ground and four levels below. Facilities include the Aoyama Theater and the Aoyama Circular Theater, a sports area, a swimming pool, roof garden play hall, computer playroom, fine arts studio, audiovisual library, music room, child care room, a well-child clinic and more, not to mention restaurants, hotel accommodations and conference halls. Open weekdays 1–5:30 P.M., weekends and holidays 10 A.M.–5:30 P.M., and closed Mon. To date it's the most technically advanced, creatively designed children's center in the world.

Sunshine International Aquarium, 10th and 11th floors, World Import Mart, Sunshine City in Ikebukero; Tel. 989–3466. Women divers feed the fish at 30-minute intervals. Open daily 10 A.M.–5 P.M. As all signs are in Japanese, pick up an English-language pamphlet on entry. Admission fee ¥1,200.

Tama River Cycling Course, 8-13 Naka Rokugo 4-chome; Tel. 731–9388. Free bicycles for adults and children over 10. Open daily 9:30 A.M.–4 P.M.

Tama Zoo (Tama Dobutsu Koen), 300 Hodokubo; Tel. 0425–91–1611. Animals run free, separated from the spectators by a moat. You can ride through the lions' park in a bus. Open 9:30 A.M.–5 P.M. Closed Mon.

Tokyo Disneyland, 1-1 Maihama, Urayasu-shi, Chiba; Tel. 0473–54–0001. A spin-off of the original Disneyland, but with the advantage of more recent technology. A direct shuttle bus from Tokyo Station costs ¥600 one way. Special tickets covering entrance fee and rides range from ¥2,600 to ¥4,500. Open 9 A.M.–10 P.M. in the summer, and 10 A.M.–6 P.M. in the winter.

Tokyo Metropolitan Children's House (Tokyo-To Jido Kaikan), 1-18-24 Shibuya; Tel. 409–6361. A children's center with a theater for performing arts and films, a museum, playroom, and some rides. Open 9 A.M.–4:30 P.M. No fee.

Toshimaen Amusement Park, 3-25-1 Mukoyama; Tel. 990–3131. The oldest amusement park in Tokyo has all of the thrill rides, the tranquility of a Japanese garden, plus seven swimming pools. Several price structures are available such as entry plus pool for adults for ¥3,000 and ¥2,000 for children; entry plus all rides, entry plus seven rides, etc. Open 9 A.M.–5 P.M. and until 9 P.M. July and Aug. From Ikebukero train station, take the Seibu Ikebukuro on track 2. A direct train runs every 15 minutes. Ask a fellow passenger, "Toshimaen yuki?" to be sure it's the right train.

Ueno Zoo Aquarium, Ueno Park; Tel. 828–5171. Over 500 species of fish can be found in this four-story aquarium. As the name implies, the zoo is in Ueno Park. Open 9:30 A.M.–4:30 P.M. Admission fee ¥200.

Yoyogi Park Cycling Course, 2-1 Yoyogi Kamizono; Tel. 469–6081. Free bicycles for children under 15 available for 30-minute rides. Open 9 A.M.–4 P.M. Closed Mon.

ESCORTED TOURS. In the interest of seeing the most in a limited time, many tourists opt for guided tours with an English-speaking guide. Japan Travel Bureau (JTB) *Sunrise Tours* features a Morning Highlight from 9 A.M. to about noon with a visit to Tokyo Tower, the Imperial Palace Plaza, Asakusa Kannon Temple with its store-lined lane, Nakamise, and then on to the Ginza where the tour disbands. The cost is ¥3,000 for adults, children 6–11 ¥1,500.

The JTB one-day tour, 9 A.M.–5 A.M., features the Tokyo Tower, Imperial East Garden, Asakusa Kannon Temple, a Japanese-style barbecue lunch at Chinzanso Garden Restaurant, Tasaki Pearl Gallery, and the Meiji Shrine. The cost is ¥11,000 for adults and ¥9,000 for children 6–11.

The *Japan Gray Line* has an all-day tour from 8:45 A.M. to 5:45 P.M. that takes in the Tokyo Tower, the Imperial East Garden, Asakusa Kannon Temple, lunch at Ginza Kushinobo Restaurant, Imperial Palace Plaza, National Diet Building, Tasaki Pearl

Gallery, Meiji Shrine, NHK Broadcasting Center, and the Ginza shopping center. The cost is ¥8,300 for adults and ¥6,000 for children 6–11.

For reservations and further tour group information call: *Fujita Travel Service* at 573–1417; *Hato Bus* at 435–6081; *Japan Gray Line* at 436–6881 or 433–5745; *Odakyu Travel Service* at 345–1461; *Sunrise Tours* at 276–7777 and/or *Tobu Travel Co. Ltd.* at 281–6622. The area code for Tokyo is 03. If calling from Tokyo, it's not needed.

INDEPENDENT TOURS. Armed with a map and a spirit of adventure, it's possible to strike out on your own. Perhaps something in the introduction caught your fancy. You can always ask directions from the front desk of your hotel; if taking public transportation, it's best not to travel at rush hours, although that's an experience in itself.

The Japan National Tourist Organization is a wonderful help. If you are interested in touring a factory, and often they are willing to accommodate individual tourists, JNTO will give you the names, addresses, and telephone numbers. Another good bet is the *Home Visit*. For a glimpse of typical Japanese home life, drop into the Tokyo Information Center the day prior to the date you'd like to visit and they will make the necessary arrangements. Also, an enterprising gentleman with a tour guide's license offers a daily, personalized Tokyo walking-tour service, area by area exploration, for ¥1,000 per person. Contact Mr. Ota at (0422) 51–7673 after 7 P.M. for information and booking.

The Japan Broadcasting Corporation (NHK) Center is open to the public every weekday between 8:30 A.M. and 6 P.M. It's accessible from Shibuya and Harajuku stations on the green JR Yamanote line, but check your map for the exact location. Reputed to be the world's best, you can see the control rooms, sets, and their large Studio 101. Ask for the *kenga-ku* (visitor's course). It's self-explanatory, but if you're more comfortable with an English-speaking guide, call 465–1111. If your interest in NHK is more than cursory, call 464–0114 or 464–0115 to make special arrangements.

A tour of a Japanese newspaper plant might be of interest. The **Asahi Shimbun** (545–1031) and the **Mainichi Shimbun** (212–0321) arrange guided tours daily. Reservations must be made in advance as groups are limited in size. These enterprises go beyond the publishing of nationally distributed daily morning and evening newspapers—they also publish weeklies, monthlies, and annuals, English-language dailies, magazines, and books. To better cover the news, they have fleets of helicopters, radio, and television networks. In addition, they have other spin-offs such as real estate and tourism agencies and other affiliated companies. Japanese newspaper companies also feel the responsibility of promoting cultural exchanges with other nations and sponsor many in the area of art, sports, education, health, and welfare programs. If you make your reservations to tour the plant well in advance, English-speaking guides are available.

The Tokai Steamship Company operates a two-hour cruise in Tokyo Bay from July 1st through August 31st. It's a floating beer hall with variety shows. The ship leaves Takeshiba Pier at 7 P.M. The cost is ¥3,300 for adults and ¥1,000 for children.

For a different boating experience, try *yakatafune,* river boats. In the traditional Edo style, the cabin is tatami-covered. Slip out of your shoes and sit on the tatami in front of a low table and cruise along the Sumida River just as the samurai did. Tempura is served in generous portions along with sake and beer. The cost is about ¥5,000 per person. Usually a group of friends will hire the boat, but call Amisei K.K. at 844–1869 for the possibilities. The boarding pier is at Asakusa, a few steps from the Ginza subway line's Asakusa's Station.

The Diet Building is interesting, but with new security regulations, it's necessary for you to apply to your embassy and then await permission to enter. Alternatively, you can visit the **Parliamentary Museum** any day except Sun. 9:30 A.M.–3:30 P.M., admission free. A large-scale model of the Diet Building is equipped with an audio/color slide system operated by push buttons. Pictures are flashed on the screen with a simultaneous English-language narration giving the history of the Parliamentary system in Japan.

The State Guest House, the former Akasaka Detached Palace, is not open to the public, but is worth looking at from the street. Built in 1909 as the residence of the then Crown Prince, it is a Japanese version of Buckingham Palace, or perhaps Versailles. This was the site of the 1980 Summit Meeting. It's near Yotsuya Station.

PANORAMIC VIEWS. A number of the larger hotels have top-floor lounges or restaurants with panoramic views. Many high-rise buildings have viewing platforms and charge admission fees.

The Kasumigaseki Building near Toranomon Station on the Ginza line overlooks the Palace Plaza. Open 10 A.M.–9:30 P.M., admission fee ¥400.

The World Trade Center Building across from the JR Hamamatsucho Station has a view of Tokyo Bay. Open 10 A.M.–9:30 P.M.

Tokyo Tower, built so it was one foot taller than the Eiffel Tower, is open 9 A.M.–6 P.M., admission fee ¥950.

On the west side of Shinjuku visit the 51st floor of the **Sumitomo Building** or the **NS (North South) Building's** top floors for a glorious view of the city with Mt. Fuji in the background, free of charge.

CONVERSATIONAL LOUNGES. If you're interested in meeting Japanese in an informal, friendly atmosphere, these lounges are the answer. Usually they are tea or coffee shops, and foreigners are either admitted free or charged a minimum fee. The Japanese pay a higher fee.

Comm'inn, 5th Fl Arai Bldg., 1-3 Minami Ebisu; Tel. 710–7163. Foreigners ¥350.

The Corn Popper International, a three-minute walk from Ebisu Station; Tel. 715–4473. Foreigners ¥350. Free coffee, tea, and popcorn. Open daily 5 P.M.–midnight, and on weekends from 1 P.M.–midnight. Paperback-book-exchange shelf, laser disc movies, darts, and other attractions.

BATHHOUSES. There was a time when the local bathhouse was the social center for the Japanese. Although most residences today have private bath facilities, some 2,200 bathhouses are still left in Tokyo. Most can be found in the older neighborhoods, and can be identified by their tall smoke stacks. The fee is ¥270. Remember, in the Japanese bath, you wash first before entering the communal tub. The faucets are found on the lower wall with low stools and portable wash basins. In most places you must bring your own towel, soap, and shampoo. A *sento* is the public bathhouse, an *onsen* is where the water is from a hot spring. You might ask at your lodging if there is a neighborhood sento.

Asakusa Kannon Onsen, 2-7-26 Asakusa; Tel. 844–4141. Experience the classic Japanese hot spring bath. Open daily 6 A.M.–6 P.M. Fee ¥400.

Tsubame-yu, 3-14-5 Ueno; Tel. 831–7305. Open Tues.–Sun., 6 A.M.–11 P.M. Closed Mon. Regular sento, ¥270.

Ginza-yu, 1-12-2 Ginza; Tel. 561–2550. Open Mon.–Sat. Closed Sun.

SAUNAS. Saunas are popular in Japan. They are more expensive than the bath, but they generally supply towels, soap, hair dryers, etc. Massages are usually available at additional cost.

Akasaka Tokyu Sauna, 4th floor, Akasaka Tokyu Plaza, 2-14-3 Nagatacho; Tel. 580–2311. Men only. Mon.–Sat. 11 A.M.–10:30 P.M.; Sun. and national holidays, 11 A.M.–9:30 P.M. Sauna ¥2,700, massage, ¥5,300 for 30 minutes, ¥7,900 for one hour.

Do Sports Plaza Bl, Sumitomo Building, 2-1-6 Nishi Shinjuku; Tel. 344–1968. Open daily 10 A.M.–10:30 P.M. Closed Aug. and Dec. 31–Jan. 1. Sauna ¥2,500. Massage, ¥3,300 for 40 minutes.

Gaien, 4-23-6 Sendagaya; Tel. 403–3264 for men, and 403–8565 for women. Open 10 A.M.–11:30 P.M. Closed Jan. 1–3. Sauna, ¥1,800. Massage, ¥2,500 for 35 minutes, ¥4,700 for 1 hour.

Isetan Ladies Sauna, Isetan Kaikan Building, 3-15-7 Shinjuku; Tel. 356–2734. Open 10 A.M.–8 P.M. Closed Wed. Sauna, ¥2,800, but if entering after 6 P.M., Mon.–Fri., ¥1,800.

SHOPPING. A trip to a Japanese department store is just different enough to be a memorable experience even if you don't love to shop. If you arrive when the store opens, you will be personally welcomed by the managers and the clerks, bowing and bidding you good morning. Throughout the day, young uniformed women, positioned at the escalators, welcome each customer.

Many of the department stores are owned by railroad companies and are strategically placed at large stations. In the basement you'll always find a food market to accommodate commuters. Their deli counters feature whole roasted chickens, salads, and other prepared foods and offer interesting possibilities. Samples are usually given out for the adventurous. You'll also find reasonably priced restaurants in these stores, often on the top floor.

The larger department stores also act as cultural centers with galleries of their own in addition to art collections and other exhibitions from abroad. Many have facilities to keep the shoppers' children amused. Most all have a shoe repair shop, usually in the basement.

Most department stores are open from 10 A.M. to 6 P.M.

They close on different days so you'll always find some stores open in the center of the city. Check at the information counter for an English store map. If you'd like an English-speaking guide, inquire at the information desk. Some of the leading department stores are: **Daimaru,** above Tokyo Station; **Mitsukoshi's** main store, **Takashimaya** and **Tokyu** in Nihombashi; **Hankyu, Matsuya, Matsuzakaya, Mitsukoshi, Printemps,** and **Seibu,** in Ginza; Tokyu main store, in Shibuya; and in Ikebukuro Isetan, **Odakyu, Seibu, and Tobu.**

Tokyo has a few discount stores that cater to the residents. They carry furniture, clothing, appliances, and a wide variety of useful merchandise for everyday domestic life. There just might be something of interest to a visitor in one of the following: **Kobutsu No Daimaru,** 19-17 Maruyamacho, tel. 462–0781; **Kimuraya,** 2-1 Surugadai, Kanda, tel. 294–7531; **Sampei Store,** 3-22-14 Shinjuku, tel. 352–1634, and **Tokyo Hyakka Funabashiya,** 1-17-8 Midori, tel. 634–4541.

Prices are fixed in Japan, but there are still a few places where you can bargain, such as Tax-free centers. Give it a try. Be sure to have your passport with you to take advantage of the tax saving. **The Amita Japan Taxfree Center** (JTC) near Kamiyacho subway stop on the Hibiya line has seven floors of Japanese merchandise. On a smaller scale there is **George Silk** near the Akasakamitsuke subway station. It's a little shop, but packed with goodies.

Some of the major stations have underground shopping malls. Try the maze under Shinjuku Station; you'll also find plenty of reasonable restaurants in the complex. And too, because land is scarce and pricey, buildings often house a number of individually owned shops. There's the **Alpha** fashion building in Ikebukuro's Sunshine City; **Tokyu Hands,** an emporium for do-it-yourself fans that has a wealth of merchandise for crafts and hobbies; **From 1st** in Minami Aoyama has boutiques and restaurants; **Bell Commons** in Kita Aoyama has boutiques and a health club on the top floor; **La Foret** in Harajuku is filled with trendy boutiques; **Parco** in Shibuya has three separate buildings: Parco 1 for inexpensive boutiques, Parco 2 for Japanese designer boutiques, and Parco 3 for interior furnishings.

Japanese folk crafts are unique and worth checking out. You'll find a number of shops around the city carrying such items, but to give you a working list: **Crafts Center,** 2d fl. Plaza 246, 3-1-1 Minami Aoyama, tel. 403–2460; **Ishizuka,** 1-5-20 Yaesu; tel.

275–2991; **Kyoto Center,** 1st fl. Kyoto Shimbun Ginza Bldg.
8-2-8 Ginza; tel. 572–6484; and **Oriental Bazaar,** 5-9-13
Jingumae; tel. 400–3933.

There are shops tucked everywhere throughout Tokyo. The
International Arcade, utilizing space under the tracks near the
Imperial Hotel, is a discount center housing individually owned
shops. A few steps away is the other end of the spectrum—the
Imperial Hotel's plush arcade of shops such as **Cartier, Gucci,**
etc. Many other hotels have shopping arcades as well. There are
tiny stalls and shops, remnants of Tokyo's black market days, in
Ameyoko, the district along the tracks between Ueno and
Okachimachi. They've tried to herd these small establishments into
a building, but many cling to their right to hawk on the street,
adding color to the neighborhood.

Antiques

The antique buff will be delighted with the range of antiques in
Tokyo. In fact, such items make marvelous souvenirs, bringing the
country and its culture to life.

Japan doesn't offer too much in the way of furniture. The
lifestyle precludes much that the Westerner thinks essential.
Storage space, however, is essential the world over. *Tansu* (chests)
are Japan's elegant answer to the problem. Beautifully made and
decorated with wrought metal, they come in all shapes and sizes.
Most were custom made: chests to be carried by two porters for the
bride; water-tight chests for the sea captain; staircase chests that
actually were the staircase, kitchen chests, etc. Unless you're
traveling by ship, transportation could equal the price of the chest.
But you may comfort yourself with the thought that a good antique
only increases in value.

Panel screens were used for privacy and to keep drafts at bay. In
the past, those with a great show of gold foil were designed to
reflect light in dark houses or castles. Today they are often hung on
the wall as large paintings. Japanese ceramics, whether blue and
white Imari, elaborately decorated Kutani or the strikingly bold
Nabeshima, are wonderful finds. Prices range from a few hundred
yen for a sake cup to a sizeable fortune. Lacquerware, *netsuke* (the
carved toggles attached to an item tucked into the obi), statues,
textiles, and a number of other exotic articles make exciting
purchases. Most antique dealers are in the business because they
love their merchandise, and they are quite willing to give you
background information on a piece.

The following shops all have English-speaking staffs.

Curios Fuso, 1st fl. Akasaka New Plaza, 7-6-47 Akasaka; Tel. 583–6945. Open Mon.–Sat. 10 A.M.–6 P.M.

Edo Antiques, 2-21-12 Akasaka; Tel. 584–5280. Open Mon.–Sat. 10 A.M.–6 P.M.

The Gallery, 1-11-6 Akasaka; Tel. 585–5019. Behind the American Embassy. Open 10 A.M.–6 P.M. Mon.–Sat., 11 A.M.–4 P.M. on holidays. Closed Sun.

Cameras

Cameras are a particularly good buy in Japan. The quality is excellent and the price range is wide. Camera shops can be found all over the city, but Shinjuku has the best prices. Check to see if the shops have a duty-free section and show your passport for additional savings beyond the discount prices.

Bic Camera, 1-11-7 Higashi Ikebukuro; Tel. 988–0002. Open 10 A.M.–8 P.M. daily.

Doi Camera, 1-18-27 Nishi Shinjuku; Tel. 348–2241. Open 10 A.M.–9 P.M. daily. Year-round discounts with seasonal specials.

Sakuraya Camera, 3-17-2 Shinjuku; Tel. 354–3636. Open 10 A.M.–8 P.M. daily. Year-round discounts, but special bargains in Feb.

Yodobashi Camera, 1-11-1 Nishi Shinjuku; Tel. 346–1010. Open 9:30 A.M.–8:30 P.M. daily. The largest camera shop in the world. Discounts up to 50 percent.

Doi, Sakuraya and Yodobashi all have branch stores on both sides of Shinjuku Station.

Akasaka Camera, 3-1-1 Akasaka; Tel. 585–6284 or 585–8736. Open 8 A.M.–8 P.M. every day except Sun. 10 A.M.–5 P.M.

Ginza Orient, 8-9-13 Ginza; Tel. 574–6121/2. Open 10 A.M.–7 P.M. Mon.–Sat., 11 A.M.–6 P.M. Sun.

Kimura Camera, 1-18-8 Nishi Ikebukuro; Tel. 981–8437. Open 8 A.M.–8 P.M. daily. Specializes in secondhand cameras.

Telescopes, opera glasses, microscopes, and lenses are all good buys and are all on the tax-free list for tourists. You'll have to show your passport to take advantage of the tax-free price.

Cloisonné, Coral, and Damascene

Shippo, as cloisonné is called in Japan, means seven precious stones. When you see the glowing colors, you'll understand why.

Cloisonné is made by putting enamel glass on a metal base, firing it at a high temperature and then polishing it to a high gloss. The art came to Japan from China via Korea in the 6th century. Since then, they've expanded the color palette and developed new techniques. Accessories, vases, trays, pictures, and covered containers all make lasting souvenirs.

Aoki, known internationally for its top-quality enamel pigments has a Ginza shop as an outlet for top artists and artisans in the field. Their selection for unique, one-of-a-kind pieces can't be topped. The shop is in the Asahi Bldg., 6-6-7 Ginza; Tel. 571–2255. Open 11 A.M.–7 P.M. Closed Sun. and holidays. *Ando* at 5-6-2 Ginza, tel. 572–2261 also has a large selection of quality cloisonné.

Damascene is decorated metal with inlays usually of gold or silver. Many attractive accessories are made of damascene and the price is quite reasonable. Coral, mostly from Okinawa, has become quite fashionable recently, partially because it combines so prettily with pearls. Both damascene and coral can be found in the **Amita Japan Taxfree Center,** 5-8-6 Toranomon; Tel. 432–4351. Also carried in other stores catering to the tourist.

Dolls

Japanese dolls are not used for playing as they are in Western countries. They convey a religious and talismanic message to the Japanese adult and child that the outsider cannot fathom. Elaborately robed and accessorized, the figures depict legendary or historic characters. They are treasured and kept in glass cases.

On Hina Matsuri, the third day of the third month, *Hina* dolls, which represent the Emperor, the Empress, and their court, are on display with miniature lacquer furnishings. These sets are handed down from mother to daughter. They are meant to be admired, and to instill respect for the hereditary institution and customs.

Kokeshi dolls, basically a cylindrical piece of wood topped with a round head, are more of an abstract doll, and are popular souvenirs. *Haniwa,* the clay figures modeled after those which surrounded the gravesites of the ancient nobility, still retain an air of mystery suggestive of magical powers.

You'll find other types of Japanese dolls, but don't expect a cuddly baby doll. Department stores have a good selection as does the **Amita Japan Taxfree Center** at Kamiyacho. They're also available in arcades.

Electric Appliances and Electronics

The development of the integrated circuit revolutionized the electronic industry. Audio/video components were brought down to size without sacrificing professional performance and tourists are zeroing in on these small marvels to tuck into their carry-on luggage. There are stereo cassettes the size of a cassette tape, a CD player that can fit in your hand, or a TV set you can put into your pocket.

Akihabara, Japan's largest wholesale/retail electronic market-place, is also the largest discount center. Discounted prices do not mean inferior merchandise here. They are top-quality bargains. You'll find all of the known brands accompanied by a guarantee. With over 600 stores and stalls operating in the neighborhood and all of the major manufacturers involved, competition is stiff. In this fast-paced industry, new models are continuously introduced and you can find the previous models reduced as much as 35 percent, a savings well worth consideration. Some of the smaller shops, eliminating the costly overhead, offer even better prices. Communication may be a problem here. Head for a place that has a duty-free center to find an English-speaking clerk. Bring your passport to cash in on the tax saving.

To reach Akihabara, take the JR Yamanote green train or the blue Keihin Tohoku line to Akihabara. It's right there. Most places are open 10 A.M.–7 P.M. Some of the shops in Akihabara with duty-free centers are: **Hirose,** 1-12-1 Soto Kanda, tel. 255–5931; **LAOX,** 1-2-9 Soto Kanda; tel. 255–9041; **Nishikawa Musen,** 1-15-6 Soto Kanda, tel. 253–4787/8; **Minami Denki Kan,** 4-3-3 Soto Kanda, tel. 255–8030; **Yamagiwa,** 3-13-10 Soto Kanda, tel. 253–4311; and **Yamamoto,** 1-15-15 Soto Kanda; tel. 255–0814.

Outside of Akihabara, try the **Amita Japan Taxfree Center** at Kamiyacho. They have one floor for electronics. Also check **Sundry** in the International Arcade, 1-7-23 Uchisaiwaicho; Tel. 591–8668. Across the street is the **Nishi Ginza Arcade,** 2-1-1 Kyodaku Yurakucho, which has five more electronic shops. All are tax free and willing to give a rock-bottom price.

Kimono and Traditional Clothing

Japanese *kimono* make beautiful gifts for both men and women. However, the price tag can run into millions of yen. The style of kimono has changed little with the years; the difference is based on the fabric and design. They are one-of-a-kind and take from one to two years to make. The construction itself is relatively simple. A bolt of kimono fabric measures 14 inches wide and 12 yards long. Regardless of the wearer's size, the fabric is cut in eight pieces leaving no material left over. The seams are all hand sewn. For cleaning, it is dismantled and then reassembled. The garment is wrapped around the body and held in place with a sash *(obi)*. The obi is usually elaborate and can equal the cost of the kimono.

Recognizing that tourists rarely indulge in the expense of a kimono, the industry has adapted. Kimono for tourists now come in washable materials with brightly colored patterns and obis. *Tabi,* the split-toed socks, and *zori,* the thonged sandal, are also available in Western sizes. If you are interested in buying, try the **Oriental Bazaar,** 5-9-13 Jingumae, tel. 400–3933; **Amita Japan Taxfree Center,** 5-8-6 Toranomon; tel. 432–4351; **K. Hayashi** in the International Arcade, 1-7-23 Uchisaiwaicho; tel. 591–9826; and **George Silk,** 2-12-8 Nagatacho, tel. 580–5350.

Used kimono sell for a fraction of the cost. Many take the kimono apart and fashion Western clothes out of the fabric. The obi is pressed into use as a table runner, cut into place-mat sizes, made into pillows and other ingenious items for today's lifestyle. The *uchikaki,* or wedding robe, makes a striking wall hanging. And the men's black silk formal kimono make super dressing gowns. **K. Hayashi** has a great selection and **Oriental Bazaar** also has them. **Takashimaya** and **Daimaru** department stores have biannual sales of their rental wedding finery in March and September.

Happi coats, originally hip-length dark blue cotton jacket worn by firemen, carpenters, and other workmen, are worn at matsuri (festival) time by the people carrying the portable shrine. These too have been "foreignized" and today come in a whole range of colors in practical wash and wear, also in thigh length. They make great beach coats and they are good to wear over jeans. Available in tourist shops.

Yukata is a summer kimono made of cotton, traditionally blue and white. It also serves as night wear and you'll find it for your convenience in most Japanese hotels. Yukata is very popular and is sold all over town in the summer months. Be careful about size though, these are made for Japanese. Yukata made in Western sizes are available in some department stores and in stores catering to tourists year-round. They're inexpensive and make great gifts to bring back home.

Furoshiki is a large square of fabric, traditionally silk or cotton, but today often of synthetic material. The Japanese still use them for carrying parcels, foreigners use them for scarves, blouses, etc. The colors and designs are intriguing. Inexpensive and lightweight, they make good gifts. Anyplace that sells kimono sells furoshiki.

Bangasa is the Japanese oiled paper and bamboo umbrella. These are not only fun to have, but are also small works of art. In addition to the size that's used for protection from rain or snow, there's a super size that is used in outdoor tea ceremonies that makes an exotic garden umbrella. Prices start at ¥2,500. Available at most folk craft stores, the folk craft section of department stores, and at specialty shops. **Idaya,** 1-31-1 Asakusa, tel. 841–3644 always has bangasa in stock, and **Hasegawa Hakimonoten,** 2-4-4 Ueno, tel. 831–3933, usually has them.

Lacquer

Japanese lacquer is the finest in the world. The sap of the deciduous tree *Rhus verniciflus* is used as a protective coating on wooden objects. Layer after layer must be meticulously applied; the process is not only time-consuming, but hazardous. If the lacquer touches the skin, a painful rash results. Finally the lacquer is buffed to a high luster. When gold or silver particles are applied in intricate design, it is called *maki-e*.

Many articles are made of lacquer, such as covered soup bowls, trays of all sizes, stationery boxes, or boxes of any size or shape. Anything from a pair of chopsticks to a large piece of furniture can be lacquered. Antique stores often have fine old pieces of lacquerware. Also check department stores, craft centers, **Oriental Bazaar, JTC,** and **Inachu** 1-5-2 Akasaka, tel. 582–4451.

Paper and Paper Products

Japanese paper *(washi)* is something special—so special that Rembrandt used it. Washi is handmade; the long fibers beneath the bark are pounded and steamed, but remain uncut. Because it is porous, it takes well to dye, and brilliant colors are possible. The craftsmen are innovative in design and use, and washi makes a wonderful gift. It is used for mobiles, desk accessories, paper wallets, and lanterns.

If you'd like to see the centuries-old practice of paper making, take the Tojo line from Ikebukuro Station to Ogawa-machi. In about an hour and 15 minutes, you'll be in the center of a country town where literally hundreds of families make paper. They are very friendly and welcome visitors. You might want to visit the Oji

Paper Museum in the northern part of Tokyo. Once the site of Japan's first Western paper mill (1875), Oji pays homage to the art of Japanese paper making with a museum that has an impressive array of exhibits and a film on the process of making washi. The museum is open 9:30 A.M.–4:30 P.M., closed Mon.

Folk craft shops, department stores, and all of the stores catering to tourists have a selection of items made of washi. **Washikobo,** 1-8 Nishi Azabu, near Roppongi Station, deals exclusively in washi and has a wonderful selection of this highly developed traditional art. **Haibara Company,** 2-7-6 Nihonbashi, tel. 272–3801 has a wealth of handmade papers, wallpaper, cards, fans, etc. and has been in business since 1803. **Isetatsu** has branches at 2-18-9 Yanaka, tel. 823–1453 and in the Soft Town Aoyama Bldg., 3-1-24 Jingumae, tel. 497–5305.

Ceramics

Pottery shards found in Japan have been dated some ten thousand years old. With a history like that you can well imagine that Japanese ceramics are something special. You won't be disappointed.

Shopping for tableware is an adventure. Japanese sets come in five—soup bowls may be one shape, the rice bowl another, the fish dish yet another, and each in different design. The Japanese do not like all the pieces to be the same and the dishes themselves assume more importance in Japan than they do in the West.

The department stores are great for browsing. You'll find Western and Japanese ware in both pottery and porcelain. You will also find shops in every neighborhood including antique stores. Hotel arcades usually have tableware shops. Check the **Fujiou and Toyo Porcelain** in the Imperial Hotel Arcade and **Goto Trading Co.** in the Tokyo Hilton and the **Noritake** shop in the Hotel New Otani. Also try **Koshida Satsumaya** in Sukiyabashi Shopping Center, 5-4 Nishi Ginza, **Shimura's** at 6-3-2 Jingumae, and **Tachikichi** at 5-5-8 Ginza. Don't neglect the folk craft shops and those catering to tourists. You'll have no problem finding excellent shops. If you are really feeling adventurous, you might wish to explore the wholesale districts of Tsukiji on the Hibiya subway line, and Tawaramachi on the Asakusa subway line.

Provincial Specialties

Each of Japan's 39 prefectures have folk craft unique to the area. It's rare that anyone has the time to visit every one, but they are all represented in Tokyo. Twelve of the prefectures exhibit on the 9th floor of the Daimaru department store. You can enter at the Tokyo Station, Yaesu side. The rest of the prefectures have their showrooms in the Kokusai Kanko Building just outside the Yaesu exit. If the particular item you fancy is not for sale, the staff can tell you where you can buy it.

Textiles

Japan has a wonderful array of fine fabrics of excellent quality, but there are few cheap buys. However, the wholesale fabric district centers around Nippori Station on the JR Yamanote line and some of the shops there do sell retail.

Silk kimono fabric is exquisite, but remember it comes only in 12-yard lengths a scant 14 inches wide. It is possible to make Western wear out of it, but it takes some skill and ingenuity. Yukata fabric, in a galaxy of designs, basically blue and white cotton, comes the same way. The kimono section in department stores carries these fabrics. Every neighborhood in the city has a kimono shop with roll after roll of intriguing fabrics. An interesting shop, **Blue and White**, 2-9-2 Azabu Juban; tel. 451–0537, has fascinating items made for the most part of yukata material and also sells it by the meter. Another shop in Roppongi, **Tomoya,** tel. 479–1176 (call for directions to the shop) has clothing fashioned of kimono and yukata fabrics and also sells it by the meter.

Handwoven material colored with natural dyes has an undeniable charm and is durable. Many of the pieces are an artistic statement and are used as hangings, others are sturdy enough for upholstery, but the majority come by the meter for apparel. **Shibui Fabrics,** Nishii-so 1-1, 1-49-10 Ohara, tel. 485–0275, has yardage of authentic tsumugi, shijira, kasuri, and other traditional Japanese material. Custom-order designs are also available. Call first, as the showroom is by appointment only.

Japan Folk Crafts Museum (Nihon Mingeikan) 4-3-33 Komaba; Tel. 467–4527. Closed during Jan. and Feb. It's a fascinating museum and they have a small shop on the first floor with traditional handwoven material for sale. Natural dyes, mostly indigo.

Kanebo, Ginza Cygnas, 5-3-3 Ginza; Tel. 564–5281. Silks in standard widths.

Kinkado, 1-24-5 Minami Ikebukuro; Tel. 971–1211.

Nuno Functional Textile Shop, Axis Bldg. Bl, 5-17-1 Roppongi; unusual textures in mostly natural, neutral tones.

Tokyu Hands, 12-18 Udagwacho in Shibuya; Tel. 476–5461. A do-it-yourself store with a large selection of fabrics. Tokyu Hands also has a store in Ikebukuro near Sunshine City.

Wacoal Fabric House, 1st fl. Shibuya Parco Bldg. Part 1; Tel. 496–9516. Upholstery and drapery fabrics.

Toys

Department stores all have large sections devoted to toys. Folk craft shops are also a good source, but you may find today's children too sophisticated for the simple toys of yesterday. Japan's largest toy store is **Hakuhinkan,** 8-8-11 Ginza; tel. 571–8008. In Harajuku, **Kiddyland,** 6-1-9 Jingumae, tel. 409–3431, also has a great selection. For the electric train buff, department stores carry HO gauge equipment as does the hobby shop **Tenshodo,** 4-3-9 Ginza; tel. 562–0021. Hobby and craft stores offer other possibilities for youngsters. Check out **Aile Ken** 4, 5-10-22 Roppongi; tel. 402–0004 or 403–0004; **Hobby Sakura,** 1-13-13 Jingumae, tel. 470–6588; **Joy Plaza,** 3-16-14 Sotokanda; tel. 251–1154; and **R/C Model Shop Asami,** Yamada Bldg. 4th fl, 4-4-2 Sotokanda; tel. 251–4051.

Watches

Japan gives Swiss watches a run for the money. They're all of top quality and range from inexpensive to pricey designer models. **Seiko** and **Citizen** are the leading manufacturers, but by no means the only ones in the field. You'll find them in every department store, arcade, duty-free center and discount store.

Woodblock Prints

Japan has been a recognized leader in the field of graphic art since early traders brought woodblock prints to Paris, the 19th-century world's art center. At first they were used as wrapping for ceramics—it made perfect packing material for pieces that were shipped abroad. Nevertheless, they were quickly identified by the knowledgeable as an exciting artistic endeavor.

Some of the prints from the old Japanese masters are around, but mainly as collector's items since the price is prohibitive. However, many good reproductions are available. Contemporary Japanese prints represent modernity while embodying an exquisite sense of traditional sensitivity. They're always a good buy and can be easily transported. Better yet, they can be safely rolled in a postage tube and mailed.

In addition to woodblock prints, there's a whole range of

printing processes practiced in the media: metalcut, linocut, stonecut, collagraph, etching, engraving, dry point, mezzotint, aquatint, lithograph, mimeograph, silk screen, serigraph, and combinations of these processes.

Graphics are easy to find. Almost all of the hotel arcades have a shop specializing in them; tourist centers also have stacks to choose from. Many antique shops will have a selection. Some shops worth visiting are: **S. Watanabe Wood Cut Color Print,** 8-6-19 Ginza, tel. 571–4684; **Yoseido Gallery,** 5-5-15 Ginza, tel. 571–1312 or 571–2471; **Matsushita Associates,** 6-3-12 Minami Aoyama, tel. 407–4966; and **Sakai Kokodo Gallery,** 1-2-14 Yurakucho, tel. 591–4678 for traditional and modern originals and reproductions. For original contemporary prints, the Tolman Collection in a former geisha house, 2-2-18 Shiba Daimon, tel. 434–1300, is worth a visit.

SPORTS. Popular sports in Japan range from the traditional sumo (Japanese wrestling), kendo (Japanese fencing), judo and karate to imported baseball, soccer, rugby, tennis, golf, volleyball, bowling, and other sports. Tickets are not always available for the professional games as companies often buy large blocks to entertain customers, but it's worth checking.

Sumo. This indigenous sport, full of pageantry, has been a favorite for centuries. Two grossly overweight opponents, topknotted and stripped except for a silk loincloth, face each other in a 4.5-meter dirt ring. The first to push, trip, throw, or lift his adversary out of the ring is the winner. Wrestlers are matched despite weight differences. Currently the heaviest weighs in at 510 pounds, with the lightest at about 245. It's quite a show—the prematch rituals take longer than the actual match. The wrestlers rinse their mouths to purify themselves and then toss salt into the ring to purify it. They glare at each other from a crouching position and stomp the ground ferociously. Presiding over the bout is a referee garbed in gorgeous traditional attire. Sumo is televised nationally and is followed avidly by men and women, Japanese and foreign residents alike. Six 15-day tournaments are held annually, three in Tokyo (January, May, and September) at the Kuramae Kokugikan, 1-3-28 Sumidaka Yokoami, near Ryogogu Sobu line station. For booking call 622–1100.

Judo, karate, and **aikido dojos** are everywhere in Tokyo. These traditional martial arts are not only physical sports, but treated as a spiritual discipline. You can watch judo practice

sessions at *Budokan,* 2-3 Kitanomaru Koen, tel. 216–1781, where
the Olympic judo events were held. Judo can also be seen at
Kodokan Judo Hall at 1-16 Kasugacho, tel. 811–7151. Watch
karate at the *Japan Karate Association* at 1-6-1 Ebisu Nishi, tel.
462–1415. *Aikido World Headquarters* is in Shinjuku-ku, 102
Wakamatsu cho, tel. 203–9236. Lessons in **T'ai Chi,** the Chinese
exercise, are available in Tokyo at the *YMCA Athletic Gymnasium*
in Kanda.

Baseball is practically a year-round sport in Japan. The 12 pro
teams are divided in two major leagues. Franchised teams in Tokyo
include the *Yomiuri Giants* (the most popular team in Japan) of the
Central League and the *Nippon Ham Fighters* of the Pacific
League. Both share Korakuen Stadium. There's also the *Pacific
League Yakult Swallows* who play at Meiji Jingu Stadium. The
seven-month pennant race culminates in October when the two
league champion teams clash in the Japan Series. Baseball receives
great TV coverage, and not just of the major leagues. The All
Japan High School Tournament has one of the highest, if not the
highest, TV ratings in the nation.

You'll find many public **swimming** pools in Tokyo, both
outdoor and indoor. Check the English Telephone Directory under
Stadiums and Swimming Pools. You'll find the facilities available
in each ku (ward) with addresses and telephone numbers. These
are all at minimal cost. Tennis courts are also listed in this
category.

Hikers can trek down the historic Tokaido, the artery that
connected Edo with the shogunal court and Kyoto, seat of the
Imperial court. The 438-mile section between Tokyo and Osaka
has been developed as a nature trail with government-subsidized
lodges and campsites along the way to provide overnight accommodations.

A **cycling** route has been laid out that extends the 975-mile
stretch from Boso Peninsula east of Tokyo to Wakayama south of
Osaka. If you are interested and want to rent a bicycle, call the
Bicycle PR Center at 586–0404. They speak English.

Tennis has become very popular in Japan since, some years
ago, the Crown Prince had an *omiyai* (arranged meeting) with
Michiko Shoda on a tennis court in Karuizawa. Soon after, they
became engaged and were wed. Today there are 500 tennis courts
in Karuizawa. Not everyone has found a handsome prince, but it
certainly popularized the game. It is hard to get on public courts.

Reservations may take months in Tokyo and it's expensive. It is possible to book courts the same day during weekdays at the Shinagawa Prince Hotel. From 6 A.M. to 6 P.M. it's ¥7,000 an hour, minimum.

Golf is in the same category. Reservations must be made one to two months in advance, fees are high and credit cards are not accepted.

Check with the Tourist Information Center on **fishing** facilities near Tokyo.

Entertainment and Nightlife

For a city that has long had a reputation for sin and gaiety, Tokyo closes up surprisingly early. This is a crucial fact to bear in mind when planning a night out. With the last subways leaving at midnight, and the last surface trains around half an hour later, Tokyo is all but dead by midnight. That doesn't mean, however, that there isn't plenty to see and do before the clock strikes twelve.

The first thing any visitor should do in Tokyo at night is walk through one or more of its busy sections, such as Shibuya, Akasaka, or Roppongi. Probably no city in the world presents such an air of vitality between the hours of 6 and 11 P.M. Certainly no other city has Tokyo's combination of Oriental color and Western sophistication.

THEATER AND MUSIC. Japan has a rich and ancient theater tradition and no visit to Tokyo is complete without a visit to the **Kabuki.** The principal theaters—the *Kabuki-za,* the *Shimbashi Embujo,* and the *Meiji-za*—are modern structures occupying a position in Tokyo akin to that of opera houses in a European city.

A Kabuki program is a long drawn-out affair running from about 11 A.M. to 10 P.M., with intervals for meals and snacks in the numerous restaurants inside the theaters. But very few people attend a full program from beginning to end. Japanese Kabuki lovers will often select just one celebrated act of a famous play and drop in for an hour to see how their favorite actor performs the leading role. All major troupes provide some kind of English synopsis of the play's action.

Even older than Kabuki is **Noh,** a highly formalized dance drama with strong Buddhist underpinnings. Many foreign visitors find it dauntingly esoteric, but it has a timeless dignity that can be fascinating. An example of the city's best Noh theaters is the *Suidobashi Noh Gaku-do.*

Many successful Broadway or West End musicals come to Tokyo (in Japanese versions with Japanese cast) soon after their first run. *The Fiddler on the Roof* and *Cats* are two shows that have enjoyed outstanding success.

The Takarazuka Theater, opposite the Imperial Hotel, specializes in a type of lachrymose musical peculiar to Japan, in which all the roles are played by women. Two nearby theaters, the *Teikoku Gekijo* and *Nissei Gekijo*, specialize in Western-style drama. The National Theatre *(Kokuritsu Gekijo)*, near Nagatacho subway station, has a regular program of Kabuki and seasonal presentations of **Bunraku,** the classic puppet theater of Osaka.

Tokyo has a very active music scene, including several of its own symphony orchestras (the best is probably the *NHK Symphony*) and is constantly being visited by foreign artists, orchestras, and opera and ballet companies. The new *Suntory Hall* is the city's best theater, while *Bunka Kaikan* in Ueno and *NHK Hall* in Shibuya are runners-up. The local English-language press carries information about concerts and other events.

CABARETS, NIGHTCLUBS, AND DISCOTHEQUES. Beware of the plush cabarets that cost the visitor a fortune. Beware also of the bars and clubs plastered with signs reading ''No Tip: Drinks only ¥500.'' Both can get you into a lot of trouble. Club hostesses are very costly creatures. For an economical night on the town, head in the direction of a busy railway station such as Shibuya or Shinjuku and try the *yakitori-ya* (shop selling grilled chicken on skewers) and similar unpretentious *nomi-ya* (pubs) under the arches.

Check that the cover charges in the entries listed below have not increased. In many clubs, plates of nuts, and charm have to be paid for, whether you want them or not. But it's the other extras, especially hostess rates, that can be calamitous.

Cover Charge ¥1,000–¥4,000

Elysees Matignon, Roppongi; basement of TSK Bldg.; plush but reasonable. **Byblos,** Akasaka-Mitsuke; pay in cash with each order. **Mugen,** next door to Byblos; has the same cash rule. **Crazy Horse,** Monami Bldg., Shinjuku; popular pub-cum-discotheque. **El Cupid,** Chiba Bldg., Roppongi; features Philippino trio. **After Six,** Zonan Bldg., Roppongi; jazz pub with reasonably priced snack food. **Lollipop,** Nittaku Bldg., Roppongi; live Motown and twist music.

Cover Charge up to ¥1,000

Top of the Roppongi, Hotel Ibis; cocktail lounge, piano show. **Topkapi,** Roppongi Square Bldg.; turkish bellydancers. **Pub Crescent,** near Ginza Dai-Ichi Hotel. **Pub Suntory,** Mori Bldg., Namiki Dori; live music. **Suntory Cellar,** Roppongi; live music. **Chaps,** Shimojo Bldg., Roppongi; American C&W singer.

BEER HALLS. If you're a beer drinker, you'll feel at home in Japan, where beer halls are sprinkled throughout the city. Lion has a whole chain of beer halls where you pay only for the beer; no tax, no tips, or service charge. There's the **Lion Akasaka,** Akasaka Parco Bldg., 2-14-34 Akasaka, tel. 583–8828; **Lion Ginza** 5-chome, Sapporo Ginza Bldg., 5-8-1 Ginza; tel. 571–5371; **Lion Shibuya,** Daigai Bldg., 2-3-2 Dogenzaka; tel. 462–1756; **Lion Shinjuku,** 3-28-9 Shinjuku; tel. 352–6606. Others include the **Pilsen** in the Kohjunsha Bldg., 6-8-7 Ginza, tel. 571–2236; **Tivoli** in the Yurakucho Denki Bldg., 1-7-1 Yurakucho; tel. 214–7920; and the **Azumabashi Beerhouse,** 1-23 Azumabashi; tel. 622–0530. In the summer months a number of rooftop beer halls open, many with live music.

CINEMA. First-run movie houses in Tokyo show American, British and Continental films soon after or even before they are seen in the West. The charge for unreserved seats is about ¥1,500, but for popular movies, it's standing room only. Tickets are sold whether there are seats or not. We recommend reserved seats, possibly obtained at the front desk of your hotel, but certainly at the box office. The English-language newspapers list the films and give the times of performance. The *Tokyo Weekender* provides directions to the theaters in English and the address in Japanese for the taxi driver or a passerby in case you missed it.

Movie theaters are scattered throughout the city, usually in clusters such as in Ginza, Shibuya, Shinjuku and Ikebuburo.

For cheap movies, try *Shimbashi Bunka,* tel. (03) 431–4920, ¥500–¥700; *Ginza Namiki-za,* tel. (03) 56–3034, ¥600–¥800; *Gotanda Toei,* tel. (03) 491–0810, ¥700; *Iidabashi Kasaku-za,* tel. (03) 269–1511, ¥500–¥700.

CHIBA-KANTO

By Hollistar Ferretti

Considered the frontier in ancient times, Kanto has become the most heavily populated area of the country. It's also Japan's largest plain.

The New International Airport located at Narita in the Boso Peninsula provides visitors the opportunity to see another side of Japan. Some travelers prefer to recoup from jet lag by leisurely exploring the area before going on to Tokyo; others choose to tour through the countryside, visiting mountainside villages and shoreline fishing hamlets. If you are traveling with children, it's worth the detour.

Chiba Prefecture, which covers the whole of the Boso Peninsula, has a number of attractions. Ancient tomb and shell mounds give evidence of early inhabitancy. Before the Edo era, when the country was sealed off from outside commerce, Chiba City and Kisarazu were important seaports. During the Edo period, Boso was divided into three fiefs ruled by feudal lords.

If you have only a few hours to spare, it's still possible to see a bit of Narita. Originally a temple town, today it is the home of many of the workers employed at the airport. The thousand-year-old Naritasan Shinshoji Temple draws some 10 million pilgrims a year. Built to house the statue Fudo carved by the revered Bonze Kukai, it was transported to the site from Kyoto by the priest Kansho in A.D. 940. The copper-roofed Main Hall was completed in 1968; it remains true to traditional architectural lines. The compound also has a pagoda and a 300-year-old belfry.

Naritasan Park, located nearby, is a fine example of a landscape garden built on a hillside. The Naritasan Museum displays temple artifacts and other objects found in the northern part of the peninsula. Open 8:30 A.M.–4 P.M. Closed Monday and holidays.

If you have time, a 15-minute train ride from Narita Station will take you to Sakura. Here the recently opened National Museum of Japanese History, situated on the Sakura Castle site amid restored historical settings, offers a comprehensive exhibit of ancient, medieval, and early modern Japanese cultural history. Open 9:30 A.M.–4:30 P.M. Closed Monday.

The Boso Peninsula is not all museums and temples, however. There are wonderful beaches for all water sports, scenic mountain trails, and some areas where the lifestyle is still very traditional. In fact, this would be a good place to visit a Japanese home since many of the residents open their doors to visitors. Submit your request in writing to the Narita City Information Office at the JR Narita Station, 839 Hanasaki-cho, Narita City, Chiba Prefecture; Tel. (0476) 24–3198.

The Japan National Tourist Office Tourist Information Center in the Narita Airport Terminal Building and the Chiba Tourist Association, c/o Kanko Bussan Center, 1-7-12 Fujimi, Chiba City, have detailed maps and information about the area and you can plan your own tour to fit your interests. Train and bus routes crisscross the area for easy access. We'll touch on a few of the attractions.

Shibayama is an hour from Narita by bus and worth a visit. The Shibayama Nioson Temple, built in 781, houses a black Deva statue that was carved by an Indian priest and came to Shibayama by way of China. Some 950 ancient tomb mounds are in the area. The Haniwa Museum, also on the grounds, has replicas of the clay figures that once surrounded the tombs. Open 9 A.M.–5 P.M.

In another corner of the peninsula, near Sanukimachi is Mt. Kano (353 m). Jin-Yagi Temple, reputedly founded by Prince Shotoku in the 7th century, is close to the peak of the mountain. It's possible to stay overnight in the temple. For more information, call (0439)37–2351. Not far from the temple is the Kujikutani Observatory. On yet another slope of Mt. Kano is Mother Farm, which has an orchard, domestic animals, etc. Barbecues are served along with fresh milk and homemade ice cream. It's a great spot for kids, and lodgings are available. Call (0439) 37–3211 or, if you're in Tokyo, 431–7241 for reservations.

Mt. Nokogiri rises above Hota Beach on Tokyo Bay. You can ride an aerial cable car to the summit. After enjoying the view, take the hiking trail to Nihonji Temple, where there is row after row of Buddhist statues—1,500 if you're counting. Here you'll see the largest stone statue of Buddha in Japan, which stands 31 meters high. At Nihonji you can practice Zen meditation anytime 8 A.M. –5 P.M.

A one-hour train trip from Goi takes you into the heart of the peninsula, through lovely mountain scenery. Yoro Valley offers great camping, hiking, and fishing. Yoro Onsen is a mineral spa and there are rural inns with fine accommodations.

Ibaraki Prefecture is just north of Chiba on the Pacific Ocean. During the Edo period, the city of Mito was the seat of an important branch of the Tokugawa family and became a center for scholars. The scholarly air persists, not in Mito, but in the prefecture as Tsukuba Academic New Town, founded in 1973 on a concept of reform within the Japanese university system. Tsukuba is better known to tourists as the site of the Tsukuba Expo. Kairakuen, in Mito, is one of Japan's famous gardens landscaped with lagoons, lakes, and sandy beaches. Another tourist attraction is Fukuroda Falls, where the water falls in a series of four cascades. The site is spectacular in the fall. Fukuroda Hot Springs is nearby.

West of Ibaraki is the Tochigi Prefecture. Probably the most noted landmark here is Nikko, the site of the Toshogu mausoleum. There are other attractions for the visitor as well. The Nasu Highland area is a favorite for summer holidays since the elevation helps to keep it cool. The mountainous land is beautiful and there are hot springs, golf courses, tennis courts, and a number of interesting excursions. The Emperor has a summer villa here.

In southeastern Tochigi, the town of Mashiko is known for its folk craft pottery. Ancient shards have been found on the site. In the Edo era it was known for its kitchenware, but it went into a decline until the master potter, Shoji Hamada, chose to settle there. Hamada put Mashiko on the map, attracting other potters and serious students. Shoji

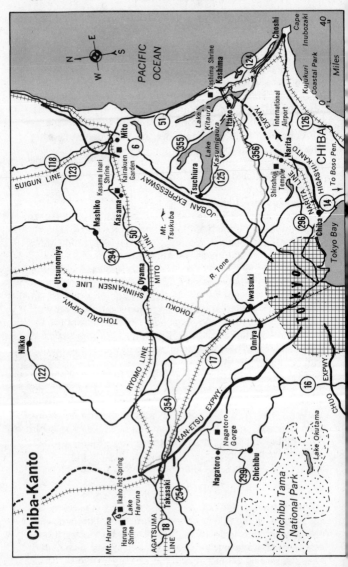

Hamada is no longer living, but his son carries on in his fine tradition. The family homestead is an old transplanted farmhouse. The Mashiko Reference Collection is open daily except Mondays. Hamada pottery tends to be expensive, but handsome pottery pieces in every price range can be found in many of the shops throughout Mashiko.

Saitama Prefecture, south of Tochigi, at one time the center of sericulture as well as silk spinning mills, today seems more like a continuation of Tokyo. The Chichibu-Tama Park is a preserve of natural beauty that includes many natural wonders such as the stalactites in a 1,640-foot-deep cave at Nippara. Two famous mountain shrines, the Mitsumine Shrine and the Mitake are training centers for Shugendo, a mountain ascetic sect.

The town of Chichibu itself has retained the spirit from the days when it was part of the thriving silk industry—especially in early December as it comes alive with one of the three largest festivals in Japan. This is called the Night Festival of Chichibu and dates back more than 300 years. Ninety-five of the Festival's floats have been designated Important Folk Properties.

Bonsai Mura, located outside of Omiya, is a village of dwarfed trees and plants. Westerners are intrigued by the skill required to raise a perfectly shaped miniature tree to maturity. It's a great surprise to find foot-and-a-half-sized apple trees bearing normal-sized fruit or to see a wee wisteria vines with blossoms. Some of the plants have been handed down through generations. One pine tree is 700 years old! Not everyone in the village has specimens of this caliber, but each and every plant requires special attention.

PRACTICAL INFORMATION FOR CHIBA-KANTO
How to Get There

When you land at Narita airport, you are in Chiba Prefecture. If you are coming from Tokyo, take the JR *Sobu* line at Tokyo Station's underground platform 2 or 3 to Chiba City. Here you can transfer to the *Uchibo* line and continue down the west coast of the Boso Peninsula all the way to Awa-Kamogawa on the east coast.

Some of the Sobu trains go on from Chiba to Choshi on the east coast. To continue down the east coast, change at Naruto to the Togane line. Check the timetable for the semi-express. The *Tokai Kisen Co.* hydrofoils leave Tokyo's Takeshiba Pier several times daily for Takeyama and Katsuyama. Reservations are suggested; Tel. 463–1131.

The Seibu line's *Red Arrow Express* from Ikebukuro takes 83 minutes to Chichibu. Reservations are necessary. To get to the Nasu Highlands you can take the *Tohoku Shinkansen* (Aoba) from Ueno Station to Nasu Shiobara, a 70-minute ride, or the *Tohoku* northeast bound limited express to Kuroiso station (two hours).

Where to Stay

HOTELS. A rash of new, modern hotels have sprung up in Narita, though for the most part they tend to be pricey. They accommodate passengers with early morning flights or late arrivals, but their main revenue comes from housing flight crews and catering local social functions. Their swimming pools and deluxe features lure Tokyoites for an occasional long weekend. We've left the posh establishments off of our list, and included those that are more moderately priced. ⬤ = Highly Recommended.

Chiba Grand, 7-2 Chiba Minato, Chiba City, 260; Tel. (0472) 41–2111. Single, ¥5,000. Twin, ¥11,000. Located in the heart of the city, in front of Chiba Harbor Park.

Chiba Keisei, 14-1 Hon Chiba cho, Chiba City 280; Tel. (0472) 22–2111. Single, ¥5,000. Twin, ¥11,000. Three minutes from Chiba. In the middle of the Keiyo Industrial zone.

Chiba New Park, 7-3 Chiba Minato, Chiba City, 260; Tel. (0472) 42–1111. Single, ¥7,000. Twin, ¥13,500. Visitors to Disneyland often choose to stay here.

Hotel Saitama Tei, 2-16-9 Urawa City, 336; Tel. (0488) 24–0811. Single, ¥5,300. Twin, ¥8,800. This business hotel faces the Prefectural Government office.

Kashima Central, 4-7-1 Ohnohara Kamisu cho, Kashima gun, 314-01; Tel. (0299) 92–5511. Convenient to the Kashima Industrial area.

Kisarazu Park, 3-2-30 Nitta Kisarazu, Kisarazu City, 292; Tel. (0438) 23–3491. Single, ¥5,300. Twin, ¥9,000. Close to Kisarazu port. Comfortable atmosphere.

⬤**Narita Holiday Inn,** 320-1 Tokka, Narita City, 286-01; Tel. (0476) 32–1234. Single, ¥10,000. Twin, ¥16,000. Five minutes from Narita International Airport. Swimming pool. Spacious rooms. Children under 12 admitted free.

YOUTH HOSTELS. The average cost for the following is about ¥3,500 per person daily, including two meals. Although these accommodations are single, hostels are usually situated in some spot of natural beauty.

Chiba Prefecture

Inubo-so, 10292-10 Inubosaki, Choshi, 288; Tel. (0479) 22–1252. A three-minute walk from Inubo Station.

Tateyama Youth Hostels, 1132 Fura, Tateyama City, 294-02; Tel. (0470) 28–0073. Beautiful flower garden on the grounds. Thirty minutes by bus from Takeyama Station.

Gumma Prefecture

Haruna Kogen Youth Hostel, 845 Haruna san Namanohara Harunacho, 370-33; Tel. (02737) 4–9300. Near Lake Haruna and the ropeway to top of Haruna Fuji. Good fishing and bicycling.

Ibaraki Prefecture

Mito Tokuda Youth Hostel, 1127-2 Nikoda, Tomobecho, Nishi Ibaraki gun, 309-17; Tel. (02967) 7–3113. Twenty minutes by bus from Tomobe Station. Good location for Mito and Oarai beaches.

Tsukuba Sanso, 692 Tsukuba, Tsukuba-cho, 300-43; Tel. (0298) 66–0022. In Mt. Tsukuba, 10 minutes by bus from Tsukuba Station.

Saitama Prefecture

Hanno Youth Hostel, 1370-2 Futayanagi, 357; Tel. (04297) 2–4018. Ten-minute bus ride from Hanno Station followed by a seven-minute walk. Near Nakuri River.

Chichibu Youth Hostel, 3755 Otaki, Otaki mura, 369-19; Tel. (0494) 55–0056. Good base for mountain hiking.

Tochigi Prefecture

Nasu Kogen Youth Hostel, 213 Yumoto, Nasu cho, 325-04; Tel. (02877) 8–1615. Thirty-five minutes by bus from Kuroiso Station. Good base for climbing the Nasu mountain chain.

JAPANESE-STYLE. The following rates include two meals.

Daishin, 10-22 Chuo Cho, Choshi City, 288; Tel. (0479) 22–4190. Per person, ¥8,000–¥12,000. Near Choshi's Fisherman's Wharf.

Grand Hotel Isoya, 10292 Inubosaki, Choshi City, 288; Tel. (0479) 24–1111. Per person, ¥13,000–¥25,000. Offers a view of the rising sun from the bath. In summertime, there's an open-air bath near the breaking surf.

Kinoshita, 1325 Tsuchiya, Narita 286; Tel. (0476) 22–0800. Per person, ¥5,000. Four minutes from Narita Station.

Kisarazu Onsen, 2-3-5 Fujimi Kisarazu City, Chiba, 292; Tel. (0438) 22–2171. Per person, ¥11,000–¥14,000. Near the heart of city. All rooms face Tokyo Bay with Mt. Fuji in the distance.

New Daishin, 10292 Inubosaki, Choshi City, Chiba, 288; Tel. (0479) 22–5024. Per person, ¥10,000–¥20,000. Big Japanese garden. Good view of Inubo Point and Pacific Ocean.

Ohmiya, Narita, 286; Tel. (0476) 22–0119. Per person, ¥7,000–¥8,000. A 15-minute taxi ride from Narita Airport.

Seikaiya Ryokan, 407 Amatsu, Amatsu Kominato, Chiba 299-54; Tel. (04709) 5–2711. Per person, ¥9,000–¥20,000. Near Awa-kominato Station.

KOKUMIN SHUKUSHA. These accommodations, known as People's Lodgings, are built by local governments under the guidance of the Ministry of Health and Welfare. The idea is to encourage people to get out and enjoy some leisure time at an affordable price. They're found in national parks and other scenic spots. The cost is between ¥4,400 and ¥5,000, and includes two meals. Bookings can be made through any JTB office. If you speak or write in Japanese, you can do it directly.

Chiba Prefecture

⬤**Hatoyamaso,** 787-2 Kenbutsu, Tateyama City, 294-03; Tel. (04702) 9–1141. Take the Uchibo Line Tateyama Station; bus is available from the station. Near fields of cultivated flowers and a nice beach. Former Prime Minister Hatoyamaso's villa.

Ichinomiya So, 2512 Sendokyu, Ichinomiyamachi, Choseigun, 299-43; Tel. (0475) 42–2626. Bus available from Station Kazusa Ichinomiya. Nice beach for swimming and surfing.

Inubo Hotel, 10315 Nagasaki cho, Choshi City, 288; Tel. (0479) 22–3205. Good ocean view.

Kujukuri Centre, 4908 Magame, Kujukuri machi, 283-01;

Tel. (0475) 76–4151. Bus available from the Oami Station. Located in an agricultural town.

Ibaraki Prefecture

Shirahoso, 419-1, Tennomisaki, Asomachi, Namekata-gun, 311-38; Tel. (02997) 2–0831. Twenty minutes by taxi from the Itako Station Kashima line. Beautiful iris in June. Two important shrines located nearby.

Saitama Prefecture

Chichibu Ryokamiso, 707, Komori, Ryokami-mura, 358; Tel. (0494) 79–1078. Set in the mountains where priests train.

Iruma Green Lodge, 1387-1 Busshi, 358; Tel. (0429) 32–1131. Seibu line's Busshi Station. In the Musashino Plain, where there are tea plantations and other cultural sights including temples.

KOKUMIN KYUKAMURA. Known as People's Vacation Village, this is another government project to encourage vacations, usually set in remote scenic places. It is not popular with foreigners, probably because it's hard to get reservations. If you're interested, it's best to make arrangements through the Tokyo Tourist Information Center.

Kokumin Kyukamura, 725 Kenbutsu Kaigan, Tateyama City, Chiba, 294-03; Tel. (0470) 29–0211. Near Sunosaki Lighthouse and Tenjoji Temple. ¥6,000 per person with two meals.

Sports

During the *summer* months, there are water sports, such as fishing, swimming, surfing, scuba diving, and boating, as well as facilities for mountain climbing, hiking, jogging, cycling, and horseback riding. In the *winter* months, both indoor and outdoor skating rinks and ski slopes are available. At Shinrin-Koen Park in Saitama ken, you can rent bicycles and tour Asia's biggest forestry park. To get there, take the Tobu Tojo line from Ikebukuro Station to Shinrin-Koen Station. Closed Mondays.

SHONAN

◆

By Hollistar Ferretti

Shonan, a term not commonly used today, refers in general to Kanagawa Prefecture, the area from Yokohama including the Miura Peninsula, the land fronting the Sagami Bay and extending to the Tanzawa Range. There's lots to see here, particularly in Yokohama, which was Japan's first international port. Kamakura, seat of the first Shogunal government in this area, is a charming city that should also be on your priority list. The sandy beaches, coves, and natural yacht harbor make the Miura Peninsula a good site for water sports, and the unspoiled natural scenery of the Tanzawa Range make that area a good stop for hiking and nature enthusiasts.

In comparison with other cities in this ancient land, Yokohama is a relative newcomer and yet it has had a profound impact on the development of the country. Although the Shogunal government signed a treaty with Townsend Harris stipulating that Kanagawa would be an international port and residence for foreigners, the Shogun had second thoughts. Kanagawa was a flourishing town, a busy crossroad on the Tokaido, the artery between Edo and Kyoto. There was growing resentment against foreigners immigrating to Japan, and so it was thought best to keep the unwelcome foreigners out of the way. Yokohama, a lonely hamlet on the side of the Ooka River, was chosen in its place. Despite the objections of the parties involved, swamps were drained, wharves, warehouses, and houses were built—all in less than a year. With no other available options, the first foreign settlers moved in.

Silk was the main export and fortunes were made with

this commodity, both for Japanese and foreign traders. It has been said that Japan's industrial economy was launched on this gossamer thread. If the Sankeien Garden is any indication, that may well have been true. This magnificent garden was formerly the private garden of a magnate who secured a sizable share of the silk market. It is now open to the public.

Yokohama soon developed into Japan's major trade and shipping gateway. However, the whole prosperous structure of the settlement was destroyed in the fire of 1886. It was rebuilt only to be leveled again in the Great Kanto Earthquake of 1923. Survivors sorted through the rubble and began anew. The debris, dumped into the harbor along Kaigon dori (Waterfront Street), was eventually turned into today's Yamashita Park. By the end of World War II, Yokohama was once again leveled. With an assist from the occupation forces, the citizens of Yokohama once more put the pieces back together. Today it is second only to Tokyo in size and is not only the country's foremost port, but one of the major ports in the world.

Alas, there's little left of the early days for tourists to see, but Sankeien Garden is a remnant of the old grandeur. Sankeien features a collection of old, traditional Japanese buildings set in the kind of Japanese garden you dream of. Silk merchant Tomitaro Hara had them moved from other parts of the country to his own estate. Six of the ten buildings are designated Important Cultural Properties. Among them, there's a three-story pagoda built in 1457, part of a palace built by Tokugawa Yorinobu in 1649; a teahouse built by the third Shogun, Iemitsu; a sanctuary of the Tokei Temple in Kamakura; and a 17th-century thatch-roofed farmhouse.

There are some other attractions in Yokohama worth visiting. The Prefectural Museum is housed in one of the few buildings that withstood the earthquake of 1923. At one time, it had been the head office of the Yokohama Species Bank, Japan's first modern foreign exchange bank. A few hours in this wonderfully comprehensive museum will give you a feeling for Japanese culture and history. The Yokohama Archives of History tells its history in 19th-century woodblock prints. The Silk Center spells out the story of silk. Chinatown, once referred to as Blood Town because of rowdy sailors, has scores of restaurants and souvenir shops. For more elaborate shopping, tour Motomachi, a street of sophisticated shops; Isezaki cho, a mall of more mundane merchandise; and the great underground complex at Yokohama Station. For a change of pace, you might want to take a harbor tour.

Kamakura, seat of the first effective centralized government, is a vital metropolis known also as a cultural center for artists, writers, and philosophers. Yoritomo Minamoto (1147–1199) chose the site because it was a natural fortress, surrounded by hills on three sides and fronted by Sagami Bay. One of the major attractions is the Hachimangu Shrine, a shrine to the Minamoto clan's patron god, Hachiman. The wide avenue running from the seashore through the center of town on up to Hachimangu was constructed by Yoritomo when he learned his wife, Masako, was pregnant. His heir was to be carried in state to the shrine for the dedication ceremony. To this day it is called Wakamiya Oji (Young Prince Avenue).

The Daibutsu, Great Buddha, is another impressive sight. Cast in bronze, the 93-ton statue is 11.4 meters in height. Although originally conceived by Yoritomo, it was not completed until 1252, long after he died. To view the tallest wooden statue in Japan, visit the Hasedera Temple. The standing figure of Kannon, covered in gold leaf, is said to date back to the 8th century.

This is but a sampling of what's in store. The city has some 65 Buddhist temples and 19 shrines and is about one hour from Tokyo. To get there, take the JR Yokosuka line from Tokyo, Shibuya, or Shinagawa and get off at Kamakura.

Other areas in the region worth a visit are Hiratsuka, noted for Tanabata Matsuri (the Star Festival), which takes place July 7th–11th; and Odawara, once the stronghold of the powerful Hojo clan. The original castle has been restored and presents an unforgettable sight in the cherry blossom season.

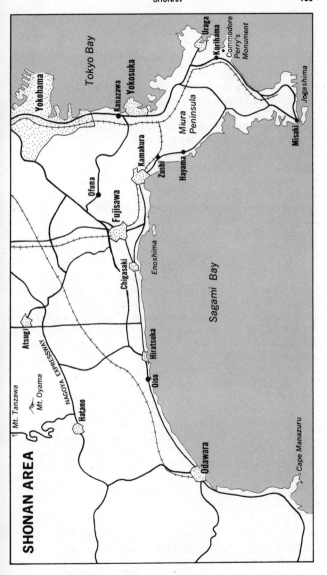

PRACTICAL INFORMATION FOR SHONAN

How to Get There

To reach Yokohama from Tokyo Station, you can take the JR *Yokosuka* line or the *Keihin Kyuko* express. It takes about 20 minutes from Shinagawa to Yokohama Station. If you want to stop at one of the other stations in Yokohama, such as Kannai (for Isezaki cho Mall) or Ishikawacho (for Motomachi or Chinatown), you'd be better off taking the local train, the blue *Keihin Tohoku* line. Otherwise you will have to change at Yokohama. The Yokosuka line stops at Kamakura, Zushi, Yokosuka, and Kurihama. The *Tokaido Main Line* is a more expensive express that also stops at Yokohama, Atami, Oiso, and Odawara on its way to Kyoto. The *Keihin Kyuko,* a private line that you can get at Shinagawa Station, is the cheapest and fastest way to get to Yokohama and it travels down the Miura Peninsula to Misaki.

Useful Addresses

TOURIST INFORMATION. The Kanagawa Prefectural Tourist Association, 1st floor of the Silk Center Bldg., 1 Yamashita cho, Naka-ku; Tel. (045) 681–0007, has detailed information about the area as does the **Yokohama International Tourist Association,** in another office of the Silk Center on the 1st floor; Tel. (045) 641–5824. Also check the information counter at the Yokohama train station and the Shin Yokohama Station for the Shinkansen.

In Kamakura, the **Kamakura City Tourist Office** is at the east exit of the Kamakura Station. City maps indicating places of interest are free of charge at these centers. If transportation is not listed for a particular place you want to visit, ask the clerk for directions. In some cases, taxi travel might be the best mode.

Tourist Bureau, Yokohama City Hall, 1-1 Minato machi, Naka ku; Tel. (045) 641–1441.

For home visits, apply at the Tourist Information Centers. There is no charge for this.

Immigration Office, 37-9 Yanashita-cho, Naka-ku, Yokohama, 231; Tel. (045)681–6801.

EMERGENCIES. To report a **fire** or summon an **ambulance,** dial 119. Speak slowly and distinctly. To reach the **police,** call 110.

INTERNATIONAL ORGANIZATIONS. Missions to Seamen, 194 Yamashita, Naka-ku, Tel. (045) 662–1871.

United Seamen's Service, 3, Honmoko Futo, Naka-ku, Yokohama; Tel. (045) 623–2231/7.

YMCA, 1-7 Tokiwacho, Naka-ku, Yokohama; Tel. (045) 662–3721.

YWCA, 225 Yamashitacho, Naka-ku, Yokohama; Tel. (045) 681–2903.

Where to Stay

HOTELS. The following moderate and inexpensive hotel accommodations, including business hotels, have been organized according to location.

Yokohama

Aster, 87 Yamashita cho, Naka-ku, 231; Tel. (045) 651–0141. Single, ¥5,500. Twin, ¥11,000. Conveniently located in front of the Marine Tower near Yamashita Park.

Bund Hotel, 1-2-14 Shin Yamashita, Naka-ku, 231; Tel. (045) 621–1101. Single, ¥5,500. Twin, ¥13,900. A 75-year-old hotel with a harbor view. The Shell Room Supper Club on the 7th floor provides one free drink as a service for guests. Within walking distance to Motomachi and Yamashita Park.

Hotel Rich, 1-11-3 Kita Saiwai, Nishi-ku, 220; Tel. (045) 312–2111. Single, ¥9,110. Twin, ¥18,700. Five minutes on foot from Yokohama Station. Relatively new, well-appointed hotel situated in a good area for shopping.

Hotel Sun Route, 2-9-1 Kita Saiwai, Nishi-ku, 220; Tel. (045) 314–3111. Single, ¥7,310. Twin, ¥13,900. A seven-minute walk from Yokohama Station. Business hotel offering a pretty view from its Chinese restaurant.

Satellite Hotel, 76 Yamashitacho, Naka-ku, 231; Tel. (045) 641–8571. Single, ¥6,350. Twin, ¥12,460. Five minutes by taxi from Sakuragicho to this business hotel located near Chinatown. Pro baseball players stay here when playing at Yokohama stadium.

Shin Yokohama, 3-8-17 Shin Yokohama, Kohoku-ku, 222; Tel. (045) 471–6011. Single, ¥6,350. Twin, ¥11,000. Three minutes on foot from the Shinkansen ("bullet" train) Yokohama Station, and Yokohama line city subway. Has a waterfall in the lobby, live music, and a sky restaurant.

Yokohama Tokyu Hotel, 1-1-12 Minami Saiwai, Nishi-ku, 220; Tel. (045) 311–1682. Single, ¥14,750. Twin, ¥21,700. Near the west exit of Yokohama Station. Convenient for business and shopping.

Yokosuka

Hotel Yokosuka, 2-7 Yonegahama, Yokosuka, 238; Tel. (0468) 25–1111. Single, ¥5,500. Twin, ¥10,000. Within walking distance of the Keihin Kyuko line, Yokosuka Chuo Station. Businessmen and relatives of Americans stationed at the Yokosuka Naval Base often stay here.

Kamakura

Kamakura Park, 33-6 Sakanoshita, Kamakura, 248; Tel. (0467) 25–5121. Single, ¥11,000. Triple, ¥15,000. Faces Yuigahama beach in an old part of this ancient capital.

Zushi

Zushi Nagisa Hotel, 2-10-18 Shinjuku, Zushi, 249; Tel. (0468) 71–4260. Single, ¥11,000. Twin, ¥12,000. This 61-year-old wooden hotel faces Zushi beach.

YOUTH HOSTELS. Prices for the following listings range from ¥1,100 to ¥3,250 and include two meals. If you do not have a membership card from your own country, contact the Japan Youth Hostel, Inc. in Tokyo (03) 269–5831 to apply for a youth hostel membership.

Kanagawa Youth Hostel, 1 Momijigaoka, Nishi-ku, Yokohama, 220; Tel. (045) 241–6503. Near Sakuragicho Station. Convenient location.

Youth Hostel Nihon Gakusei Kaikan, 27-9 Sakanoshita, Kamakura, 248; Tel. (0467) 25–1234. Good base for both Kamakura and Enoshima.

Shonan Youth Hostel, 3-3-54 Naka Kaigon, Chigasaki City, 253; Tel. (0467) 82–2401. Near Chigasaki beach. Views of Mt. Fuji.

Lake Sagami Youth Hostel, 266 Yose Sagamiko-cho, Tsukui-gun, 199-01; Tel. (04268) 4–2338. Air-conditioned. Located by the lake, has a good picnic area, boating, hiking.

JAPANESE INN. These accommodations usually have a small Japanese garden, a communal bath, and a futon bed on a tatami floor. Two 'meals are served, and tax and service charge are included.

Kaihinso, Kamakura, 249; Tel. (0467) 22–0960. Per person, ¥13,000–¥22,000. Near Yuigahama Station on the Enoden train line.

Shindo-Tei, Zushi, 249; Tel. (0468) 71–2012. Per person, ¥9,000–¥13,000. Near JR Zushi Station.

S P L U R G E S

The Hotel Yokohama, 6-1 Yamashitacho, Naka-ku, 231; Tel. (045) 662–1321. Twin/double, ¥19,900 and up. Five minutes by taxi from Sakuragicho Station. Relatively new, expensive, but well appointed. Across from Yamashita Park.

FUJI-HAKONE-IZU

By Hollistar Ferretti

Mount Fuji, geisha girls, and cherry blossoms have symbolized Japan in the minds of many for ages. Today's geisha are but a remnant of Japanese culture; the cherry blossoms' beauty hasn't diminished, but it is fleeting. Fuji, however, endures, at once suggesting strength and beauty. The sight of snowcapped Fuji on a clear winter's day is breathtaking and inspires a wonderful feeling of tranquility.

The 12,388-foot Mt. Fuji is a dormant volcano, last active on Dec. 4, 1707. Six trails lead to the summit, each named after the starting place at the foot of the mountain: Gotemba, Subashiri, Yoshida, Funatsu, Hoji, and Fujinomiya. If coming from Tokyo, the climber usually takes the Yoshida trail. On each of the trails, there are ten stations on the way to the top, and at each you'll find stone or wood huts offering toilet facilities, futon (mattresses) on the tatami mat for resting, and refreshments—all at a price that rises with the elevation. You can have your walking staff (purchased at the beginning of the climb) branded with the sign of the station. You'll have a great souvenir as well as proof of your ascent. It is wise to bring sandwiches and a canteen along with layered, warm clothing and sturdy hiking boots. Tennis shoes will be torn to shreds on the hike.

The official season for climbing Mt. Fuji is during July and August. It is possible to do so at other times of the year, but the facilities are closed and weather is also a deciding factor. The intrepid climber may well start from the foot of the mountain. Those looking for a shortcut will take the bus to the fifth station, where you can rent a horse and traverse the next two stations on horseback rather than foot.

Once you've decided on your approach, you must choose your strategy. It takes from seven to nine hours to scale Fuji. Some prefer to begin the ascent late in the day and continue the climb, arriving at the summit by daybreak the following morning. The second method is to start in the early afternoon and climb to the 7th or 8th station, bed down for the night, awaken before dawn and reach the summit before daybreak. These are the most popular climbing plans. A third, worth considering, is to leave Tokyo early morning, take the bus to the fifth station and climb to the summit. You can spend the night in a hut and descend after sunrise. Sunrise viewed from the top is an exhilarating experience. The descent time can be cut in half, or to as little as two hours by using the "sand slide," a four-mile stretch near the Gotemba trail.

PRACTICAL INFORMATION FOR FUJI
How to Get There

TO FUJI SAN. During the climbing season, a bus leaves from Hamamatsucho Bus Terminal, stops at the Shinjuku Bus Terminal, and then goes directly to the fifth station. From Hamamatucho it's a three-hour trip. The bus runs from mid-July to the end of August; from mid-April to early November, only on Sundays and holidays. The fare is ¥2,300 from Hamamatucho and ¥2,100 from Shinjuku. You can make reservations through major travel agents or by calling Fuji-kyuko Reservation Center at 374–2221.

Another approach is to travel to Gotemba, beginning of one of the trails to the top of Fuji san, by the Tomei Expressway bus from Shinjuku. It takes two hours to Gotemba and then on to Togendai.

TO THE FUJI LAKES COUNTRY. A two-hour train ride from Tokyo brings you to the Fuji Five Lakes: Lake Yamanaka, Lake

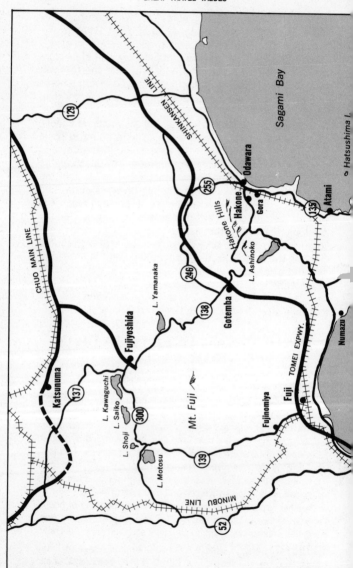

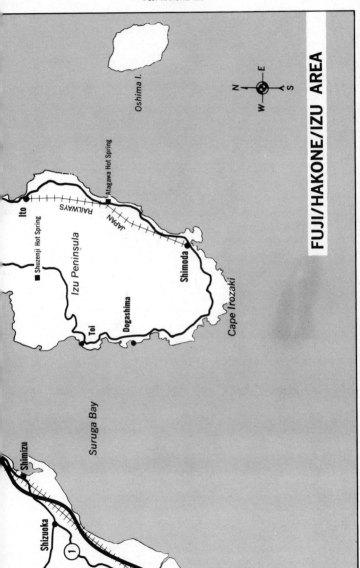

FUJI/HAKONE/IZU AREA

Kawaguchi, Lake Saiko, Lake Shoji, and Lake Motosu. The area is a summer favorite for Tokyoites since it's close enough to get to on weekends. Swimming, boating, fishing, and hunting are readily available. Check on licenses for the latter two. Hills, lakes, ponds, forests, caves, and waterfalls are all accessible.

Buses provide good transportation within the area. Fuji Kyuko and Keio Teito run buses every hour from Shinjuku to Lake Kawaguchi; it takes about an hour and 45 minutes. The JR Chuo train, Fuji Kyuko, has several direct runs to Kawaguchi. If you don't catch a direct train, you will have to change at Otsuku Station to the Fuji express line. For Lake Yamanaka, take the Odakyu line from Shinjuku to Gotemba and from there bus to the lake. To travel by car, take the Chuo Jidosha (auto expressway).

Where to Stay

HOTELS. This resort area is within easy reach of Tokyo and is highly popular with the Japanese. It is difficult to book accommodations for weekends, and as a resort area, hotels are expensive. Many companies maintain vacation houses for employees and absorb a major portion of the expense. The charges to the employee are minimal, making this a wonderful fringe benefit.

The listings below represent the more moderately priced lodgings. In addition to the rate quoted, add a 10 percent tax and a 10–20 percent service charge (in lieu of tipping).

Fuji Lake Hotel, 1 Funatsu, Kawaguchi; Tel. (0555) 72–2209. Single, ¥15,000. Twin, ¥20,000. A four-minute walk from Kawaguchi Station, Fuji Kyu line. Offers boating and fishing on the grounds.

Hotel Grand Fuji, 8-1 Hirakakine honcho, Fuji City; Tel. (0545) 61–0360. Single, ¥7,550. Twin, ¥8,750.

Hotel Mount Fuji, 1360-83 Yamanaka; Tel. (0555) 62–2111. Single, ¥18,500. Twin, ¥33,700. On the Oide hill, 1,100 meters above sea level. View of Mt. Fuji in the distance and Lake Yamanaka below. A 25-minute bus ride from Fuji Yoshida Station.

GUEST HOUSE. This is not a usual category, but this guest house, a cross between a minshuku and a pension, is such a find for the budget traveler that we wanted to give it special mention.

Fuji-Hakone Guest House, 912 Sengoku, Hakone, Kanagawa, 250-06; Tel. (0460) 4–6577. Japanese-style. Family atmosphere, but with privacy, and a natural hot spring bath. The cost is ¥4,500 per person, ¥8,000 for two, and ¥11,000 for three. Breakfast is optional at ¥600. There are restaurants in the vicinity. It's also close to Gotemba, for those wanting to climb Mt. Fuji.

PENSIONS. Privately owned lodgings that can usually accommodate from eight–10 guests in Western-style rooms. These are rarely found in the big cities, but are found near resort areas. They will often have a theme—American, Swiss, French, etc. The word *pension* is French and most food is in this style. Prices usually include two meals and when they don't, an optional breakfast will be offered at a reasonable price. These are not hotels and service is minimal, but they are ideal for people traveling on a budget.

Call any of the following numbers, in Tokyo, for locations of pensions in the area you want to visit.

Japan Pension; Tel. (03) 407–2333.

Nippon Pension Association (Kyokai); Tel. (03) 262–0350.

Puchi Pension Group; Tel. (03) 563–1821. In Osaka, (06) 222–1005.

HAKONE

A visit to Hakone is well within a day's trip from Tokyo, but if you want to enjoy the major attractions at a leisurely pace, an overnight stay is recommended. Located in the crater of an extinct volcano, the area of Hakone includes Mt. Kami, Mt. Koma, Mt. Futago, Lake Ashi, sometimes called Lake Hakone, and a number of hot springs. The description may not sound exceptional, but the scenery is spectacular, the air is clean and fresh and it has a lot to offer.

Miyanoshita is a thriving spa town frequented by foreigners. The famous Fujiya Hotel is a favorite and for good reason. This just might be worth a night's splurge. Check it out and see if you agree. There's an English-speaking staff, a hot spring bath, swimming pools, tennis courts, good food, and dancing. It costs ¥19,000 and up for a twin. The Tokyo reservations number is 271–1511. About a mile away, the Hotel Kowaki-en, without the 100-year-old pedigree, is a delightful hotel with good facilities. Prices from ¥18,500 and up. The Tokyo telephone reservation number is 943–2111.

A three-minute walk from the Chokoku-no-Mori Station brings you to the Hakone Open-Air Museum, an outdoor sculpture museum. Works include those of Rodin, Bourdelle, Moore, and Zadkine. They also have an indoor Picasso Gallery. An admission fee is charged.

If you stop at Gora Station, you'll see a French-style rock garden, brick paved promenades and a gigantic fountain pond. The park is particularly attractive in cherry blossom season, though there is an admission fee.

At Koen-Kami Station you will find the Hakone Art Museum featuring ceramics, displaying a comprehensive collection of pottery and porcelain. There's also the added attraction of an exquisite moss garden, a bubbling stream, and a bamboo grove.

From Sounzan, take the ropeway over Owakudani (Valley of Greater Boiling), the site of the last volcanic activity in the Hakone mountains. There's a great view of Fuji san from here. Check out the Natural Science Museum for a detailed description of the geological features, fauna, and flora of Hakone. Admission fee.

At Togendai Station, leave the cable car and board a boat for Hakone-machi on Lake Ashinoko. On a clear day you can see Mt. Fuji reflected in the waters of Lake Ashi. Once in Hakone-machi, check out the ancient Cedar Avenue that runs between Hakone-machi and Hakone-moto. This was once part of the old Tokaido. A five-minute walk takes you to a replica of the Tokugawa checkpoint. Life-sized figures in feudal costumes now stand on the historical site.

Visiting the Hakone Shrine is a worthwhile pilgrimage. Founded in the 8th century, the present shrine was rebuilt in 1667. This shrine figures prominently in ceremonial rites of Kosui-sai observed July 31st when thousands of lighted lanterns are set afloat on the lake.

One of the most appealing aspects of the Hakone region is that it's easy to do the tour on your own. From Moto- Hakone you can catch a bus to the Shinkansen Station at Odawara and ride the "bullet" train back to Tokyo.

PRACTICAL INFORMATION FOR HAKONE
How to Get There

The *Odakyu's Romance Car* takes 92 minutes from Shinjuku to Yumoto Station (¥1,280 one way, reservations necessary). They leave every half hour, starting at 9:30 A.M. They also have 7:30 and 8:50 A.M. trains if you want an earlier start. *Odakyu's Express Train* takes 1 hour and 35 minutes to Odawara; the price is ¥550 and trains leave every 15–30 minutes. You can board the *Hakone Tozan Railway* at Yumote Station—though it's probably Japan's smallest, slowest line. The two-car train zigzags its way up the mountain, crossing ravines and gorges and passing through tunnels, and stopping at many spa towns on its way to Gora Spa.

The Hakone Tozan Railway offers a discount ticket, called Hakone Free Pass, which allows you to use the Hakone Tozan railway, bus, cable car, ropeway, the Okakuyu highway bus (between Togendai and the Tomei Gotemba Expressway interchange), and the Hakone excursion boat as many times as you want. These tickets may be purchased at the Odawara Railway station or at the Hakone Tozan Information Center at Odawara Station. The price is ¥4,390 for adults from Shinjuku station, ¥2,200 for children, or ¥3,400 for adults from Odawara and ¥1,700 for children. The Romance car ticket from Shinjuku is not included.

The Izu Hakone Railway also issues a discount ticket. This one, called Hakone Wide Free, allows unlimited use of the Izu Hakone bus, cable car, ropeway, and excursion boat, and with the coupon you can get a 10–15 percent discount at the following: Hakone-en Aquarium, Hakone Checkpoint, Hakone Picnic Garden, Owakudani Natural Science Museum, and Fuji Hakone Land. The price of this coupon is ¥2,900 for adults, and ¥1,450 for children. They are available at Odawara Station.

Where to Stay

ACCOMMODATIONS. The following listings include hotels, ryokan and minshuku, and are organized according to location.

Yumoto Onsen Spa

Hoei-so Ryokan, 227 Yumoto, Hakone; Tel. (0460) 5-5763. Rooms start at ¥13,000 and include two meals, tax and service charge. Features a lovely garden with seasonal flowers.

Suizanso Ryokan, 694 Yumoto, Hakone-machi; Tel. (0460) 5–5757. Rooms start at ¥10,000 and include two meals, tax and service charge. The modern six-story building blends in with the natural scenery. Situated on the Hayakawa River.

Miyanoshita Onsen Spa

Fujiya Hotel, 359 Miyanoshita, Hakone; Tel. (0460) 2–2211. Twin, ¥19,100 and up. Tax and service charge included. A grand, century-old hotel with a great atmosphere and all modern facilities. Worth the splurge.

Gora Onsen Spa

Hakone-taiyo-sanso Kokumin Shukusha, 1320 Gora, Hakone; Tel. (0460) 1–3388. ¥4,850 and up, including two meals.

Ishikura Ryokan, 1300 Goro, Hakone; Tel. (0460) 2–2471. ¥10,000 and up, including two meals. Attractive rock garden. Near Hakone Gallery and Open-Air Museum.

Sengokuhara Onsen Spa

Fuji-Hakone Guest House Minshuku, 912 Sengoku-hara, Hakone, Kanagawa, 250-06; Tel. (0460-46577). ¥4,500 without meals. Breakfast ¥600. Privately owned, but more like a Japanese pension. A relaxed family atmosphere. The owners speak English. Natural hot spring bath, a coin laundry and optional breakfast. Near Lake Ashinoko, a 50-minute ride from Odawara Station by bus from lane 4 to Senkyoro-mae; fare ¥800.

Hakone Kanko Hotel, 1245 Sengokuhara, Hakone; Tel. (0460) 4–8501. Twin, ¥15,280 and up; tax and service charge included. On a hillside with an overview of the Sengokuhara plain. Many recreational facilities.

Hyoseki-kaku Ryokan, 1290 Sengokuhara, Hakone; Tel. (0460) 4–8531. ¥13,000 and up, including two meals. Located on 100,000 square meters of land, surrounded by mountains. Beautiful Japanese garden.

Hotel Kagetsu-en, 1244-2 Sengokuhara, Hakone; Tel. (0460) 4–8621. Single, ¥7,200. Twin, ¥12,000 and up. Tax and service charge included. Comfortable atmosphere with a view of Lake Ashinoko. Ten-minute walk to Togendai Ropeway.

YOUTH HOSTEL. Hakone Sounzan Youth Hostel, 1320 Gora, Hakone-machi; Tel. (0460) 2–3827. Per person ¥3,200, including two meals. Membership card necessary.

What to See and Do

FESTIVALS. Prominent festivals in the area include: *O-Shiro Matsuri,* May 3, at Odawara Castle Park, celebrated with a feudal procession and retainers. *Torii Matusui,* August 5th, a huge wooden torii gate built on the water is burned and a thousand lighted lanterns are floated. *Daimonji Yaki Festival,* on August 16th, on Mt. Myojo; great blazing torches spell out the character "DAI" on the hillside. A fireworks display and folk entertainment are held near Gora Station; and on November 3rd, the *Daimyo Gyoretsu* or Feudal Lord's Procession takes place at Hakone-Yumoto with a costume parade.

HOT SPRING BATHS. You don't have to check into a hotel to enjoy a hot spring bath. "Onsen-kyodo-yokujo" means a public hot spring bath and you'll find them located in Yumoto, Tonosawa, Ohiradai, Miyanoshita, Ninotaira, Gora, and Miyagino. Except for two places in Yumoto and one in Miyagino, the spas are all indoors. The price ranges from ¥200 to ¥500 per person.

RECREATIONAL FACILITIES. Hakone Komaga-take Snow Land. The ski slopes are covered with artificial snow and there's a snow playground for children. Rental equipment is available. Open from the end of December to mid-March.

Gora Kokusai Ice Skating Rink. Open from the end of November to mid-March. Outdoor rink. Rental skates.

Odakyu Hakone Athletic Garden. An outdoor exercise course. Open 9 A.M.–5 P.M. daily, except for Tues., Dec.–Feb. and rainy days.

Bicycle Rentals. Rent bicycles at *Hakone-en,* ¥1,000 for two hours. There's a cycling course between Hakone-en and Kojiri. You can also rent bicycles at the *Hakone-Kojiri Lodging Center,* one hour ¥400, or one day ¥2,400.

Boat rentals. On Lake Ashinoko at Kojiri, Moto-Hakone and Hakone motor boats, rowboats, and pedal boats are for rent. Chauffeured motor boats for one to five persons cost ¥6,000 around the lake, ¥4,000 half-way around. Rowboats range from ¥500 to ¥600 for thirty minutes. Pedal boats cost ¥1,500 (two people) for thirty minutes.

IZU PENINSULA

Atami, the famous hot spring spa, is often a decided disappointment to the tourist. It's crowded with resorts and hotels and has a glitzy, Coney Island atmosphere. But don't write it off completely. The sight of a castle perched on a promontory captures the imagination, the plum garden is exquisite in mid-December when in bloom and a delight to meander through at any time, and Himenosawa Park is the biggest rhododendron garden in the country. There is also the recently built MOA Museum. Set high on a hilltop overlooking Sagami Bay, it offers both a spectacular view of the wonders of nature and a comprehensive sampling of Japan's cultural heritage. The sophisticated technology employed in the edifice and in the facilities is an ingenious engineering feat. Of the museum's 3,500 pieces of art, three have been designated National Treasures, 53 Important Cultural Properties and 47 Important Art Objects. All exhibits have English titles.

You'll be impressed with the teahouse and its equipment made of gold, a replica of the portable one that Hideyoshi took to Kyoto to perform tea ceremony for Emperor Ogimachi. As you will note in this lavish display, the charismatic general did things with a decided flair. If this is your first introduction to tea ceremony, don't be misled. The tea ceremony is akin to communion, performed in a room that does not distract from the aesthetic experience. The museum also has a teahouse where you may enjoy a modified version of the tea ceremony. The tea garden is beautiful. They also have a traditional Noh stage with modern innovations.

Leaving Atami, you might consider taking the bus that runs along Route 36 around Izu Peninsula. If you've not been in the area, it's a good way to see the shoreline, even if you take it only to Ito. This is the site where Will Adams built Japan's first Western ships between 1605 and 1610. If you remember the novel *Shogun*, you may recall that the foreign character was modeled after Will Adams. Ito remains a fishing village that attracts tourists in the summer.

Farther down the coastline, Shimoda, Izu's big summer resort, has wonderful sandy beaches. Shimoda also has its fair share of history. In Shimoda's Ryosenji Temple, the

Kanagawa Treaty of 1854 was signed. Two years later American Consul Townsend Harris, the first foreign envoy to Japan, lived in Gyokusenji Temple. The Black Ship Festival held in Shimoda every May celebrates these events.

PRACTICAL INFORMATION FOR IZU

How to Get There

From Tokyo station you can take the JR *Tokaido* line for a 90-minute ride to Atami. The *Shinkansen Kodama* reaches Atami in 60 minutes. From Atami you can take a bus that follows Route 36 around the Izu Peninsula, or board the Izu train line. Alternatively, the Odoriko train leaves from Tokyo and goes through Izu without changing trains.

Where to Stay

The appeal of beaches, hot springs, and the proximity to Tokyo make most accommodations in this region expensive. If you have your Youth Hostel membership card, check that possibility. Also there are pensions in the area, and a few ryokan.

YOUTH HOSTELS. The cost is about ¥5,000 per person. Membership cards are necessary.

Ito

Amagi Harris Court, 28-1 Nashimoto, Kawazu cho, Kamo gun; Tel. (05583) 5–7253. Named after Townsend Harris. Ten minutes by bus from Kawazu Station, Izukyu line.

Komuroyama Koen, 1260-125 Kawana, Ito City; Tel. (0557) 45–0224. 15 minutes by bus from JR Ito Station.

PENSIONS. Those listed here welcome foreigners, speak some English, have baths and furnish towels. The rate for one night, on the basis of two to a room, are around ¥5,000 without meals and ¥7,500 with two meals. Some honor credit cards.

Ito

Jogasaki Kawakami Pension, 785-3 Futo, Ito, 413-02; Tel. (0557) 51–3683. A 15-minute walk from Futo Station of the Izu Kyuko line. American Express and VISA accepted.

Pension Palette, 614-156 Ike, Ito, 413-02; Tel. (0557) 54–1365. Five minutes by taxi from Izu Kogen Station on the Izu Kyoko line.

Pension Sun House Yahatano, 224-1, Yawatano, Ito, 413-02; Tel. (0557) 54–1365. A five-minute taxi ride from Izu Kogen Station on the Izu Kyoko line.

Pension Marin Hills, 976 Yoshida, Ito, 414; Tel. (0557) 45–4537. A 20-minute bus ride from JR Ito Station. Visa accepted.

Pension St. Paulia, 662-100 Yukawa, Ito, 414; Tel. (0557) 36–8556. A 20-minute walk from JR Ito Station.

Shimoda

Pension Minami Izu, 2184 Ihama, Minamiizu, Kamo-gun, 415-05; Tel. (05586) 7–0878. A 50-minute bus ride from Shimoda Station. American Express honored.

Dogashima

Pension Seagull, 521 Nishina, Nishiizucho, Kamo-gun, 410-05; Tel. (05585) 2–0082. A 50-minute bus ride from Shimoda Station.

RYOKAN. These are Japanese-style lodgings of moderate price.

Shimoda

Izumiso Ryokan, 1-13-7 Nishi Hongo; Tel. (05582) 2–3080. Per person, ¥8,000–¥20,000 including two meals. A five-minute walk from Izukyu Shimoda Station. Consists of four major buildings connected by corridors. Commands a view of Mt. Negugata.

Katsuya Ryokan; Tel. (05582) 2–2126. Per person, ¥8,000–¥15,000 including two meals. Three-minute walk from Izukyu Shimoda Station. Good food and service.

Rendaiji-so, 305 Rendaiji, Shimoda; Tel. (05582) 2–3501. Per person, ¥13,000–¥25,000 including two meals. Ten minutes from Izukyu Shimoda Station by bus. Located at Rendaiji spa in a Japanese building. Every room has a garden view.

Izu Nagaoka

Nanzan so, 1056 Nagaoka; Tel. (05594) 8–0601. Per person, ¥10,000–¥55,000 including two meals. Five minutes by bus from Izunagaoka Station. Rotenburo, open-air hot spring. Rooms are semidetached with a garden view.

Yasudaya, 28 Kona; Tel. (05594) 8–1313. Per person,

¥13,000–¥25,000 including two meals. Five minutes by bus from Izunagaoka Station. All rooms face south with a view of the Amagi mountain chain.

Izu Kogen

Kukumin Kyukumura Irozaki, 199-4, Irozaki Minami, Izumachi; Tel. (05586) 5–0537. Per person, ¥4,500 including two meals. A 20-minute bus ride from Izukyu Shimoda Station. Clean with bare essentials.

NIKKO

◆

By Hollistar Ferretti

Nikko's fame is deserved. Here mountainous terrain, waterfalls, rivers, hot springs, lakes, and volcanoes combine in a dramatic effect. The first temple founded in this glorious wilderness was by Priest Shodo-Shonin in 766. Over the centuries, pilgrims have sought and found a spiritual renewal in Nikko, which has been an important religious center throughout Japanese history. In 820, Kobo Daishi visited these beautiful mountains and changed the name from Niko zan to Nikko, meaning "light of day."

This holy ground was chosen as the mausoleum for Ieyasu Tokugawa, the man who brought unity and peace to the country and established the shogunal government that lasted for 250 years. Although he had requested that his remains be taken to Kurozan, they were transferred to Nikko the year after his death and a magnificent temple was erected to receive them. The lavish Toshogu Temple is a fitting monument to a man of such genius, political acumen, and historical influence. In 1645 the Emperor Go Kommyo conferred the posthumous title of *Tosho daigongen* upon Ieyasu. During the Meiji era the Toshogu Temple (Buddhist) was designated Toshogu Shrine (Shinto), an interesting change to fit Meiji political strategy.

A visit here is quite an experience, and you'll find a wealth of English literature available at the shrine office. But, just to prepare you, the following are a few of the highlights.

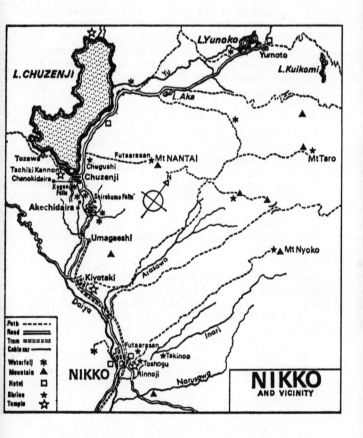

NIKKO
AND VICINITY

The Shinkyo, a sacred bridge, is a 15-minute walk from the station along Nikko Street. The vermilion-lacquered bridge, spanning the Daiya River, is used only at the time of the Tokugawa Shrine Festival. A cedar-lined avenue, 23 miles in length with 13,000 Japanese cedars, leads the way to the shrine. Rinnoji Temple's Sambutsudo houses three gigantic statues, the Thousand-Handed Kannon on the right, Amida in the center and the Bato Kannon on the left. Sambutsudo also has a bronze pillar containing ten thousand holy sutras.

The Toshogu Shrine, dedicated to Ieyasu (1542–1616) and built by his grandson Iemitsu, is a combination of Buddhist and Shinto architectures. A huge Shinto stone torii is the first entrance to the shrine; to its left is a red- and gold-lacquered Buddhist pagoda. The main entrance to the shrine is the Niomon Gate, the Gate of Two Deva Kings, who are Buddhist guardians of the temple. Be sure to look under the eaves of the Sacred Stable for the carved "Hear no evil, see no evil, and speak no evil" monkeys. A ten-minute walk from the shrine brings you to Nikko Botanical Garden and the Nikko Museum. These are also worth seeing.

Northwest of Nikko, at the foot of Mt. Nantai, is Lake Chuzenji. The lake was formed by a volcanic eruption that blocked the Daiya River. At the eastern shore the water spills over a 318-foot drop. This is the famed Kegon Falls. Alongside the main fall are 12 minor falls. When frozen in winter, it's spectacular. An elevator takes visitors to the bottom of the gorge for a view of the falls.

Mt. Nantai is the second highest peak in the area. The path from Chuzenji to the semicircular crater at the top is about a five-hour climb and is thickly wooded all of the way to the top.

PRACTICAL INFORMATION FOR NIKKO AND CHUZENJI

Where to Stay

HOTELS. The following moderate and inexpensive hotels have been organized by location.

Nikko

Kanaya Hotel, 1300 Kamihatsuishi-cho, Nikko, 321-14; Tel. (0288) 54–0001. Single, ¥7,000. Twin, ¥11,000. Five minutes by taxi from Nikko Station. Established over a century ago, it has a nostalgic air. Swimming pool.

Green Hotel, 9-19 Honcho, Nikko, 321-14; Tel. (0288) 54–1756. ¥8,000–¥12,000 with two meals. 10 minutes by taxi from Nikko Station. Neatly arranged garden. Bath from mineral spring.

Nikko Lakeside Hotel, 2482 Chugushi, Nikko, 321-16; Tel. (0288) 55–0321. Twin/double, ¥16,000. 30 minutes by taxi from Nikko Station. Close to Kegon Falls. Tennis courts.

Chuzenji

Chuzenji Hotel, 2478 Chugushi, 321-16; Tel. (0288) 55–0333. ¥10,000–¥15,000 including two meals. 30 minutes by taxi from Nikko Station. Biggest hotel in area, located in between Mt. Nantai and Lake Chuzenji.

Chuzenji Kanaya Hotel, 2482 Chugushi, 321-16; Tel. (0288) 55–0356. Twin, ¥11,000. 40 minutes by taxi from Nikko Station. Located at the foot of Mt. Nankai, near Lake Chuzenji. Tennis courts.

RYOKAN. For further information and listings for these comfortable, Japanese-style inns, check with the JNTO. They can usually provide names of ryokan where some English is spoken. The prices quoted below include two meals.

Nikko

Konishi Ryokan, 1030 Kamihatsuishi-cho, Nikko, 321-14; Tel. (0288) 54–1101. Per person, ¥10,000–¥15,000. Five minutes by bus from Nikko Station. A 120-year-old inn with a cozy atmosphere. The inside bath is in the midst of rocks.

Fukudaya, 1036 Kamihatsuishi-cho, Nikko, 321-14; Tel. (0288) 54–0389. Per person, ¥10,000–¥14,000. Three minutes by taxi from Nikko Station. Lovely mountain view.

Chuzenji

Ichiryukaku Bekkan, 2478 Chugushi, Chuzenji, 321-16; Tel. (0288) 55–0383. Per person, ¥8,000–¥15,000. 30 minutes by taxi from Nikko Station. Situated high enough to see Lake Chuzenji and surrounding forests. Excellent Japanese food.

Hashimoto Hotel, 2480 Chugushi, 321-16; Tel. (0288) 55–0310. Per person, ¥9,000–¥14,000. 30 minutes by taxi. Convenient to all scenic attractions, including Kegon Falls.

PENSIONS. This type of accommodation is relatively new to Japan and ideal for the budget traveler. The lodgings are run in a Western fashion; the name is derived from the French. They are small, maybe eight–10 rooms, privately owned, usually found in the country near some sporting facilities. In these regions, it's skiing. Two meals, an American breakfast and French dinner, are included. For further information on pensions in these and other parts of the country, contact the *Japan Pension Center* in Tokyo, Tel. 407–2333, or check with the JNTO office in Yurakucho. ◉ = Highly Recommended.

Nikko

◉**Turtle,** 216 Takumicho, Nikko, 321-14; Tel. (0288) 53–3168. Per person, ¥5,850–¥6,180. All meals are served on Mashiko-ware. Homey atmosphere.

Green City, 1773 Kujiya cho, Nikko, 321-14; Tel. (0288) 53–4744. Per person, ¥8,550–¥8,900. American-style house; features Swiss country dishes.

Chuzenji

Pension Toge, 2546 Yumoto, 321-16; Tel. (0288) 62–2571. Per person, ¥6,000. Located near ski slopes. Homemade specialties make use of the mountain vegetables.

YOUTH HOSTELS. Economical lodgings, often located in scenic spots. Many require valid membership card, so check with the Youth Hostel Association in your country.

Nikko

Nikko Youth Hostel, 2854 Tokorono, Nikko, 321-14; Tel. (0288) 54–1013. Per person, ¥1,600. Good location for Toshogu. Winter skiing and skating nearby.

Daiyagawa Youth Hostel, 1075 Nakahatsuishi-cho, Nikko, 321-14; Tel. (0288) 54–1974. Per person, ¥2,850. By the Daiyagawa River.

JAPAN ALPS

◆

By Peter Popham

This large area of central Honshu embraces both mountain and coastal scenery, and several of the nation's most interesting and traditional provincial cities. Within easy reach of the capital, it is a very popular area for recreation of all sorts, including tennis, swimming and theater-going.

The most famous of several medieval post towns in the area is Karuizawa, which is probably the most popular summer resort in the country. Quiet during the cooler seasons, the town comes to life during the heat of summer, and many of Tokyo's most fashionable stores open branches here for the season.

The cities of Takayama and Kanazawa epitomize the unique appeal of this quarter of the country. Takayama, though prosperous and fully modernized in terms of roads, hotels, etc., still retains some of its ancient character in the middle of town, where a number of old merchants' houses have been preserved and may be visited. The annual festivals held in mid-April and mid-October, are among the most splendid and elaborate in the country.

Kanazawa is larger and more hectic than Takayama but still deserves its "little Kyoto" tag. Formerly the seat of the Maeda family, the wealthiest of all the provincial barons of the Edo period (1603–1868), the city was untouched by World War II and contains whole streets lined with the old houses of the samurai, winding streets with earthen walls, and traditional craft workshops, ideal for strolling and picture taking. In the center of the city is the remains of an

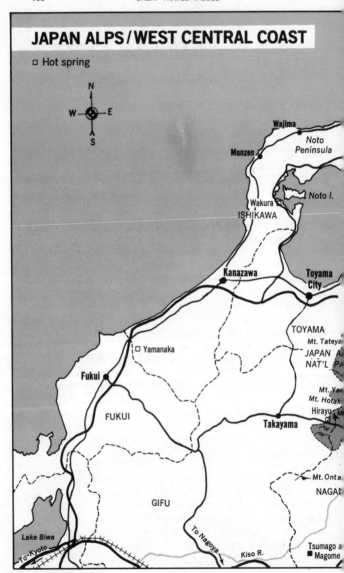

JAPAN ALPS / WEST CENTRAL COAST

□ Hot spring

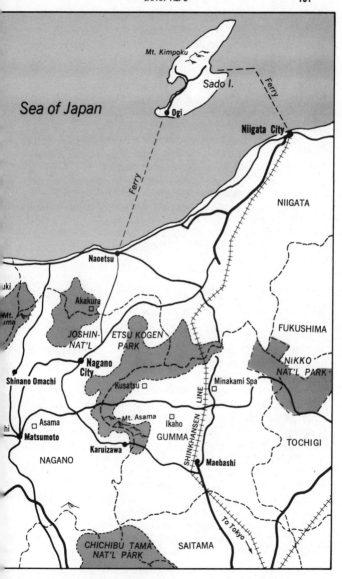

enormous castle that burned down in 1881; adjoining is Kenrokuen, one of Japan's three most celebrated landscape gardens. *Kenroku,* or "Six Combinations," refers to the park's features—vastness, solemnity, careful arrangement, venerability, scenic variety, and coolness. On one side of the garden are the Prefectural Art Museum and *Seisonkaku,* the ancestral villa of the Maedas, where many of the family treasures are displayed.

The furthermost attraction in this part of Japan is Sado-ga-Shima, Sado Island, which is separated from the city of Niigata by a broad channel of turbulent water. A former place of exile for political enemies of the government, site of the long-exhausted gold mines that gave Japan its ancient and unmerited reputation as a country possessed of enormous wealth, Sado is a quiet, severely depopulated island of natural beauty and a strong character. A native school of puppetry and an internationally famous troupe of "demon drummers" make the island their home.

PRACTICAL INFORMATION FOR JAPAN ALPS
How to Get There

By Train. There are five separate railway lines serving this large area from Tokyo and through the mountains. There are, however, no striking travel bargains.

The *Shinkansen Joetsu Line* links Ueno Station in central Tokyo with Niigata, thus bringing Sado Island within comfortable reach of the capital. "Bullet" trains cover the distance in about two hours. To reach Kanazawa, change at Nagaoka from the Shinkansen to the regular express service. The total journey time is a little under five hours.

The Joetsu Honsen (trunk line) runs north from Tokyo's Ueno through Takasaki, up to Iwappara and on to Niigata. This economical service has been deliberately run down by Japan Railways in an effort to get more people riding the more expensive "bullet." For example, if you left Ueno in Tokyo at 11 A.M. you would arrive in Niigata more than seven hours later, after waiting nearly two hours for a connection at Mikami. The trip would cost you ¥5,200. For an extra ¥4,400 the "bullet" train covers the same distance in one hour 50 minutes!

The Shinetsu line also runs from Ueno to Takasaki but then branches off to the west through Karuizawa and Nagano, terminating at Naoetsu. Ueno to Karuizawa takes just under two hours, to Nagano just under three hours. A couple of trains per day go on through Toyama to Kanazawa, covering the distance in a little under seven hours.

The most southerly of the lines is the *Chuo line,* which leaves from Tokyo's Shinjuku Station and terminates at Matsumoto, in the heart of the region, between three and 4½ hours later.

Takayama is most directly accessible from Nagoya via the *Takayama line,* which ends at Toyama. Some trains continue on to Kanazawa. The fastest service from Nagoya to Takayama takes about 2½ hours.

By Air: All *Nippon Airways* and *Japan Airlines* operate daily flights from Tokyo (Haneda) to Kanazawa.

By Bus: The only inexpensive and useful route into the area is the bus service of the private *Seibu Bus Co.* Departing from Ikebukuro Station in northwest Tokyo six times a day, Seibu buses cover the distance to Niigata in just five hours for a fare of ¥5,000. The service operates all year round and reservations can be made in Tokyo, Tel. (03) 989–2525 (in Japanese). The first bus of the day is 9:05 A.M., the last 11:35 P.M.

Facts and Figures

This large area covers the following four prefectures: Nagano, population 2,140,000, area 13,584 square km.; Ishikawa, population 1,152,000, area 4,1970 square km, Toyama, population 1,120,000, area 4,252 square km.; Niigata, population 2,490,000, area 12,579 square km.

Telephone area codes in the region are as follows: Karuizawa: 0267; Matsumoto: 0263; Kamikochi: 0263; Takayama: 0577; Kanazawa: 0762; Niigata: 0252.

USEFUL ADDRESSES. All the prefectures in the region have tourist offices in Tokyo that can answer detailed questions about the area. Addresses and phone numbers are as follows:

Nagano (for questions about Karuizawa, Kamikochi, Matsumoto, Nagano City, etc.): Kokusai Kanko Kaikan, 8-3, Marunouchi 1-chome, Chiyoda-ku, Tokyo; Tel. 214–5651.

Gifu (for questions about Takayama): Tetsudo Kaikan, 9-1, Marunouchi 1-chome, Chiyoda-ku, Tokyo; Tel. 231–1775.

Ishikawa (for questions about Kanazawa): same address as for Nagano (above); Tel. 231–4030.

Niigata (for questions about Niigata and Sado Island): same address as Nagano (above); Tel. 215–4618.

Toyama: address as for Nagano (above); Tel. 231–5032.

Getting Around

The railway lines described in "How to Get There" (above) are the simplest way to travel the cities and towns in this region. In addition, the *Hokuriku Honsen* (Hokuriku trunk line) provides the best link between the cities of Kanazawa, Toyama, and Niigata. To get from Kanazawa to Niigata takes a little over four hours.

The destination boards are difficult for foreigners to understand and therefore put a limit on the usefulness of buses. Cars may be rented in major centers such as Kanazawa and Niigata, and also in Karuizawa.

The channel between Niigata and Sado Island is crossed by Boeing jetfoils in 55 minutes. The conventional ferry takes 2½ hours, but is perhaps more appropriate to the island's slow-paced charm. In the depth of winter, between January and March, the channel can be very rough and the island is often cut off.

The most varied method of transportation is provided by the spectacular Tateyama-Kurobe Alpine Route. This is reached by traveling from Matsumoto to Shinano-Omachi via JNR's *Oito Line* (one hour). From there you travel successively by bus (twice), cable car (twice), trolley bus, bus, cable car, and finally train to Toyama. The whole route provides magnificent views and is described in detail in a Tourist Information Center leaflet.

The Noto Peninsula is best explored by bus, though there is also a limited train service.

Much of the region is great for exploring by foot or by bicycle. Mountaineers will like several of the higher peaks in the Alpine range, especially Shirouma, Tateyama, and Ontake. You can also walk up the 8,389-foot Mt. Asama outside Karuizawa (a live volcano), or climb the rather difficult Mt. Shirane (10,472 feet, and also active). Cycles may be rented at Karuizawa, Takayama, and Kanazawa. Rental shops are generally close to the main railway station.

Where to Stay

The price categories for the accommodations in this region are based on the following rates per person, per night, *Moderate,* ¥6,000–¥10,000; *Inexpensive:* ¥4,000–¥6,000; *Low Budget,* ¥4,000 and under. ● = Highly Recommended.

Hotels

Moderate

●*Kanazawa:* **Holiday Inn Kanazawa,** 1-10 Horikawa-cho, Kanazawa; Tel. (0762) 23–1111. Includes shopping arcade, beauty salon, tea ceremony room, wedding hall, parking facilities, 181 rooms. One-minute walk from Kanazawa Station.

Hotel New Kanazawa, 2-14-10 Honmachi, Kanazawa; Tel. (0762) 23–2255. 10-year-old, 10-story concrete hotel in the middle of town, and a two-minute walk from the train station.

Niigata: **Niigata Silver Hotel,** 1-1-25 Benten, Niigata City, Tel. (0252) 45–7111. Features bar, lounge, restaurant arcade and stores. Close to the city center, opposite Niigata Station. 98 rooms.

Niigata Station Hotel, 1-2-10 Benter, Niigata City, Tel. (0252) 243–5151. 150 rooms. Large modern business hotel in the heart of the city.

●*Takayama:* **Takayama Green Hotel,** 2–180 Nishi Noishiki-cho, Takayama; Tel. (0577) 33–5500. This hotel has a five-story Japanese-style annex, a large communal bath (as well as individual ones attached to rooms), a beauty salon, electronic game corner. 184 rooms. A three-minute ride from the station.

Inexpensive

Kanazawa: **Kanazawa Plaza Hotel;** 11-18 Konohanamachi, Kanazawa City; Tel. (0762) 23–1510. Three-minute walk from the station.

Toyama: **Toyama Station Hotel;** 1-4-1 Takara-machi, Toyama City; Tel. (0764) 32–4311. Centrally located business hotel with 70 rooms. A minute walk from the station.

Nagano: **Nagano Palace Hotel;** 132 Minami Sekido-cho, Nagano City; Tel. (0262) 26–2221. Modestly scaled business hotel in the heart of the city. 30 rooms. Close to station.

Takayama: **New Alps Hotel;** 6-59 Hanasatomachi, Takayama; Tel. (0577) 32–2888. 75 rooms. Plain, decent business hotel near the train station.

Ryokan

Inexpensive

⊜*Kanazawa:* **Hotel Shinboya;** 1-12-3 Hikosomachi, Kanazawa City; Tel. (0762) 21–6650. A small, well-located ryokan oriented to the needs of foreign guests. 15 rooms.

⊜*Takayama:* **Ryokan Asunaro,** 2-9-2 Hatsudacho, Takayama; Tel. (0577) 33–5551. 30-room ryokan recommended for overseas visitors by Japan National Tourist Organization. Telex 4822–239. American Express, Visa, JCB, DC, MasterCard honored.

Ryokan Hakuun, 67 Horibatacho, Takayama; Tel. (0577) 34–0700. 15 rooms, recommended by Japan National Tourist Organization. Telex 4822–230. A five-minute car ride from the station.

Nagano: **Hotel Fujiya;** 80 Daimoncho, Nagano; Tel. (0262) 32–1241. Relatively small, well-located ryokan. 24 rooms. American Express honored. Telex 3322–517.

Low Budget

Kanazawa: **Ryokan Murataya:** 1-5-2 Katamachi, Kanazawa City. Intimate ryokan (11 rooms); American Express, MasterCard, Visa honored.

⊜*Sado:* **Sado Seaside Hotel;** 80 Sumiyoshi, Ryotsu, Sado Island; Tel. (02592) 7–7211. Small countrified ryokan with 14 rooms, close to the beach. American Express honored.

Minshuku

Inexpensive

Kanazawa: **Toyo,** 1-18-19 Higashiyama, Kanazawa; Tel. (0762) 52–9020. Typically small family minshuku with just five rooms. A five-minute ride from the station.

Takayama: **Ipponsugi;** 3-Hachikenmachi, Takayama; Tel. (0577) 32–5384. The name means "One Cedar Tree." Eight rooms.

Hatanaka, 1-78 Sowamachi, Takayama; Tel. (0577) 32–1309. 11 rooms; good central location, walking distance from station.

Noto: **Sannanmi,** 2-95-2 Hanami, Notomachi, Fugeshi-gun; Tel. (0768) 62–3000. Eight rooms. Bay view.

Karuizawa: **Shiozawa-sanso,** 530 Shiozawa, Karuizawamachi, Kita-Saku-gun, Nagano Pref; Tel. (0267) 45–6270. An unusually large minshuku with 32 rooms. Tennis.

Pensions

Moderate

Karuizawa: **Love-Thirty,** Nagakura, Karuizawamachi, Kita-Saku-gun, Nagano Pref; Tel. (0267) 45–3270. Splendid New England-style pension in wooded setting. Guests may try out the owner's collection of old sports and mini cars.

Good Morning, Nagakura, Karuizawamachi, Kita-Saku-gun, Nagano Pref; Tel. (0267) 46–1670. L-shaped wooden structure with terrace. Rental bicycles, skiing in winter, hiking in summer.

Youth Hostels

Low Budget

Kanazawa: **Kanazawa YH,** 37 Suehiro-cho, Kanazawa City; Tel. (0762) 52–3414. 120 beds. Japanese-style day room, Western-style lounge, wooded setting.

Takayama: **Hida-Takayama Tenshoji YH,** 83 Tensho-jimachi, Takayama City; Tel. (0577) 32–6345. Beautiful old temple building in its own grounds. 150 beds in Japanese-style rooms.

Toyama: **Toyama YH,** 3377 Matsushita, Hamakurosaki, Toyama City; Tel. (0764) 37–9010. Small hostel surrounded by tall conifers. 50 beds in Japanese-style rooms.

Sado Island: **Kazashima-kan YH,** 397 Katanoo, Ryotsu-shi, Sado Island; Tel. (02592) 9–200. Small hostel, 29 beds in Japanese-style rooms. Close to the sea. Closed Jan.–Apr.

Where to Eat

Decent, wholesome Japanese food is available in every town and village in the region, but this is not generally an area of Japan known for gourmet cuisine. Kanazawa, the region's most refined city, is the exception: its native *kaga* cuisine, grilled on a net over a special stove of white pipe clay, demands to be tried. We recommend the following:

Zeniya, Tel. (0762) 33–3331. Dinner costs ¥5,000 and up. Excellent *kaga.*

Otomoro, Tel. (0762) 21–0305. A charmingly traditional restaurant. Dinner is a minimum of ¥4,000 per person and reservations are essential.

What to See and Do

MAJOR ATTRACTIONS. Hyakuman-goku Festival, Kanazawa.

An elaborate festival that features a costume parade through the city's streets. Participants dress as feudal lords, vassals, firemen, lion dancers, etc. to commemorate the long and enlightened rule of the Maeda clan over the city. The festival is held each year in mid-June. Check with the Tourist Information Center for exact dates.

Kenrokuen, Kanazawa. A beautiful landscaped garden in the center of Kanazawa. The park is open 6:30 A.M.–6 P.M except Nov.–Mar., when it opens 8 A.M.–4:30 P.M. Entrance fee is ¥300.

Takayama Festival, in Takayama City. Held twice yearly, in Apr. and Oct. On both occasions the city's gorgeously decorated and ancient floats are paraded through the streets. Lion dancers, drummers, and all manner of ancient costumes add to the spectacle.

Torch Festival of Asama Spa, at Asama Onsen in Matsumoto City. Torches of all sizes are lit at Misa Shrine's sacred flame and paraded in the streets. At dawn the torches are thrown into the river and the festival comes to an end. One of the region's most spectacular traditional events, held in early Oct.

Other Attractions. Noh Theater, Kanazawa. Full-scale professional productions are given on the first Sun. of every month, but classical Japanese dance and music, either in rehearsal or actual performance, can be enjoyed here practically every day. The theater is south of Kenrokuen Park.

Notojima Marine Park located on Notojima Island, just off the Noto Peninsula. The park includes large aquaria, a dolphin pool, fishing facilities, a monorail, tennis courts, and a race track for kids. Open 9 A.M.–4:30 or 5 P.M. year-round; adults ¥800, children ¥200.

MUSEUMS. Utsukushigahara Plateau Museum near Matsumoto. An open-air sculpture museum featuring panoramic view of the Northern Alps. One hour 40 minutes by bus from Matsumoto Station. Open 9 A.M.–5 P.M. Admission ¥800.

Ukiyo-e Art Museum, Matsumoto. Houses a famous collection of pre-modern woodblock prints. A taxi ride from Matsumoto Station. Open 10 A.M.–5 P.M., closed Mon. Admission ¥500.

Takayama Yatai Kaikan Hall, Takayama. If you can't be in Takayama for the spring or autumn festivals, you can at least admire the floats on display at this exhibition hall. Open 8:30 A.M.–5 P.M. Mar.–Nov.; 9 A.M.–4:30 P.M. Dec. to Feb. Admission ¥380.

Ishikawa Prefectural Art Museum, near Seisonkaku Villa at Kenrokuen Park in Kanazawa. The best permanent collection of Kutani pottery, dyed fabrics, old Japanese-style paintings and other Kanazawa handicrafts. Admission is ¥300 to ¥1000, depending on the exhibit.

Honda Museum, Kanazawa. Collection of art objects, armor, and household objects belonging to the Honda family, chief retainers of the ruling Maeda family in feudal times. Open 9 A.M.–5 P.M. Closed Thurs. Admission ¥500.

HISTORICAL SITES. Matsumoto Castle, Matsumoto. Built in 1504, this is one of the best-preserved castles in the country. Offers fine alpine views from the upper floors. Open daily 8:30 A.M.–4:30 P.M.; adults ¥400, children ¥210 (includes admission to the nearby Folklore Museum).

Hida-no-Sato Village, Takayama. One of Japan's largest and best collections of ancient buildings, including several of the multi-story thatched A-frame farmhouses for which the mountain villages around Takayama are renowned. Open 8:30 A.M.–5 P.M., 4:30 P.M. in winter. Admission ¥500 for adults.

Ninja-dera, Takayama. This "temple of the secret agents" is famous for its incredible number and variety of tricks and devices for foiling assailants. Open 9 A.M.–4 P.M., but reservations are necessary. Call (0762) 41–2877. Admission ¥400.

Monzen, Noto Peninsula: **Sojiji Temple,** Monzen. An urbane and spacious temple close to Noto's wild west coast, this is the former headquarters of the Soto sect of Zen Buddhism.

Sodayu-ko Gold Mine, Aikawa, Sado Island. Formerly one of the most productive gold mines in the Orient, now featuring mechanized figures that demonstrate the mining process.

ESCORTED TOURS. Japan Travel Bureau operates a five-day *Sunrise Tour* of Takayama and Kanazawa every Tues., Apr.–Oct. The cost is ¥150,000 for adults. The tour includes many of the region's most interesting spots previously mentioned in this chapter. A descriptive leaflet is available from JTB offices.

SHOPPING. The best items to shop for are regional craft products. In the Nagano Prefecture Wasabi, look for the delicious Japanese equivalent to horseradish, and *shinshu soba* (buckwheat noodles). In Takayama, local *sake, miso* (fermented bean paste), wallets, and other textile articles. In Kanazawa, check out the *Kutani* pottery, items carved from paulownia wood, gold and silver leaf products, dolls, Wajima lacquerware, and *Kaga-yuzen* silk fabrics.

SPORTS. Japan is the best place in Asia for **skiing,** and this region has some of the best slopes, notably Shiga Heights and its sister slopes at Sun Valley. There's also Ishiuchi and Yuzawa, which are nicknamed ''Skiing Ginza'' to convey their fashionable and expensive appeal. Naeba, another skiing resort, is popular among Japanese royalty. **Skating** is also a popular winter sport. There are five skating rinks in Karuizawa and three decent public **golf** courses. This is not, however, a significant area of the country for spectator sports. The one exception is the annual outdoor **sumo wrestling,** held on the evening of September 25th at Hakui, Noto Peninsula.

Entertainment and Nightlife

A thriving nightlife exists in towns such as Takayama and Kanazawa, but for the foreign visitor it is pretty much virgin territory. A world of bizarre experiences awaits the traveler bold enough to test the waters. There are tiny hostess bars with deafeningly loud music, *karaoke* bars where the customers take turns crooning into a microphone . . . it's all good material for a novel, or at least a few lively postcards.

◆

S P L U R G E S

The Kinjoro, Hashiba-cho; Tel. (0762) 21–8188. A 100-year-old inn noted for its excellent food. The cost of lodging (not including meals) is ¥27,000–¥35,000 per person.

◆

NAGOYA AND ISE-SHIMA

by Peter Popham

———————————◆———————————

Nagoya's history dates back to 1610, when the Shogun Tokugawa Ieyasu, founder of the dynasty that ruled Japan until 1868, made it one of his strategic castle towns. Like much of the rest of the city, the castle itself was destroyed in wartime air raids. An impressive replica now stands on the same spot.

A modern and somewhat anonymous city of more than two million inhabitants, Nagoya is laid out on a grid and is the center of a vast industrial area whose best-known industry is automobiles. It is also the home of Noritake China and Ando cloisonné, and tours of these factories are among the area's more unusual sightseeing possibilities. Also worth a visit and very close to Nagoya is Inuma, which can be reached in less than 45 minutes by train from Nagoya Station. Its 16th-century castle commands a fine view of the lower stretch of the Kiso rapids. The nearby outdoor museum called Meiji Mura brings together more than two dozen architectural relics of the Meiji era (1868–1912).

The eight-mile stretch of the Kiso River from Imawatari down to Inuyama has been called the Japanese Rhine because of its resemblance to stretches of the German river. Visitors may enjoy shooting the rapids in hired boats,

NAGOYA

CHUO MAIN LINE

Yada R.

(41)

SHINKANSEN LINE

(22) Nagoya Castle

Noritake China Factory

Nagoya RR Station

Miyako Hotel

Meibetsu Grand Hotel

KANSAI MAIN LINE

Chunichi Stadium

Tokugawa Art Museum

Nitaiji Temple

Higashiyama Zoo & Botanical Garden

Atsuta Shrine

(1)

Nagoya Race Track

TOKAIDO MAIN LINE

SHINKANSEN LINE

(23)

Port of Nagoya

OUTSIDE NAGOYA

Seki

(156) (248)

Gifu

(21)

Inuyama

Ichinomiya

CHUO

EXPWY.

Meiji Mura

Nagoya Airport

TOMEI EXPWY.

Nagoya

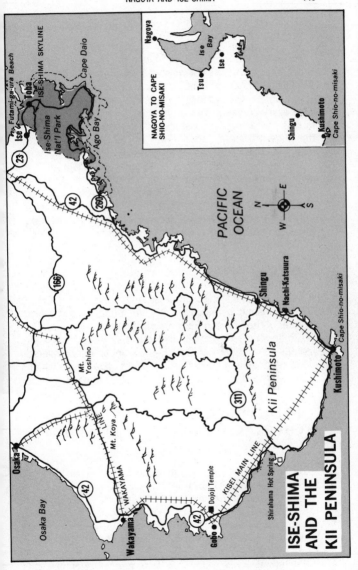

ISE-SHIMA AND THE KII PENINSULA

viewing the cherry blossoms in spring, or doing some cormorant fishing in the summer.

The Ise-Shima National Park includes all of what was once called the province of Shima. At its heart are the Great Shrines of Ise, the most sacred shrines of Shinto—Japan's national religion. In keeping with Shinto ideas about purity, the wooden shrines are rebuilt on adjacent sites every 20 years. The simple beauty of the architecture touches the hearts of most visitors, as does the majesty of the huge groves of cedar trees that surround them. The next scheduled reconstruction is in 1993.

The small town of Toba, the home of Pearl Island, is a convenient base for exploring the Ise Peninsula. On Pearl Island you can see the process of cultivating artificial pearls, developed by the pearl king, Kokichi Mikimoto. Although these pearls put many pearl divers out of work, some can still be seen at Toba, diving for sea vegetables.

Two important religious centers in the area are Mt. Koya and Mt. Yoshino, both of which have hosted communities of Buddhist monks for many centuries. The former is particularly worthy of a visit, and features a great complex of temples, monasteries, cemeteries, schools, and a museum established by Kobo Daishi, the Buddhist saint and founder of the Shingon Sect. Its most remarkable feature is the mile-long avenue of mausoleums, where some of Japan's most illustrious families lie under moss-covered stone pagodas in a grove of magnificent cedar trees, which surround the Oku-no-in, tomb of the saint himself.

PRACTICAL INFORMATION FOR NAGOYA AND ISE-SHIMA
How to Get There

By Train. The simplest and most attractive route into the area from Tokyo or Kyoto/Osaka is by Shinkansen "bullet" train. The fastest trains, called *Hikari,* cover the distance from Tokyo in about two hours, the slower *Kodama* about 2½ hours. From Osaka, Hikari trains take one hour, Kodama trains 1½ hours. The fare from Tokyo is ¥10,100 (including special express fare), from Osaka ¥5,900.

The private *Kinki Nippon Railways* runs a slower but less

expensive service between Kintetsu Namba (in central Osaka) and Kintetsu Nagoya (in central Nagoya). Trains take two hours and 14 minutes and the fare is ¥2,930.

By Bus. If money is more of a problem than time, the best way to go to Nagoya is by highway bus, operated by Japan Railways. The trip from Tokyo to Nagoya costs ¥4,500, but takes six hours, three times as long as the train. Four buses leave per hour between 7 A.M. and 7 P.M. from the Yaesu side of Tokyo Station. There is also one late-night bus that leaves Tokyo at 11:20 P.M. and arrives in Nagoya at 6:01 A.M.

The same buses run between Nagoya and Kyoto and Osaka. The trip to Kyoto takes two hours 50 minutes, the trip to Osaka three hours one minute.

By Plane. It is also possible to fly to Nagoya. Flying time from Tokyo is 60 minutes, and the airport is 45 to 55 minutes by bus from Meitetsu Bus Center, near Nagoya JR Station.

Facts and Figures

Nagoya has a population of more than two million, and covers an area of more than 320 sq. km.

USEFUL ADDRESSES AND PHONE NUMBERS. The Nagoya area code is 052. *Nagoya Central Post Office*, located near JR station; Tel. (052) 564–2003. *Nagoya Overseas Telegraph and Telephone Office* (KDD); Tel. 203–3311. *Lost Property* (city bus and subway); Tel. (052) 961–1111. *Nagoya Prefectural Hospital:* Shiroyama Hospital, Tokugawa Yama-cho, Chikusaku 4-1-7; Tel. (052) 763–1511.

Getting Around

Nagoya has a fast and efficient subway system, with three lines traversing the city in several directions. This is the quickest and easiest way of getting about, except in rush hours. A subway map (with destinations using the Roman alphabet) appears in ''Your Guide to Nagoya,'' a helpful pamphlet published by the city and available at the tourist information office in the station.

The bus service is good but difficult for travelers to use because destinations are written only in Japanese.

To hire a car, contact one of these offices: *Nippon Hertz Rent-a-Car*, Tel. (052) 551–1976; *Toyota Rent-a-Lease*, Tel. (052) 586–1318; *Nissan Rent-a-Car*, Tel. (052) 451–4123.

Outside Nagoya City, the Nagoya-Ise Shima area is well served by JR lines, private railway lines, and long-distance buses. To go from Nagoya to Inuma take the private *Meitetsu Inuyama Line* from Shin-Nagoya (New Nagoya) Station, near the JR tracks. It takes about 33 minutes. Another Meitetsu line from Nagoya passes through the "Japanese Rhine" (River Kiso) area and stops at Meiji Mura, the museum of historical architecture.

For trips to the scenic spots south of Nagoya, use the lines of the private *Kintetsu Railway*. To travel to Ise, Toba, and Kashikojima, take the Kintetsu line from Nagoya via Yokkaichi. The express is extremely comfortable, reasonably priced, and covers the distance in just over an hour.

Where to Stay

HOTELS. Price categories are based on the following rates per person, per night; *Moderate* ¥6,000–¥10,000 and *Inexpensive* ¥4,000–¥6,000. ● = Highly Recommended.

Nagoya

Moderate

Ekimae Mont Blanc Hotel, 3-14-1 Meieki, Nakamura-ku, Nagoya; Tel. (052) 541–1121. 272 Western-style, nine Western-cum-Japanese-style rooms. Large, functional hotel in highly strategic location. American Express, MasterCard, Visa honored. Telex 445–4335. A two-minute walk from Nagoya Station on JR Tokaido-Shinkansen line.

Hotel Kiyoshi, 1-3-1, Heiwa, Naka-ku, Nagoya; Tel. (052) 321–53. 87 Western-style rooms. Telex 443–7070. Plain and simple, immaculately clean. Close to the Higashi-Betsuin Station on the Meijo subway line.

●**Lions Plaza Nagoya,** 4-15-23 Sakae, Naka-ku, Nagoya; Tel. (052) 241–1500. 219 Western-style rooms. Well managed; one of a large chain. American Express, MasterCard, Visa honored. Telex 4424–193 HLPLAZA N. A three-minute walk from Sakae Station on Higashiyama subway line.

Nagoya Central Hotel, 2-1-15 Marunouchi, Naka-ku, Nagoya; Tel. (052) 203–5511. A short walk from the Marunouchi Station. 78 Western-style rooms. Designed for business travelers, but welcomes tourists too. American Express, MasterCard, Visa honored.

●**Nagoya Green Hotel,** 1-8-22 Nishiki, Naka-ku, Nagoya; Tel. (052) 203–0211. 105 Western-style rooms. Functional, compact, but more stylish than average. Telex 442–250. Five minutes by bus or car from Nagoya Station.

Toba

Moderate

Toba Hotel International, 1-23-1 Toba, Toba-shi, Mie Prefecture; Tel. (0599) 25–3121. 124 Western-style rooms. A famous resort hotel with facilities for golf, boating, fishing, and bathing.

RYOKAN. Price categories are based on the following rate per room (two people are expected to share one room) and include two meals: *Moderate* ¥6,000–¥15,000; *Inexpensive* under ¥6,000.

Nagoya

Moderate

Ryokan Meiryu, 2-4-21 Kami-Maetsu, Naka-ku, Nagoya; Tel. (052) 331–8686. 24 Japanese-style rooms. Parking available.

⊖**Satsuki Honten,** 1-18-30 Meieki-Minami, Nakamura-ku, Nagoya; Tel. (052) 551–0052. 10 Japanese-style rooms, one Japanese-cum-Western-style room. Intimate ryokan with old-fashioned service. Parking available. Not far from Nagoya Station.

Inexpensive

Oyone Ryokan, 2-2-12 Aoi, Higashi-ku, Nagoya; Tel. (052) 936–8788. 18 Japanese-style rooms. American Express honored. A short walk from Chigusa Station.

Inuyama

Moderate

Geihanro, 41-6 Aza Kitakoken, Oazainuyama, Inuyama; Tel. (058) 1–2205. 57 Japanese-style rooms. Conference rooms, wedding hall, parking facilities. Expect delicious and elaborate traditional meals. A short drive from Inuyama-yuen Station.

Toba

Moderate

Kogaso, 237-1 Toba, Toba City; Tel. (0599) 25–2170. 44 Japanese-style rooms. Conference rooms, game room, parking facilities.

Sempokaku, 2-12-24 Toba, Toba City; Tel. (0599) 25–3151. 71 Japanese-style rooms. Swimming pool, gateball field, conference rooms, wedding hall, parking facilities. Too large to be very personal, but a good place to watch the Japanese at play.

Ise City

Inexpensive

Saekikan, 6-4 Honmachi, Ise; Tel. (0596) 628–2017. 29 Japanese-style rooms, American Express, Diners Club, MasterCard, Visa honored. Telex 499–509.

Kashikojima

Moderate

Ryokan Ishiyama-so, Kashikojima, Akomachi, Shima-gun; Tel. (05995) 2–1527. 12 Japanese-style rooms, parking. Accustomed to foreign guests.

Yunoyama Spa

Moderate

Hotel Yunomoto, Oaza Komono, Komono-machi, Mie-gun; Tel. (05939) 2–2141. 31 Japanese-style rooms. Hot spa bath, conference rooms, parking facilities. A good example of an *onsen* (hot spa) ryokan. Annexed to Grand Hotel Koyo.

YOUTH HOSTELS. The following accommodations are considered *Low Budget* and cost under ¥4,000 for a single room.

Nagoya

Nagoya Youth Hostel, 1-50 Kameiri, Tashiro-cho, Chikusa-ku, Nagoya; Tel. (052) 781–9845. 92 beds in Western-style rooms. This modern hostel is centrally located but set in its own wooded grounds. Not far from Higashiyama Koen Station.

Youth Hostel Aichi-ken Seinen Kaikan, 1-18-8 Sakae, Naka-ku, Nagoya; Tel. (052) 221–001. 60 beds in a mixture of Western- and Japanese-style rooms. More like an office block than a hostel in appearance; near the heart of the city.

Gifu

Gifu Youth Hostel, 4716-17 Kamikanoyama, Gifu City; Tel. (0582) 3–31. 60 beds in Western-style rooms. Mountainous location, good base for hiking, bird watching, etc.

Inuyama

Inuyama Youth Hostel, 162-1 Himuro, Tsugao, Inuyama City; Tel. (058) 1–1111. 92 beds in a mix of Western- and Japanese-style rooms. Modern hostel with traditional spirit featuring a common room with piano and sing-along tape machine (*karaoke*). Good hiking nearby. Self-catering facilities.

Ise-shima

Ise-shima YH, 1219-80 Anagawa, Isobe-cho, Shima-gun, Mie Pref; Tel. (05995) 5–02226. 120 beds in a mix of Western- and Japanese-style rooms. Odd pyramidal building in verdant setting. Outdoor pool filled July and Aug., rental cycles. An uphill walk from Anagawa Station takes about seven minutes.

Matsusaka

YH Atago-san, 1-4 Atagomachi, Matsusaka City; Tel. (0598) 21–2931. 30 beds in a mix of Western- and Japanese-style rooms. Traditional temple hostel in the city famed for its beef. Rental cycles, self-catering.

Inuyama Youth Hostel; Tel. (0568) 61–1111. 25 minutes on foot from Inuyama-yuen Station.

Toba

YH Kontaji; Tel. (0599) 25–3035. 15 minutes on foot from Toba Station. Only seven beds—and men only!

Mt. Koya

Henjoson-in YH; Tel. (07365) 6–2434. Reservations necessary.

Where to Eat

RESTAURANTS. Nagoya is known for *kishimen,* flat noodles akin to tagliatelli, and its high-quality chicken, but like all large Japanese cities it has a huge number of restaurants serving many different types of cuisine. In Ise, the seafood is delicious, especially the lobster. All restaurants in this category are moderately priced. ● = Highly Recommended.

Credit cards: As in Tokyo and other major cities, increasing numbers of moderately priced restaurants accept American Express, MasterCard, Visa, and other major international credit cards.

Reservations: Not expected at these restaurants—though at peak times you may want to call to check how busy they are and determine if there is a wait.

Japanese

Ayame, 3-12-22 Sakae, Naka-ku; Tel. (052) 21–5914. Specializes in tempura.

Azumazushi, 1-5-21 Sakae, Naka-ku; Tel. (052) 231–3141. Classy sushi shop located in the middle of town.

Daimyozushi, 3-14 Nishiki, Naka-ku; Tel. (052) 951–3277. Sushi shop with large menu including 30 kinds of *nigirizushi* (hand-formed sushi). Open 24 hours a day throughout the year.

●**Gomitori,** 3-9-13 Sakae, Naka-ku; Tel. (052) 241–0041. Nagoya's exotic tavern, featuring horsemeat sashimi, loaches, frogs (in season), all served in the best of taste. Another branch is located close to Nagoya Kanko Hotel.

●**Raku,** 3-9-29 Nishiki, Naka-ku; Tel. (052) 951–1152. Features old local recipe for chicken stew and lots of other chicken dishes served in refined traditional atmosphere.

Torikyu, 1-1-15 Meieki-minami, Nakamura-ku; Tel. (052) 541–1888. Another celebrated place for Japanese-style chicken, including good *yakitori*.

Chinese

Matenrou Daihanten, 2-1-1 Nishiki, Naka-ku; Tel. (052) 204–0058. Open throughout the year.

Totenko, Kokusai Center Bldg., 1-47-1 Nakano, Nakamura-ku; Tel. (052) 571–8101. Wide range of dishes including excellent seafood.

Korean

●**Pion,** Miyako Building, 2 fl., 3-17-20 Nishiki, Naka-ku; Tel. (052) 971–82/5. Open till 3 A.M., serving Korean beef barbecue (*yakiniku*) and other native dishes.

French

Shirakawa, 2-1-5 Sakae, Naka-ku; Tel. (052) 231–8877. Classy mainstream French restaurant in the heart of Sakae section.

Italian

Carina, 1-12-1 Izumi Higashi-ku; Tel. (052) 971–9034, Italian specialties served till early hours of the morning.

Eiger, Aster Plaza, 2F, 4-14 Sakae, Naka-ku; Tel. (052) 241–2958. Centrally located pasta specialist.

Indian

Akbar, 3-1-1 Sakae, Naka-ku; Tel. (052) 21–098. Curries and other Indian dishes, authentically prepared.

OUTSIDE NAGOYA. In most areas visitors are well advised to eat at their hotel or ryokan—it's probably the best place in town. In

Ise–shima, the restaurant of the **Shima Kanko Hotel** in Kashikojima has a tremendous reputation for French cuisine and lobster dishes. Tel. (0599) 43–1211.

What to See and Do

MAJOR ATTRACTIONS. Meiji Mura. This museum houses more than two dozen architectural relics from the Meiji era (1868–1912). A real steam train adds fun for children. Open 10 A.M.–4 or 5 P.M., admission ¥1,200 for adults. Take the bus from Nagoya's Meitetsu Bus Center or the Meitetsu train from Nagoya to Meiji Mura Guchi and then a bus.

Nagoya Matsuri. This is the city's biggest annual splash and lasts the whole week of Oct. 10. Historic costume processions and elaborately decorated floats brighten the streets. All manner of sideshows, citywide. No charge.

Ukai Cormorant Fishing. Enjoyed from May 11 to Oct. 15 at Nagara River in Gifu, and June 1 to Sept. 30 at Inuyama. Rent a boat (¥2,000–¥2,600), load it with friends, food and drink, and watch the trained birds pluck fish out of the river and deliver them to their masters. The fishing takes place daily except when the water is too muddy or when there is a full moon, at which times the fish do not rise. Book through JTB.

Other Attractions. Adventure World, at Shirahama. There are three sections to the park: Marine Pavilion, Animal Pavilion, and Recreation Pavilion. Separate admission is available, but admission to all three costs ¥2,800 for adults, ¥1,400 for children. Open 9 A.M.–4:30 or 5 P.M.

Fertility Festival, Mar. 15, at Tagata Shrine, 30 minutes by Meitetsu train from Nagoya, two stops before Meiji Mura. A procession in which the shrine's treasures, including the largest collection of erotic talismans in Japan, are borne through the town.

Toshogu Matsuri, grand festival of Toshogu Shrine in Nagoya on Apr. 16 and 17. Gorgeous floats and palanquins wind through the streets of the city.

MUSEUMS AND HISTORIC SITES. Museum Toba Marina, on Pearl Island in Toba. A maritime museum with various displays, including the history of men and the sea. Open 8:30 or 9 A.M.–5 P.M. Admission ¥500 for adults. Close by are two other museums: *Brazil Maru,* a liner formerly used for Japanese emigration to Brazil, and the *Toba Aquarium,* where Toba's diving ladies display their skills.

Nagoya Castle. Modern reconstruction of the 17th-century original. Open 9:30 A.M.–4:30 P.M. Admission ¥300.

Tokugawa Art Museum, near Shindeki-machi; Tel. 935–6262. Said to be the best in the city, this museum includes a huge collection of historical treasures. Open 10 A.M.–4 P.M. Closed Mon. Admission ¥300.

TRAVELING WITH CHILDREN. There are several facilities with special appeal for children.

Higashiyama Zoological and Botanical Garden, near Higashiyama subway station. More than 1,000 animals of 260 species. Open 9:30 A.M.–4:30 P.M. Closed Mon. Adults ¥300, children free.

Nagoya Municipal Science Museum, near Fushimi subway station; Tel. (502) 201–4486. Contains a planetarium. Open 9:30 A.M.–5 P.M. Modest admission fee.

Nihon Monkey Center. Meitetsu train from Nagoya to Inuyama Yuen Station, then four minutes by monorail. 1,000 monkeys of 100 different species—one of the biggest parks of its type in the world. Open 9:30 A.M.–4 or 5 P.M. Admission: adults ¥1,000, children ¥600, infants ¥400.

Little World. An outdoor ethnological museum, featuring real houses and other artifacts that illustrate ways of life of people from all over the world. Open 9:30 or 10 A.M.–4:30 or 6 P.M. Admission: adults ¥1,000, teenagers ¥800, younger children ¥500.

ESCORTED TOURS. Japan Travel Bureau runs one-day and two-day tours of the main attractions of Ise and its Pearl Island. Both originate daily in Kyoto or Osaka and terminate in Tokyo. The one-day trip costs ¥36,800, the two-day option ¥45,600.

SHOPPING. Nagoya has major department stores, regional speciality shops and two bustling underground arcades. Specialty shops include *Ando* (cloisonné), Tel. (502) 261–1808, and *Noritake* (chinaware), Tel. (502) 961–6831. *Maruzen,* Tel. (502) 261–2251, stocks English-language books. The department stores are *Mitsukoshi* (subway to Hoshigaoka); *Matsuzakaya* (subway to Yaba-cho); *Marui* (subway to Sakae); and *Meitetsu* (subway to Nagoya).

SPORTS. Nagoya's **baseball** team is the *Dragons,* and you can see them at the Chunichi Stadium. **Horse racing** takes place at Nagoya Horse Race Track and National Chukyo Track in Toyoaki Village. Kanayama Gymnasium is the venue for the mid-July **sumo** tournament. Nagoya Sports Center is open throughout the year for **ice skating.** The Shimo pool in Showa-ku is open July and Aug. for **swimming. Tennis** can be played at Sakae Tennis Courts in Higashi-ku. For **golfing,** try the Forest Park Golf Course in Kasugai City, about 18 km north of Nagoya and open to the general public. Toba, Ago, and Ise bays are all excellent **fishing** grounds, and you can hire a boat for a reasonable charge. And don't forget the cormorant fishing at Nagara River, during summer months.

Entertainment and Nightlife

Nagoya's three theaters offer modern Japanese fare that may not appeal to the foreign visitor, although major national and international performers sometimes come to the city. Details of these and other performances are available at the tourist information office at the station.

Nagoya has a good selection of beer halls, discos, and several clubs with live music, in addition to the usual abundance of late-night *snakku* (so-called snack bars that are actually tiny nightclubs) and hostess bars.

Two German-style beer halls well worth noting are: *Pilsen,* 1-4-5 Shinsakae, Naka-ku; Tel. (052) 241–2911; and *Lion,* Meichika Ichibangai, 3-14-15 Meieki, Nakamura-ku; Tel. (052) 551–3256. Of the two, Pilsen stays open the latest, closing around midnight.

Two establishments with live music deserve mention: *Lovely,* 1-10-15 Higashisakura, Higashi-ku; Tel. (052) 951–6085; live jazz four or five times a week, with top musicians from Tokyo and Osaka. *Kentos,* Kanko Bldg., 4th fl., 4-13-5 Sakae, Naka-ku; Tel. 241–8045. Open till 2 A.M. throughout the year; decor and music of the fifties.

Two of the city's most popular discos are: *Scheherazade,* Watchman Bldg., B1 fl., 3-15-21 Nishiki, Naka-ku; Tel. (052) 92–0052; and *Rajah Court,* 11-14 Sumiyoshi-cho; Sakae, Naka-ku; Tel. (052) 251–3375. Rajah Court stays open the later of the two, until 3 A.M. (Scheherazade closes around midnight).

◆

S P L U R G E S

Cormorant fishing, described above, is one of the most curious entertainments in this part of Japan. Instead of racing back to the city the same night, why not stay at one of Inuyama's excellent ryokan and have a really relaxing time of it? Overnight accommodations at the **Inuyama-kan,** for example, will cost between ¥12,000 and ¥18,000 without meals. Tel. (0568) 61–2309. There are several other ryokan in the area to choose from.

◆

KYOTO

◆

By Helen Brower

Founded in 794, when Buddhism was making its greatest inroads in Japan, Kyoto quickly became not only a government center, but a focal point of cultural and artistic activity, creating a "Golden Age" that lasted for several centuries. It remained the capital of Japan for more than 1,000 years.

A walk around the historic center, where many of the shrines and temples are located, reveals why the Japanese think of their ancient capital as a microcosm of the high points of their history and culture.

Kyoto has about 270 Shinto shrines, 1,600 Buddhist temples, and close to 60 landscaped gardens, where rocks, shrubbery, and water are carefully arranged according to philosophical and spiritual principle, laid down many years ago. These beautiful parks and gardens are delightful places to rest and regroup in between sightseeing forays.

Kyoto's handicraft tradition is justifiably famous. The Museum of Traditional Industry displays fine samples of pottery, silk-dyeing, and lacquerware. There are also individual factories where visitors can see pottery and woodblock prints being made. Admission is usually free or nominal.

Because Kyoto is arranged in a checkerboard pattern, it is relatively easy to get around on foot—just be sure to plan each day's walk in advance.

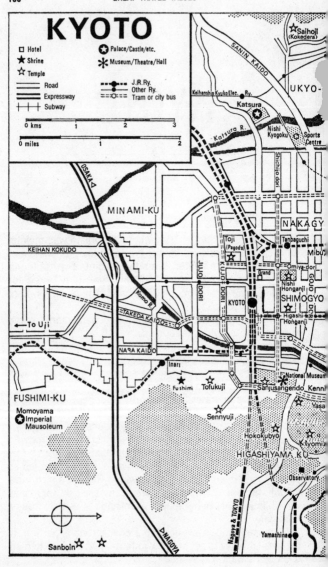

KYOTO

□ Hotel
★ Shrine
☆ Temple
★ Palace/Castle/etc.
✳ Museum/Theatre/Hall

Road
Expressway
+++ Subway

J.R.Ry.
Other Ry.
Tram or city bus

0 kms   1   2   3
0 miles   1   2

SANIN KAIDO

☆ Saihoji (Kokedera)

UKYO-

Keihanshin Kyuko Elec. Ry.

★ Katsura

Katsura R.

Nishi Kyogoku

Sports Centre

Shichijo dori

OSAKA

MINAMI-KU

NAKAGY

KEIHAN KOKUDO

Toji (Pagoda) ☆

Tenbaguchi

Mibu

Omiya-dori

Grand

Nishi Honganji

SHIMOGYO

JUJO DORI

KUJO-DORI

Kamo R.

KYOTO

Higashi Honganji

TAKEDA KAIDO

←To Uji

NARA KAIDO

Inari

National Museum

Fushimi ★

Tofukuji ☆

Sanjusangendo Kenni

FUSHIMI-KU

Momoyama ★ Imperial Mausoleum

Sennyuji ☆

Yasa

Hokokubyo ★

☆ Kiyomiz

HIGASHIYAMA KU

Observatory

Nagoya & TOKYO

Sanboin ☆   ☆

Yamashine

NAGOYA

PRACTICAL INFORMATION FOR KYOTO

How to Get There

Express trains from Tokyo to Kyoto run frequently throughout the day, and take just under three hours. The fare is ¥12,600, including surcharges. Japan Railways also operates overnight "Dream Bus" service from Tokyo to major cities, including Kyoto. The Tokyo–Kyoto service costs ¥7,800.

If you arrive at Osaka International Airport, take the airport bus that stops at major hotels in Kyoto. Travel time is about 60 to 95 minutes, and the cost is ¥730 to ¥800, depending on your destination.

Facts and Figures

AREA/POPULATION. Kyoto is a city of 1,500,000 people. It lies 27 miles north of Osaka and about 300 miles south of Tokyo, on the island of Honshu, the most important of Japan's four major islands. The area code is 075.

USEFUL ADDRESSES. TOURIST INFORMATION. *JNTO's Tourist Information Center,* 1st fl., Kyoto Tower Bldg., Higashi-Shiokojicho, Shimogyo-ku; Tel: (075) 371–5649, open 9 A.M. to 5 P.M. Mon.–Fri., 9 A.M. to noon Sat. A free publication, *The Monthly Guide,* offers details on current activities in Kyoto. It is available from the TIC office and most hotels.

Kyoto City Government Tourist Information Office, Kyoto Kaikan, Okazaki, Sakyo-ku; Tel: (075) 752–0215, open 8:30 A.M. – 5 P.M. weekdays.

For English-language tourist information in Kyoto, deposit ¥10 in a public phone and call Japan Travel-Phone at 371–5649. Your ¥10 will be returned after you call.

Medical Services: *Japan Baptist Hospital,* 47 Yamanomoto-cho, Kitashirakawa, Sakyo-ku; Tel: (075) 781–5191, has American-trained staff.

First Red Cross Hospital, Hammachi Higashiyama; Tel: (075) 561–1121.

Prefectural Medical University, Kawaramachi Hirokoji; Tel: (075) 251–5111.

Emergencies: To call the police, dial 110. To report a fire or call for an ambulance, dial 119. If using a public phone, no coin is needed. Just push the red button on the phone before dialing. *Kyoto Police Headquarters* is located at Shinmachi Shimodachiuri, Tel: (075) 451–9111, *Fire Department Headquarters*, at Teramachi Goshokoji, Tel: (075) 231–5311.

Post Office Main Building, Kyoto Kaikan, Okazaki, Sakyo-ku, Tel: (075) 365–2971/2473.

Getting Around

By Bus and Subway. Kyoto is served by five train companies, six bus firms and one subway line. You can save time and see the major attractions if you take buses numbered 201, 205, or 206 (¥160), which circle the city and pass most of Kyoto's historic landmarks.

You can also purchase a day ticket for ¥960 (¥490 for children) for unlimited travel on the city's public bus and train lines. If you plan on using public transportation frequently, you can save quite a bit off the regular fares of ¥140 to ¥170 per ride.

By Taxi. Kyoto claims to have more taxis than any other city in Japan. Fares start at ¥420, with ¥80 added for every 0.5 kilometer. The average ride will cost you about ¥1,000.

By Bike. Bicycles are a good alternative for sightseeing in Kyoto. The avenue that runs north of Sanjo Station, Kawabata-dori, has a number of bicycle rental shops, including *Keihan Rent-a-Cycle*, Tel: (075) 761–4892.

Where to Stay

HOTELS. As the most important repository of Japan's artistic and cultural heritage, Kyoto offers a wide selection of moderately priced accommodations for budget-minded art and history enthusiasts. Some are simple, but modern, Western-style hotels, and others are small, traditional Japanese-style inns. The price categories are based on the following rates: *Moderate*, ¥7,000–¥13,000 for a single, and ¥10,000–¥20,000 for a double/twin; *Inexpensive*, ¥5,500–¥8,500 for a single, ¥10,000–¥15,000 for a double/twin; and *Low Budget*, ¥4,000–¥5,000 for a single, ¥8,000–¥11,000 for a double/twin. ❤ = Highly Recommended.

Moderate

❤**Gimmond** (145 rooms), Takakura, Oike, Nakagyo-ku; Tel. (075) 221–4111. A good value for its comfortable accommodations and convenient location near downtown shopping area. Good French-Continental restaurants.

Holiday Inn Kyoto (270 rooms), 36, Nishihiraki-cho, Takano,

Sakyo-ku; Tel. (075) 721–3131. Located near the Ginkakuji Temple, the hotel has an outdoor and indoor pool, and other amenities.

● **International** (332 rooms), 284, Nijo Aburanokoji, Nakagyo-ku; Tel. (075) 222–1111. Quiet but convenient location, near Nijo Castle. Beautiful gardens. Five Western and Japanese restaurants, as well as a coffee shop.

● **Kyoto** (507 rooms), Oike Kawara-machi, Nakakyo-ku; Tel. (075) 211–5111. Central location, good choice for shopping and sightseeing.

New Miyako (714 rooms), Hachijo-guchi, Kyoto Station, Minami-ku; Tel. (075) 661–7111. Has a shopping arcade with a good selection of local handicrafts.

Inexpensive

● **Kyoto Dai-ni Tower** (306 rooms), Shichijo-sagaru, Higashinotoindori, Shimogyo-ku; Tel. (075) 361–3261. Close to Kyoto Station, offering rooms with beautiful views of Higashiyama Mountains.

Kyoto Palace-side (120 rooms), 380, Oukakuen-cho, Shimodachiuri-agaru, Karasuma-dori, Kamigyo-ku; Tel. (075) 431–8171. Next to Kyoto's Old Imperial Palace Park.

● **Kyoto Prince** (100 rooms), 43, Matsubara-cho, Shimogamo, Sakyo-ku; Tel. (075) 781–4141. Near the Shimogamo Shrine grove, where the spring Aoi Matsuri festival is held.

Sun-flower Kyoto (195 rooms), 51, Higashitennoji-machi, Okazaki. Sakyo-ku; Tel. (075) 761–9111. Located near the Heian Shrine and Ginkakuji Temple.

Low Budget

The following are small hotels, with one or more English-speaking staff members on duty.

● **Kyoto Central Inn** (2 Japanese-style rooms, 148 Western-style rooms), Shiji-Kawaramachi Nishi, Shimogyo-ku; Tel. (075) 211–8494.

Kyoto Traveller's Inn (19 Japanese-style rooms, 42 Western-style rooms), 91, Enshojicho, Okazaki, Sakyo-ku; Tel. (075) 771–0225.

Pension Higashiyama Gion (18 Western-style rooms), Sanjo Sagaru, Shirakawasuji, Higashiyama-ku; Tel. (075) 882–1181.

Pension Kitashirakawa (20 Western-style rooms), 5, Kamibettocho, Kitashirakawa, Sakyo-ku; Tel. (075) 721–5290.

JAPANESE-STYLE ACCOMMODATIONS, RYOKANS, AND MINSHUKU.

These accommodations offer a wonderful opportunity to save money and sample a traditional Japanese inn. Kyoto inns in particular are known for their fine cuisine—local families celebrating an important event often opt for a banquet in a ryokan dining hall rather than a restaurant.

The price categories are based on the following rates: *Moderate:* ¥3,500–¥4,000 singles, ¥6,000–¥9,000 twins/doubles, without meals; *Inexpensive:* ¥3,000 single, ¥5,000–¥6,000 double/twins, without meals; *Low Budget:* ¥5,000 single/twin, including two meals. ● = Highly Recommended.

Moderate

Matsubaya Ryokan (11 rooms), Nishi-iru, Higashitouin, Kamijuzuyamachi-dori, Shimogyo-ku; Tel. (075) 351–4268.

Ryokan Masuya (8 rooms), Konpira-Minami-dori-Nishi-iru, Yasui, Higashiyama-ku; Tel. (075) 561–2253.

Ryokan Mishima (8 rooms), Umamachidori, Higashiyamasen-Higashi-iru, Higashiyama-ku; Tel. (075) 551–0033.

Ryokan Rakucho (8 rooms), 67, Higashihangi-cho, Shimogamo, Sakyo-ku; Tel. (075) 721–2174.

Inexpensive

Hiraiwa Ryokan/Annex Hiraiwa (16 rooms), 314, Hayao-cho, Kaminoguchi-agaru, Ninomiyacho-dori, Shimogyo-ku; Tel. (075) 351–6748.

Riverside Takase/Kyoka Annex (5 rooms), Kiyamachidori-Kaminokuchi-agaru, Shimogyo-ku; Tel. (075) 351–7920.

●**Ryokan Kyoka** (10 rooms), Higashi-iru, Higashinotoin, Shimojuzuyamachi-dori, Shimogyo-ku; Tel. (075) 371–2709.

Low Budget

Minshuku Rokuharaya (7 rooms), 147, Takemuracho, Rokuhara, Higashiyama-ku; Tel. (075) 531–2776.

Minshuku Satomi (6 rooms), 442, Hayashishitamachi, Chion-in Sannai, Higashiyama-ku; Tel. (075) 561–8301.

●**Minshuku Tangoya** (6 rooms), Higashigawa, Nakadachiuri, Kudaru, Senbondori, Kamigyo-ku; Tel. (075) 441–7164.

Minshuku Teradaya (5 rooms), 583, Higashi Rokuchome, Gojobashi, Higashiyama-ku; Tel. (075) 561–3821.

●**Young Inn Kyoto** (10 rooms), 430–1, Bentencho,

Yaskaka Toriimae Sagaru, Kawara, Higashiyama-ku; Tel. (075) 541–0349.

YOUTH HOSTELS. The rates are based on the following: ¥2,000 for adults 19 and over, ¥1,700 for guests 12–18, and ¥1,300 for children 4 to 11.

Higashiyama (113 beds), Higashiyama-ku; Tel. (075) 761–8135.

Kitayama (43 beds), Kita-ku; Tel. (075) 492–5345.

Ohara (23 beds), Sakyo-ku; Tel. (075) 744–2721.

● **Utano** (168 beds), Ukyo-ku; Tel. (075) 462–2288.

Where to Eat

Kyoto is the birthplace of *kaiseki*, a method of food preparation and serving that originated in the Zen temples of Japan. It is considered the ultimate dining experience by many connoisseurs because the beauty and refinement of the table setting, and the arrangement of the food and the tableware are all as important as the food itself. The dishes consist mainly of seasonal fish combined with vegetables, mushrooms, and seaweed. The most elaborate *kaiseki* dinner can run from seven to 12 courses. Portions are small and courses are spaced at ample intervals, giving diners time to savor each dish. Though a complete *kaiseki* banquet can be quite costly, moderately priced alternatives are also available (see below).

Kyoto is also famous for its lightly seasoned *shojin ryori*, vegetarian dishes, created by Buddhist monks, and a variety of dishes whose main ingredient is *tofu*. *Kyo-bento,* another Kyoto specialty, is the local version of the box lunch. A filling repast that includes a selection of Kyoto's culinary specialties, it costs about ¥1,500–¥2,000 at many restaurants.

There are also many Western-style restaurants, including *McDonald's* (on Shijo-dori), *Kentucky Fried Chicken* (on Sanjo), and *Wimpy's* (near the Kyoto Station Plaza).

Price categories are based on the following: *Moderate,* ¥1,500–¥2,000 for lunch, ¥3,000–¥5,000 for dinner; *Inexpensive,* ¥900–¥1,500 for lunch, ¥2,000–¥3,000 for dinner. Reservations are generally not required for the restaurants listed below. ● = Highly Recommended.

Moderate

● **Izeki,** on the Pontocho; Tel. (075) 221–2080. Serves

kaiseki dishes in a friendly, relaxed setting, overlooking the Kamogawa River. No credit cards.

Junsei, near the Nanzenji Temple; Tel. (075) 761–2311. Specializing in tofu and vegetarian dishes. American Express, Diners Club, MasterCard, Visa.

☙**Koan,** near the Nanzenji Temple; Tel. (075) 771–2781. Vegetarian and noodle dishes. No credit cards.

Minokichi, Sanjo-agaru, Dobutsuen-mae; Tel. (075) 771–4185. An 18th-century farmhouse, decorated with folk art, serving a variety of Kyoto specialties. Major credit cards.

Natsuka, on the Pontocho; Tel. (075) 255–2105. French cuisine. American Express, Diners Club, MasterCard, Visa.

Inexpensive

A number of temples serve inexpensive vegetarian meals, such as: **Tenryu-ji** in Arashiyama, **Daiji-in** in Daitoku-ji, and **Shoteki-in,** at the Nanzenji Temple. Also, the following restaurant chains have branches around the city, and offer good, simple, low-cost meals: **Fujiya, Star Shokudo, Lipton,** and **Nagasakiya.**

Yoshikawa, at Tominokoji; Tel. (075) 221–0052. Specializes in tempura dishes. American Express, Diners Club, MasterCard, Visa.

☙**Junidanya,** at Gion Hanamikoji; Tel. (075) 561–0213. Located on the outskirts of the city. Sukiyaki and other dishes served in a homey setting. American Express, Diners Club, MasterCard, Visa.

What to See and Do

MAJOR ATTRACTIONS. The most pleasurable way to see the sights is on foot. Be sure to get a map first from the Tourist Information Center so that you can plan each day's walk in advance.

Also leave time for impromptu detours along the way. Many of the most memorable sights are not necessarily shrines or palaces. For example, you may wish to stop at a teahouse on the Old Canal to see a traditional tea ceremony, stroll along Philosopher's Walk, where one of Kyoto's most revered scholars, Ikutaro Nishida, used to take his daily constitutional, learn about Zen meditation from a master at the Sosenji Temple, or visit the house of one of Kyoto's most famous potters, Kawai Kanjiro.

Almost any time of year, there is a colorful festival in progress in one of Kyoto's shrines or temples, so be sure to check the festival calendar (also available from the TIC) to see what's on during your visit.

Ginkakuji Temple, the Silver Pavilion, in the northeastern part of the city. The Ashikaga Shogun who built the structure as his retirement home in 1489 never fulfilled his dream of seeing it covered in silver, but the name remained. The building, which later became a temple, has been designated a National Treasure.

Heian Shrine, in northeastern Kyoto, near the Zoological Gardens. Built in 1895 to mark the 1,100th anniversary of the founding of Kyoto, most of its buildings are smaller scale versions of the original Imperial Palace of Kyoto, which was erected in 794. The gardens of the shrine are especially popular for their cherry blossoms and irises when in season.

Kinkakuji Temple, the Gold Pavilion, in the northwestern part of the city. Once the mountain retreat of an Ashikaga Shogun—the grandfather of the shogun who built the Ginkakuji—the estate was converted after his death into a temple. Its name is derived from its striking gold-leaf covering, which was added by one of the original owner's descendants. The building is actually an exact replica, completed in 1955, of the original, built in 1397, which was destroyed by fire. The temple gardens and pond are especially lovely.

Kiyomizu Temple, in the northeastern part of the city. The main hall, which is now a National Treasure, was built in 1633 by the Tokugawa Shogun. Perched on the edge of a mountain, the temple is surrounded by woods and gardens. Locals and visitors flock here in the spring for the cherry trees, and in the fall, the maples. Close to the temple are shops that feature Kyoto's Kiyomizu pottery.

Nijo Castle, in north-central Kyoto, close to Nijo Station. Built in 1603, the castle was the official Kyoto residence of the powerful Tokugawa Shoguns. The castle's most famous building is the Ninomaru because of its splendid architecture and interior design and furnishings. Although many changes were made over the centuries, the castle still gives a compelling picture of how its original owners lived.

Ryoanji Temple, in the northwestern part of Kyoto. Considered one of the greatest monuments to Zen Buddhism, the Ryoanji was founded in 1473. Its deceptively simple rock garden is actually a masterful composition of stones and sand. The faithful, as well as the curious, come here to meditate.

Sanjusangendo Hall, in the northeastern part of the city, about 10 minutes from Kyoto Station. Constructed in 1266, it is most famous for the wooden statue of the Thousand-Handed Goddess, a Buddhist depiction of the Goddess of Mercy. The statue, which has been designated a National Treasure, is surrounded by more than 1,000 other images, both large and small, of the goddess.

Other Attractions. Byodoin Temple, in Uji City, south of Kyoto. Best known for the lovely Phoenix (Ho-odo) Hall built in 1053 by the Fujiwara clan. The mythological Ho-odo is shown poised, about to descend to earth. Both the Ho-odo, and an image of the Amitabha Buddha, sitting in the lotus position, are National Treasures.

Fushimi Inari Shrine, in the eastern part of the city, near Inari Station. One of the most important Shinto shrines in Japan. Founded in 711, it is best known for its 10,000 red-painted *torii,* gates standing on a hillside behind the shrine.

Higashi-Honganji Temple, near the Sanjusangendo Hall. The temple is the largest wooden structure in Kyoto. Founded in 1602 under the direction of the Tokugawa Shogunate, the present temple complex was built in 1895.

Nanzenji Temple, in the eastern part of the city, near the National Museum of Modern Art. This is best known for the Sammon Gate of the Main Hall, and the 16th-century paintings on sliding screens executed by a famous school of painters called the Kano group. Also noteworthy is the rock-and-sand garden.

Nishi-Honganji Temple, in the central part of the city, about 10 minutes from Kyoto Station. The temple was originally located at Higashiyama, east of its present site, and was moved in 1591. It is considered one of the most important sacred shrines of the Jodo-shinshu, a large Buddhist sect.

Tenryuji Temple, in the northwestern part of Kyoto. Founded in 1339 in memory of Emperor Godaigo, whose memorial tablet is housed in the Main Hall. Important artwork here includes a statue of the Sakyamuni Buddha.

Toji Temple, about a 15-minute walk from Kyoto Station. Established in 796, the structure was restored and rebuilt after fires destroyed much of it. Important art objects housed here include a 184-foot, five-story pagoda that is the tallest in Japan. On the 21st day of every month, a flea market is held on the temple grounds.

IMPERIAL KYOTO. For admission to the Imperial Palace (Kyoto Gosho), the Katsura Imperial Villa and the Shugakuin Imperial

Villa, you must first obtain permission from the Imperial Household Agency. See instructions below.

Katsura Imperial Villa, in the western part of Kyoto. Considered by many art experts and historians to be the finest example of classical Japanese architecture and landscaping, Katsura was built in the 17th century by Prince Toshihito, a brother of the emperor. The garden is one of Japan's most admired "stroll gardens," and is overlooked by a pond and several teahouses. Written permission to visit Katsura must be requested at least one month in advance by writing to the Imperial Household Agency (applications available from JNTO offices in the U.S.) at: Kyoto Gyoen-nai, Kamigyo-ku, Kyoto. Applications for Oct. and Nov. are not accepted as this is the busiest tourist season.

Kyoto Imperial Palace, in the northern part of the city. The original palace buildings, erected in 794, were repeatedly destroyed by fires. The current complex, which dates to 1855, adopted the same style as the original. The most beautiful buildings are Shishinden Hall, the ceremonial room where heads of state are welcomed; the Seiryoden Hall, originally conceived as the emperor's living room, and the Kogosho Palace, which consists of several audience chambers that are used for receptions. Tours are conducted daily at 10 A.M. and 2 P.M., except on Sat. afternoons, Sun., holidays, and from Dec. 25–Jan. 5. Tour requests must be made by calling the Imperial Household Agency at least 20 minutes in advance. Tel: (075) 211–1211. Bring your passport with you.

Shugakuin Imperial Villa, in northeastern Kyoto. The estate comprises three gardens, each with a villa. Shugakuin was built in the 17th century as a retreat for a former emperor. One of the palaces was constructed at a later date for a royal princess who became a nun and had it converted into a temple, called the Rinkyuji. Located at the foot of Mt. Hiei, the imperial villa covers 69 acres and offers beautiful views of the city and surroundings. To visit the Shugakuin Imperial Villa, follow the same procedures as outlined above for Katsura.

MUSEUMS. Costume Museum, in the central area, near Kyoto Station. Offers exhibits of Japanese costumes from ancient times until the present, displayed in chronological order. Open daily 9 A.M. –5 P.M., except Sun.

Kyoto Municipal Museum of Traditional Industry, in Okazaki Park. Exhibitions of Kyoto's and Japan's traditional arts and crafts made of silk, bamboo, lacquer, paper, and ceramics, featuring demonstrations of age-old production methods. Open daily 9 A.M.–5 P.M., except Mon.

National Museum, in the eastern part of Kyoto. Contains art objects from temples and shrines and other historical artifacts. Open 9 A.M.–4:30 P.M., except Mon.

National Museum of Modern Art, in Okazaki Park. Offers changing exhibitions of works by both Japanese and Western artists. Open daily 10 A.M.–5 P.M., except Mon.

Ryozen Hakubutsukan, about a 20-minute walk from the National Museum. Offers exhibitions on the history of the Meiji Restoration. Open daily, 9 A.M.–5 P.M.

TRAVELING WITH CHILDREN. Less frenetic than Tokyo or Osaka, Kyoto's leisurely pace, fairy-tale castles and temples, and appealing gardens make it a good choice for families.

Iwatayama Monkey Park, Iwatayama Hill. About 100 monkeys who live on Iwatayama Hill come down in groups to visit the park. You can even feed them apples and cookies if you like. Open 9 A.M.–5 P.M., daily.

Kyoto Municipal Zoological Gardens, Okazaki Park. Open daily from 9 A.M.–4 P.M. Well maintained and featuring a good representation of the world's wildlife. Also has some hands-on areas.

Shozan, not far from Kinkakuji. A full-scale recreation complex where the Japanese go on their day off. Has a Japanese restaurant, garden, swimming pool, and bowling. Open 9 A.M.–5:30 P.M., daily.

Toei Movieland, in Uzumasa. Kyoto's movie village has large open sets that re-create feudal and modern Japan. You can watch period-costumed actors filming, and walk through samurai movie sets. Open 9 A.M.–5 P.M., except July 24–26, Dec. 21–Jan. 1.

SIGHTSEEING TOURS. Half- and full-day sightseeing of Kyoto and excursions to Nara are operated by several companies, including *Japan Travel Bureau* (075) 361–7241; *Fujita Travel Service* (075) 222–0121; and *Kinki Nippon Tourist,* a Gray Line affiliate, (075) 222–1224. The TIC office (see "Useful Addresses") can also provide information on tea ceremonies, flower arranging demonstrations, and other special interest sightseeing.

Industrial Tours: *Inaba Cloisonné* allows groups of up to 50 to visit its factory in Higashiyamaku to watch the artisans at work. English- and French-speaking guides are available.

Kyoto Yuzen Cultural Hall invites visitors to see the process of dyeing. Interpreters are not always available.

Arrangements should be made through the TIC office (see "Useful Addresses"), which can also provide information on other industrial tours offered by Japan Travel Bureau and other tour organizers.

Home Visits: Kyoto was the first city in Japan to offer visits to Japanese homes by foreign tourists. The visits usually last one or two hours and take place in the evening. There is no charge for the visit, except for the student-interpreter, but it is customary to bring a small gift. Arrangements should be made at least a day or two in advance by contacting the Tourist Section, Department of Cultural Affairs and Tourism, Kyoto City Government, Kyoto Kaikan, Okazaki, Sakyo-ku, Kyoto; Tel. (075) 752–0215.

SHOPPING. Kyoto's main shopping avenue is Kawaramachi Dori. Here, and at the two nearby shopping arcades, you'll find good buys in silks, lacquerware, porcelain, pottery, and other items.

For antiques and curios, try the shops along Nawate, Shimmonzen, and Furumonzen streets. The establishments on Higashiyama Street offer a good selection of pottery.

If you're in a hurry but also want to keep a lid on shopping costs, then the one-stop shopping at the Kyoto Handicraft Center (Kumano Jinja Higashi, Sakyo-ku) is a good place to browse for everything from kimonos and Mikimoto pearls to furniture and souvenirs. You can also see crafts demonstrations here.

The Kyoto Craft Center nearby is where the Japanese go to buy contemporary crafts by Kyoto's finest designers. There are items to fit every budget.

Inaba Cloisonné (Sanjo, at the Shirakawa Bridge) may well be the most famous shop for cloisonné in Japan. There are also demonstrations.

Kanebo (Kawaramachi Shijo) offers an enormous variety of silks.

R. Kita (Shinmonzen, Higashiyama-ku) has fine antiques, Imari-ware and Kutani porcelain.

Komai Pearls (Shinmonzen, Higashiyama-ku) offers good value and service on pearls.

Nishimura (Teramachi-kado, Sanjo-dori, Nakagyo-ku) and *Mikumo Wood-Block Print Co.* (Shijo Naka-Shinmachinishi) offer a fine selection of woodblock prints.

Tachikichi (Tominokoji-kado, Shijo-dori, Shimogyo-ku) is a pottery-making shop that employs age-old methods to fashion modern ceramics. There is also a good selection of Kyoto's Kiyomizu-ware here.

Tanakaya (Sanjo-dori, Nakagyo-ku) specializes in traditional Kyoto-style dolls, dressed in full regalia.

Yamato Mingei-ten (Takoyakushi-agaru, Kaaramachi, Nakagyo-ku) specializes in folk art items such as handmade paper, textiles, ceramics, and glassware.

Department Stores. *Daimaru* (Shijo, Takakura) closed Wed.; *Takashimaya* (Shijo Kawaramachi) closed Wed.; *Fujii Daimaru* (Shijo Teramachi) closed Thurs.; *Marabutsu* (Karasuma Shichijo) closed Fri.; *Kyoto Station Department Store* (in Kyoto Station, upstairs) no closing; *Hankyu* (Shijo Kawaramachi) closed Thurs.

SPORTS. You can play **tennis** on the courts at *Nijo Castle,* for a small charge, or softball tennis on the courts of the *Imperial Palace Grounds,* also for a modest fee. *Lake Biwa,* Japan's largest freshwater lake, is good for **swimming** as well as **yachting.** Good beaches near Kyoto are *Mano, Ohmi, Maiko,* and *Kita-Komatsu,* all north of the city. **Golf** is available at the *Kamigamo* links, near the Kamigamo Shrine, but fees are high. There are five or six **races** a year at the *Yodo Horse Track,* south of Kyoto. The *Kyoto Arena* has facilities for both **ice skating** and **Ping-Pong.** You'll see early-morning **joggers** out in full force at many locations throughout Kyoto. Especially popular are the banks of the Kamo River, convenient to some of the major hotels.

Entertainment and Nightlife

If you take a stroll in the evening through the Gion and along the Pontocho, both traditional geisha quarters, you will see geisha and maiko (apprentice geisha) hurrying off to the various clubs where they entertain. You would be well advised, however, to avoid these high-priced bars and night spots. Instead, you can enjoy an evening of geisha musical entertainment (¥2,000) at the *Yasaka Kaikan Hall* (Shijo Hanamikoji). There are two shows each evening, at 7:40 P.M. and 8:40 P.M., Mar.–Nov. There are also regular performances of Japanese Bunraku puppet plays at this same hall.

Kabuki plays can be seen at *Minami-za* near the Shijo Bridge. In December, gala performances starring the country's best Kabuki performers are staged here.

Japanese Noh drama is also performed regularly in Kyoto. Shows last four or five hours and usually take place on Sat.

and Sun. The three theaters where Noh is presented are the *Oe-Nogaku-do,* at Yanaginobamba Oshikoji, the *Kongo Nohgaku-kodo* at Shijo Muromachi, and the *Kanze Kaikan* at Okazaki Enschojicho. Tickets for Kabuki and Noh plays start at ¥2,000.

Concerts are held at *Kyoto Kaikan* near Heian Shrine. Concerts of light music are given at *Maruyama Music Hall* (at Maruyama Park, outdoors) during the summer.

◆

S P L U R G E S

Ryokan Hiiragi-ya, Oike-kado, Fuyacho-dori, Nakagyo-ku; Tel. (075) 221–1136. Founded in the late 19th century to cater to samurai, the 31-room Hiragi-ya has counted among its guests Charlie Chaplin, the famous Japanese writer Yukio Mishima, and Japan's Nobel Prize-winning author, Yasunari Kawabata, as well as numerous ministers of state. Modern amenities have been discreetly added to the traditional furnishings. Each guest room has a private bath, some with stained-glass windows. English is spoken. Rooms cost from ¥35,000 to ¥50,000, including two meals.

Restaurant Nakamura-ro, Yasaka-jinja-uchi, Gion, Higashiyama-ku; Tel. (075) 561–0016. Reputed to be the oldest restaurant in Japan, Nakamura-ro traces its roots to the 16th century. The ambience, decor, and method of food preparation are all reminiscent of a bygone era. This is the place to splurge on a 12-course *kaiseki*-style banquet and to sample exquisite typical Kyoto cuisine. A complete kaiseki dinner will cost about ¥15,000. (A bento box lunch, however, with a sampling of assorted specialties, will cost only about ¥2,500.) No credit cards are accepted. Reservations are recommended.

◆

NARA

◆

By Helen Brower

Although standard tourist itineraries include Nara only as a side trip from Kyoto, a longer stay is certainly warranted for anyone with a serious interest in the history of Japan.

Lying just 26 miles to the south of Kyoto, Nara was the capital of Japan from 710 to 784. During that time, the arts as well as commerce flourished. The many Shinto and Buddhist shrines and temples from that period attest to Nara's influence as a spiritual capital. Buddhist culture reached its peak in 752 with the completion of the famous Daibutsu bronze image of Buddha in the Todaiji Temple.

Shoppers will find good buys in Nara's traditional arts and crafts, especially the local Nara-ningyo carved wooden dolls and Nara fans. Other shopping specialties include writing brushes, India ink, lacquerware, and articles made of deer horn.

Some of Japan's most spectacular festivals take place here. In January, the fireworks during the Wakakusa Yama Yaki (Burning of Dead Grass on Wakakusa Hill) light up the skies above Nara and illuminate its magnificent temples. In March, during the Kasuga Matsuri, the townsfolk dress in colorful garb of the Heian period and sacred dances are performed at the Kasuga Shrine.

Because Nara is a relatively small city, the major attractions can be seen on foot. The Nara YMCA English Goodwill Guide Association (address: Kumini, Nishioji; Tel: (0742) 44–2207) recently began offering free English guide service to visitors. (Also see "Sightseeing Tours" below, for other free guide services.)

171

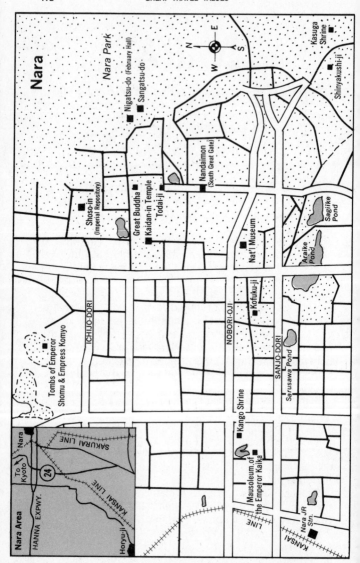

PRACTICAL INFORMATION FOR NARA

How to Get There

From Kyoto. The limited express trains of *The Kintetsu Railway* line leave every half-hour from platforms at the south end of Kyoto Station. The trip takes about 35 minutes and costs ¥780 including limited express surcharge. *The National Railway* (¥660) and the *Kintetsu* and *Keihan* bus lines also go to Nara, but take longer.

From Osaka. The trip takes about 35 minutes on the *Kintetsu Railway* and costs ¥760.

Facts and Figures

POPULATION AND AREA CODE. Present-day Nara is a town of about 250,000 people, and is the capital of Nara Prefecture. The area code is 0742.

USEFUL ADDRESSES. Tourist Information. *The Tourist Information Center,* 28, Higashi-Mukai-Naka-machi, (in Kintetsu Nara Station); Tel. (0742) 24–4858. Open 9 A.M.–5 P.M., except Dec. 29–Jan. 3. A second *TIC* office is at 23–4 Kani-Sanjo, Nara City (in Kanko Center); Tel. (0742) 22–3900. Open 9 A.M.–9 P.M., except Dec. 29–Jan. 3.

Nara City Tourist and Industry Department, Nara City Office, 1-1-1, Minami, Nijo, Oji; Tel. (0742) 34–1111.

The Nara City Information Office, windows in the Nara National Railways Station; Tel. (0742) 22–9821, and at the Kintetsu Nara Station.

Central Post Office, 5-3, Omiya-cho; Tel. (0742) 35–1611.

Emergencies. As in other cities in Japan, to call the police, dial 110. For fire and ambulance service, dial 119. *Nara Police Headquarters* is at 30, Nobori-oji; the telephone number is (0742) 23–1101. For English-language information, use the *Japan Travel-Phone,* Tel. (0120) 222–800.

Getting Around

There is frequent and reliable service by local public and private rail lines to the major attractions, many of which are clustered together in the same area. Japan Railways' *Kansai Main line* and *Sakurai line,* the *Kansai* line and the *Kinki Nippon Railways* operate in and around Nara.

Local rail fares are relatively low. For instance, the fare from Nara to Horyuji Temple, seven miles west of the city, costs ¥220 on the Kansai Main Line. If you're planning an in-depth visit of Nara and the environs, you may want to purchase the Japan Railways' Orange Card, which provides discounts for travel on its trains within a radius of 50 kilometers. Travel that would normally cost ¥5,300, costs only ¥5,000 with the Orange Card; train fare regularly costing ¥10,700, costs just ¥10,000 with the card. The Orange Card is sold at JR stations in major cities.

Where to Stay

HOTELS. Though a comparatively small city, Nara offers a good selection of hotels, both Western- and Japanese-style. The price categories are based on the following rates: *Moderate* ¥7,000–¥11,500 for singles, and ¥10,000–¥21,000 for doubles/twins; *Inexpensive* ¥4,000–¥5,000 for singles, and ¥7,000–¥10,000 for doubles/twins; and *Low Budget* ¥5,000–¥6,000 per person, two meals included. ◗ = Highly Recommended.

Moderate

Hotel Fujita (118 rooms), 47-1, Shimo Sanjo-cho; Tel. (0742) 23–8111. Convenient for sightseeing.

◗**Nara Hotel & Annex** (166 rooms), 1096, Takabatake-cho; Tel. (0742) 26–3300. Atmospheric, turn-of-the-century hotel, near Deer Park.

Inexpensive

Ryokan Hakuhoo (20 Japanese and two Western-style rooms), 4-1, Kamisanjo-cho; Tel. (0742) 26–7891. A short walk from the Kintetsu line station.

◗**Ryokan Matsumae** (12 Japanese-style rooms, all with bath), 28-1, Higashi-Terabayashi-cho; Tel. (0742) 22–3686. Centrally located, a short walk to the Deer Park, Todaiji Temple and Kasuga Shrine.

Low Budget

Furuichi Ryokan (14 Japanese-style and one Western-style room); Tel. (0742) 22–2440.

Minshuku Yamashiroya (8 rooms), 1-15, Nishinokyomachi; Tel. (0742) 33–2983.

🍂**People's Inn Nanakomichi** (29 Western-style rooms), Konishi-cho; Tel. (0742) 23–8753. Convenient to several rail lines.

🍂**Ryokan Seikanso** (15 Japanese-style rooms), 29, Higashi-Kitsuji-cho; Tel. (0742) 22–2670. Near Kasuga Shrine and Todaiji Temple.

YOUTH HOSTELS. The rates for these modest accommodations are ¥2,000 for guests 19 and over; ¥1,700 for guests 12 to 18; ¥1,300 for children 4 to 11. Meals are not included.

🍂**Nara Youth Hostel** (200 beds), Horen; Tel. (0742) 22–1334.

Naraken Seishonen Kaikan (54 beds), Handahiraki; Tel. (0742) 22–5540.

Where to Eat

There are good low-cost Japanese, Chinese, and Western restaurants on Higashi-muku-naka-machi, the arcade street to your right when you leave Kintetsu Station, and on Sanjo-dori. You can make your choice from the plastic replicas displayed in most of the windows. 🍂 = Highly Recommended.

🍂**Furusato,** Minami Hairu, Higashimuki-dori; Tel. (0742) 22–2828. Serves an inexpensive soba or udon lunch for ¥500. No credit cards.

Shizuka, Konishi-dori; Tel. (0742) 22–8092. Kamameshi lunch, ¥700. No credit cards.

Tono Chaya, Noborioji; Tel. (0742) 22–4348. A teahouse that serves a good kayu bento lunch on antique dishes for about ¥2,000. Closed Tues. Antiques are for sale here. No credit cards.

What to See and Do

MAJOR ATTRACTIONS. Deer Park. Located about 15 minutes by foot from Nara Station. Almost 1,000 tame deer roam through the park—whose real name is Nara Park. Many species of Japanese trees, including huge cedars and oaks as well as wisteria vines can be seen here. It is a good place to rest in between sightseeing visits since the park is close to the Kasuga Shrine, the Todaiji Temple, the Shin-Hakushiji Temple, and other sights.

Horyu-ji Temple. About a 45-minute ride from Kintetsu Nara

Station, Horyu-ji is referred to as the "Fountainhead of Japanese Culture." It was founded in 607 by Shotoku Taishi (the Crown Prince of Holy Virtue), whose court attracted the most learned citizens of their day. The Prince is credited with promoting the spread of Buddhism in Japan. The temple complex once consisted of 40 buildings. The Daihozoden Treasure Hall in the temple holds regular exhibitions of Buddhist art.

Kasuga Shrine. Located in the southeastern part of Nara, Kasuga was founded in 768 and is one of Japan's most important Shinto shrines. The buildings are covered in vermilion-colored lacquer. About 1,800 stone lanterns stand on the grounds and 1,000 metal lanterns are suspended from the buildings. The shrine is the site of the spring festival, the Kasuga Matsuri.

Kofukuji Temple. Located in the western part of Deer Park, the temple was founded in 710 by the Fujiwara clan. During its golden age, it consisted of as many as 175 buildings. Some of the principal structures still stand, including the Five-Story Pagoda, which dates from 1426. At 165 feet, it is the second-highest pagoda (after Kyoto's Toji) in Japan. It also contains the Kokuhokan Museum, which houses a fine sculpture collection.

The Nigatsu-do (February Hall) and the **Sangatsu-do** (March Hall) are both a short walk from the Todaiji Temple (see below). The Nigatsu-do stands on a hillside and offers a beautiful view of the Yamato Plain. The Sangatsu-do contains a statue of the male incarnation of the Bodhisattva of Compassion (usually represented as the Goddess of Mercy). The statue is made of lacquer and covered in silver, crystals, and gems.

Shin-Yakushiji Temple. About a 10-minute walk from the Kasuga Shrine, the temple was founded in 747. The main hall, which is part of the original structure, has several Buddhist statues that have been declared National Treasures.

Todaiji Temple. In the northeastern corner of Nara. Best known for its Daibutsu, the world's largest bronze statue of Buddha, measuring 53 feet in height and weighing 452 tons. Surrounding the Great Buddha Hall is the largest wooden structure in the world—161 feet high, 187 feet long and 164 feet wide. The Shosoin Treasure Repository inside houses many of Japan's most priceless art objects.

Toshodaiji Temple. Considered to be the most valuable surviving structure from the 8th century. The temple was built by a famous Tang Dynasty Chinese priest, Ganjin, in 759. In the Main Hall is an 11-foot lacquer statue of the Thousand-Handed Kannon.

MUSEUMS. Nara Museum of Ethnology, at Koriyama. Re-creates Old Japan through tableaux and old houses. Open 9 A.M.–5 P.M., except Mon.

Nara National Museum, 50, Noborioji-cho. Features important exhibitions of Buddhist art and ancient works of art. Open 9 A.M.–4:30 P.M., except Mon., and Dec. 26–Jan. 3.

Nara Prefectural Museum, a short walk from the Kofukuji Temple. Houses exhibitions of mostly contemporary works of art. Open 10 A.M.–4:30 P.M., except Tues.

Neiraku Art Museum, in the Isuien Garden. Contains major works of Chinese and Korean art and ceramics. Open 10 A.M.–4:30 P.M., except Tues.

Tenri Museum, in the village of Tenri, about a 20-minute bus ride from Nara. The town is the headquarters of the Tenrikyo Shinto sect. The museum contains about 20,000 works of art from China, Japan, and Korea, as well as Egypt, Greece, ancient Rome, Persia, and the Middle East. Well worth the trip. Open 9 A.M.–4 P.M., except Mon.

Yamato Bunka-kan, 1-11, Gakuen Minami, situated in a pine grove overlooking a lake, about 15 minutes from the city. It is best known for its Chinese ceramics, and houses the Enlarge-Jonas Netsuke Collection. Open 9 A.M.–4 P.M., except Mon., and Dec. 26–Jan. 3.

SIGHTSEEING TOURS. The following companies provide regularly scheduled sightseeing tours of Nara:

Japan Travel Bureau, Nishi-Mikado-cho (in the Kitagawa building), Tel. (0742) 23–2525. Open 9 A.M.–5 P.M., except Sun. and holidays.

Kinki Nippon Tourist Co., Higashimuki-Nakamachi; Tel. (0742) 24–0171. Open 9 A.M.–5 P.M., except Sun. and holidays.

Nippon Travel Agency, 511 Sanjo-cho; Tel. (0742) 26–7225. Open 9 A.M.–5 P.M., except Sun. and holidays.

The Sarusawa Information Center, 4, Noborioji-cho; Tel. (0742) 26–4753. Offers free guide service by English-speaking university students. Open from 10 A.M.–4 P.M., except Fri.

SHOPPING. Nara doesn't offer as many shopping opportunities as its neighbor, Kyoto, but the **Nara Prefecture Shoku Kankokan,** on Sanjo Dori, does have good values on a wide variety of traditional Nara handicraft items. These include dolls, lacquerware, fans, writing brushes, and masks. It is open 10 A.M.–6 P.M. daily, except Mon. Other shops, also on Sanjo Dori, as well as Higashimuki and Mochidono, in the center of town, offer a good selection of low-cost souvenirs and handicrafts.

◆

S P L U R G E S

Yanagi Chaya. Located just behind the Kofukuji Temple, this restaurant serves up a sumptuous luncheon consisting of exquisitely prepared local specialties, for ¥6,050. It is open 11:30 A.M.–6 P.M., except Wed. No credit cards. For reservations, call (0742) 22–4348.

Hotel Yamato Sanso (40 rooms), 27, Shosoinkita, Kawakami-cho; Tel. (0742) 26–1011. In a tranquil, wooded location on the northern outskirts of the city, not far from the Todaiji Temple. The hotel has a natural promenade, open-air bath, and tea ceremony rooms, as well as Japanese-style cottage accommodations. Rates are ¥10,000–¥12,000 for a standard twin, and ¥15,000–¥25,000 for deluxe Western- or Japanese-style accommodations.

◆

OSAKA

◆

By Helen Brower

Osaka is a bustling, modern, and surprisingly clean city of 8 million people. With their eyes on the future, the city fathers have outlined an ambitious "Twenty-First Century Plan" that aims to make Osaka the envy of other Japanese cities and perhaps even help it overtake its chief rival, Tokyo. However, Osaka's towering skyscrapers and superhighways don't tell the whole story. Perched high above the city and looking down on modern Osaka is its most famous landmark, Osaka Castle. The city is committed to an ongoing greening and beautification plan.

Osakans are known to work hard and play hard. They also love to eat, which is probably why the city offers such a mind-boggling array of culinary choices, from classical Japanese cuisine, to French country cooking and Indian curries. Though Osaka has a reputation for being an expensive city, there are money-saving ways to get the most out of your visit. Do your shopping in one of the underground arcades frequented by budget-conscious Osakans, stop for lunch at one of the reasonably priced dining spots in Umeda, and buy a day tripper's transportation pass that will give you unlimited rides on the city's buses and trains at reduced rates.

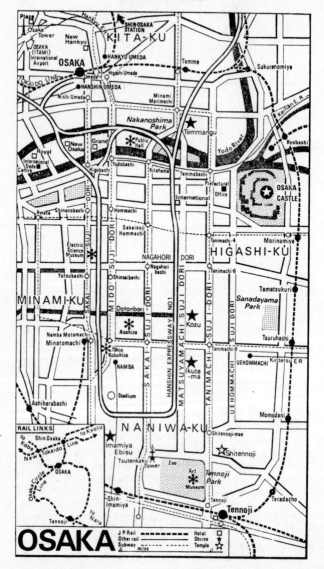

PRACTICAL INFORMATION FOR OSAKA
How to Get There

Osaka International Airport is the second busiest airport in Japan, after Tokyo-Narita. By 1992, a new, state-of-the-art airport will open on a man-made island in Osaka Bay. It will be the first airport in Japan to operate round-the-clock.

About 10 international airlines currently serve Osaka from other parts of Asia, North America, Europe, and other parts of the world. More than a dozen flights a day connect Osaka with Tokyo. From Osaka Airport to downtown Osaka (Shin-Osaka Station) takes 25 minutes by airport limousine and costs ¥360.

From Tokyo: Osaka is approximately 340 miles from Tokyo. Flights take about 50 minutes. *Japan Air Lines* (JAL) and *All Nippon Airways* (ANA) both offer frequent service.

Japan Railways' operates its *Hikari* "bullet" train service from Tokyo 39 times a day from 6 A.M. to 8 P.M. The trip takes two hours 56 minutes to Osaka. JR's *Kodama*, which operates 61 times a day from 6:10 A.M. to 10:05 P.M., takes about four hours, and the fare is ¥13,100.

In addition, the *Sunrise Holidays* division of Japan Travel Bureau offers several package tours from Tokyo that terminate in Osaka.

From Nagoya: Some JR express trains that originate in Tokyo stop in Nagoya. The *Kintetsu Electric Railways* also operates 27 trains a day from Nagoya. The journey takes two hours 13 minutes and costs ¥2,570 to Osaka's Namba Station.

From Kobe: JR operates both a superexpress train and an interurban rapid train *(kaisoku)* that takes 36 minutes from Kobe's Sannomiya Station to Osaka's Umeda Station. *Hankyu Electric Railway* serves the same route in 28 minutes and costs ¥230.

From Kyoto: JR's superexpress and interurban trains take 36 minutes from Track 4 in Kyoto Station, and cost ¥510. The *Keihan Electric Railway* express train from Kyoto Sanjo Station to Osaka Yodoyabashi Station takes about one hour and costs ¥510.

From Kyoto Kawaramachi to Osaka's Umeda Station takes about 35 minutes by the *Hankyu Electric Railway*'s limited express train, and about 45 minutes by ordinary express train and costs ¥300.

The airport limousine from downtown Kyoto to Osaka International Airport (¥730) takes 55 minutes (longer for the limo that picks up at Kyoto hotels).

From Nara: By the *Kintetsu* line to Uehonmachi Station in downtown Osaka takes about 30 minutes and costs ¥760.

Facts and Figures

POPULATION AND AREA CODE. Osaka has a population of 2,600,000 people, making it Japan's second most populous city, after Tokyo. It is situated at the mouth of the Yodo River, on the island of Honshu, and is crisscrossed by a network of canals. The area code is 060.

USEFUL ADDRESSES. Tourist Information: The *Osaka Tourist Association* has three locations in Osaka—in Osaka Station, Kita-ku; Tel. (06) 345–2189. Open 8 A.M. –5 P.M. daily. 5-16-1, in Shin-Osaka Station, Nakanoshima, Yodogawa-ku; Tel. (06) 305–3311. Open 8 A.M.–8 P.M. daily, except Dec. 31–Jan. 3. In the Kokusai Hotel, 58, Hashizume-cho, Uchi-Honmachi Higashi-ku; Tel. (06) 941–9200. Open noon–7 P.M., except Tues., and Dec. 30–Jan. 4.

Osaka Municipal Tourist Office, at the east exit of JR's Osaka Station; Tel. (06) 345–2189/6200. Open 9 A.M.–5 P.M.

Osaka Tourist Association, in the Semba Center Building, No. 2; Tel. (06) 261–3948. Open 9 A.M.–5 P.M.

Use the *Japan Travel-Phone* by dialing (0120) 222–800 for information.

Consulates: *U.S. Consulate-General*, 2-4-9, Umeda, Kita-ku; Tel. (06) 341–2754.

British Consulate-General, Hongkong and Shanghai Bank Bldg., 4-45, Awaji-machi, Higashi-ku; Tel. (06) 231–3355.

Emergencies: As in other cities of Japan, dial 110 for the police; 119 for fire and ambulance service.

Medical Services: *Yodogawa Christian Hospital,* Awajihonmachi, Higashi-yodogawaku; Tel. (06) 322-2250/4. This hospital is accustomed to handling foreign patients.

International Catholic Hospital, 5-26, Yamasakacho, Higashi-Sumiyoshi-ku, Tel. (06) 791–0939.

Osaka National Hospital, Hoenzaka-cho, Higashi-ku; Tel. (06) 942–1331, has an excellent reputation.

Getting Around

One-day transportation passes are available for unlimited rides on the municipal subway and bus lines. The cost is ¥800 for adults and ¥400 for children. Savings are considerable since regular fares range from ¥140 to ¥200. You can obtain the passes at any JR station. Although the bus service is good, route signs are only in Japanese. Your best bet is to use the subway. (Taxis are also to be avoided—Osaka is a big city and traffic is heavy.)

The main train line runs south from Shin-Osaka Station to Osaka Central Station in Umeda. From there, one branch goes east to Osaka Castle, then south, then east again. Another line serves the western part of town and the port area. The main line continues south under Midosuji Boulevard to Nanba, then divides. One branch continues southeast to the Tennoji area, while the other heads south.

The important points for the tourist are Shin-Osaka, Umeda, Shin-Saibashi, Nanba, and Tennoji, all of which are on the #1 line (Ichi-go-sen). Temmabashi (which goes to Osaka Castle) is on the #2 line (Ni-go-sen). Trains operate from 5:30 A.M.–11:45 P.M. every 2½ minutes during rush hour, and every four minutes the rest of the day.

Where to Stay

As one of Asia's most dynamic cities, Osaka's skyline is interspersed with dozens of gleaming, new hotel towers that cater to high-level executives. However, there is also a good selection of moderately priced "business hotels" (see below) that are favored by budget-minded tourists, as well as middle-level business travelers.

In Osaka and elsewhere in Japan, these hotels offer small but immaculately clean rooms, some with private bath and some with shared bath. Room service is generally not provided, but vending machines dispense soft drinks, tooth brushes, and other items for overnight guests.

Also, as the starting point of many tour packages, Osaka offers a great variety of modestly priced tourist hotels and inns.

HOTELS. The price categories are based on the following rates: *Moderate* ¥7,000–¥10,000 for singles, and ¥12,000–¥22,000 for doubles/twins; *Inexpensive* ¥5,500–¥7,000 for singles, ¥8,000–¥13,000 for doubles/twins. ● = Highly Recommended.

Moderate

Hanshin (243 rooms) 2-3-30, Umeda, Kita-ku; Tel. (06) 344–1662. Convenient location in Umeda. Has a shopping arcade and a sauna.

◓**International** (394 rooms) 58 Hashizume-cho, Uchihonmachi; Tel. (06) 941–2661. Attractively furnished; has a Japanese garden.

New Hankyu (993 rooms) 1-1-35 Shibata, Kita-ku; Tel. (06) 372–5101/6600. Well run, centrally located hotel.

Tenno-ji Miyako (151 rooms) 10-48 Hidein-cho, Tennoji-ku; Tel. (06) 779–1501. In the Tennoji Station building.

Inexpensive

Crevette Kuko (188 rooms), four minutes from Osaka Airport, 1-9-6 Kuko, Ikeda-shi; Tel. (06) 843–7201. Good, functional airport hotel.

Hotel Echo Osaka (83 rooms) 1-4-7 Abenosuji, Abeno-ku; Tel. (06) 633–1141. Near Shitennoji Temple.

Osaka Castle (122 rooms) 2-35 Kyobashi, Higashi-ku; Tel. (06) 942–1401. Overlooking the Okawa River, close to the Osaka Merchandise Mart and Matsuzakaya Department Store.

◓**Osaka River-side** (102 rooms) 5-10-160 Nakano-cho, Miyakojima-ku; Tel. (06) 928–3251. Commands a view of Osaka Castle. Good service.

BUSINESS HOTELS. The average rate for a single room is ¥6,000, not including meals.

◓**Hokke Club Osaka** (451 Western- and Japanese-style rooms) 12-19 Toganocho, Kita-ku; Tel. (06) 313–3171. About a 10-minute walk from Osaka Station.

Nankai (214 rooms) 1-17-11 Namba Naka, Naniwa-ku; Tel. (06) 649–1521. Close to Namba subway station.

Osaka World (202 rooms) 1-5-23 Sonezaki, Kita-ku; Tel. (06) 361–1100. A 10-minute walk from Osaka Station.

Toko (300 rooms) 1-3-19 Minamimoricho, Kita-ku; Tel. (06) 363–1201. Near the Minamimorimachi subway station.

JAPANESE-STYLE INNS. The price categories for the following *ryokan* are: *Moderate* ¥4,000–¥5,000/single; *Inexpensive* ¥3,000–¥4,000/single. Meals are not included.

Moderate

Chikamatsu Ryokan (8 Japanese-style rooms, 11 Western-style rooms) 7-1 Chayamachi, Kita-ku; Tel. (06) 371–5071. Well located, close to JR; Tokaido-Honseu Line and other major transportation lines.

Inexpensive

◉**Ebisu-so Ryokan** (17 Japanese-style rooms) 1-7-33 Nipponbashi-Nishi, Naniwa-ku; Tel. (06) 643–4861. Convenient to the main appliance shopping area and the National Theater.

Ryokan Masumi (10 Japanese-style rooms) 2-12-4 Miyakojima-Hondori, Miyakojima-ku. A short walk from Miyakojima Station.

YOUTH HOSTELS. The rates are as follows: ¥2,000 for guests 19 and older; ¥1,700 from 12–18 years old; ¥1,300 for children 4 to 11.

Hattori Ryokuchi (108 beds), 1-3 Hattori-ryokuchi, Toyonaka-shi, Osaka Pref.; Tel. (06) 862–0600.

◉**Osaka Shiritsu Nagai** (102 beds), 450, Higashi-Nagai-cho, Higashi Sumiyoshi-ku; Tel. (06) 699–5631.

Where to Eat

As Osaka is the leading city of Japan's Kansai region, you'll find many restaurants here serving typical regional dishes. Eel is considered a great delicacy, and some dishes, like *okonomiyaki*—a kind of cabbage pancake—is said to have originated here.

Traditional Japanese restaurants specializing in sushi, sukiyaki, and tempura are also well represented, as well as sedate English tearooms, a Continental-style wine bar and cocktail lounges that look like Madison Avenue clones.

Good, inexpensive restaurants are scattered throughout the city. Try some of the little noodle and fish restaurants in Dojima and Nakanoshima, and the sushi bars in the underground arcades. For a lark, try the eating and drinking spots in the shopping and food complex called Amerika Mura (American Village).

RESTAURANTS. There are traditional Japanese, Western, and even Eastern restaurants from which to choose, offering good value for the dollar. The price categories are based on the following: *Moderate* ¥6,000–¥7,000 per person for lunch, ¥8,000–¥16,000 for dinner; *Inexpensive* ¥4,000–¥5,000 for lunch, ¥6,000–¥11,000 for dinner. ◉ = Highly Recommended.

Japanese

Moderate

Dojima Suehiro, Dojima Grand Bldg., 2F, 1-5-17 Dojima, Kita-ku; Tel. (06) 345–1212. Specializes in sukiyaki and steaks. American Express, Diners Club, MasterCard, Visa.

Hon Fukuzushi, 1-12 Shinsaibashisuji, Minami-ku; Tel. (06) 271–3344. Sushi. Accepts Diners Club.

● **Kitahachi,** 2-25 Imabashi, Higashi-ku; Tel. (06) 231–0267. Tempura. Accepts VISA.

Minokichi Semba-ten, Yagi Bldg., 2-10 Minami-Kyutaromachi, Higashi-ku; Tel. (06) 262–4185. American Express and Diners Club.

Inexpensive

Daimi, 2-5-23 Sonezaki, Kita-ku; Tel. (06) 315–0160. Fresh eel dishes served at lunch and dinner. No credit cards.

Mizutani, Sanezaki; Tel. (06) 955–4976. Serves oden—a local, tasty vegetable stew—and other dishes. No credit cards.

● **Wakaba,** 1-4-27 Dojimahama, Kita-ku; Tel. (06) 345–5743. Good, low-priced udon (noodle) dishes with vegetables and fish. No credit cards.

Kikuya and **Yotaro** are two inexpensive restaurant chains with branches throughout the city.

Western
Moderate

● **Bistro Eventhia,** 3-3-6 Minami-Senbar, Minami-ku; Tel. (06) 243–9141. Good, reasonably priced French food. MasterCard and Visa.

Edelweiss, Soemon-cho, Minami-ku; Tel. (06) 271–0425. Serves Bavarian-German cuisine. American Express, Diners Club, MasterCard, Visa.

Hollyhock, 5-14-12 Fukushima, Fukushima-ku; Tel. (06) 453–4530. Home-made Italian specialties. American Express, Diners Club, Mastercard, Visa.

Other
Moderate

Ashoka, Osaka Dai-Ichi Hotel; Tel. (06) 346–0333. Indian food. American Express, Diners Club, Mastercard, Visa.

● **Chugoku Daihanten,** Osaka Eki-mae Dai-san Bldg., 1-1-3 Umeda, Kita-ku; Tel. (06) 344–2937. Chinese cuisine, featuring Shanghainese dishes. American Express, Diners Club, Mastercard, Visa.

Durian. About a dozen locations throughout Osaka. Indonesian cuisine.

CAFES/TEAROOMS. London Tea Room, 2-2-38 Dojima, Kita-ku; Tel. (06) 347–0107. English-style tearoom. Also serves English breakfast.

MJB Coffee House. At four locations in Osaka.

What to See and Do

In the 4th century, both the Emperors Ojin and Nintoku built palaces on the hill where Osaka Castle now stands. When hard times struck some years later, Nintoku helped the citizens by suspending taxes, and displayed the practical, solid business sense that still remains a typically Osakan characteristic.

Osaka's heyday as a great commercial center, however, didn't come to pass until the 16th century. Hideyoshi Toyotomi, the powerful warlord who built Osaka Castle, convinced a group of wealthy merchants that their businesses would thrive even more if they moved from their native Kyoto to Osaka. In fact, Osaka has been so successful as a commercial center that many visitors tend to overlook the fact that it is also the site of some of Japan's most important monuments. Besides Osaka Castle, there is Shitennoji Temple, which predates Horyuji Temple in Nara, the Sumiyoshi Shrine, founded in the 3d century, and the Temmangu Shrine, which is honored every July during Tenjin Matsuri.

MAJOR ATTRACTIONS. Osaka Castle, located in the middle of a park overlooking the city. Inside the castle is the Osaka Municipal Museum, which contains documents and memorabilia pertaining to the castle and the Toyotomi family. The castle was destroyed and rebuilt several times, first by the Tokugawa shogunate, whose forebears had also demolished it, and lastly in 1931 after it had been consumed by fire during a civil war in 1867. The present donjon is five stories outside and eight stories within. At night, until approximately 9 P.M., the castle is illuminated and can be seen from many points around the city.

Shitennoji Temple, near the Shitennoji-mae subway station. This temple was founded in the 6th century by Prince Shotoku before he built the Horyuji Temple in Nara. The temple now serves as headquarters for the Washu sect of Buddhism. The 13th-century stone torii that stand at the main entrance are the oldest of their kind in Japan. Many of the treasures contained in the temple have been declared important Cultural Properties. Shitennoji is the site of three major festivals; the Shusho-e in January, the Higan-e in spring and fall, and the Shoryo-e in April.

Sumiyoshi Shrine, near the Torii-mae Station of the Hankyu

line. A popular Shinto shrine, Sumiyoshi is believed to date back
to 202. Three of the shrine's deities are worshiped as guardians of
those who sail the seas; in fact, the stone lanterns leading up to the
shrine were donated by sailors. There are four main buildings that
have been designated National Treasures. The Otaue Matsuri (Rice
Planting Festival) in June and the Sumiyoshi Matsuri (Summer
Festival) are both celebrated here. Near the temple is Sumiyoshi
Park, one of the most popular parks in Osaka, noted for its pine
and camphor trees.

Temmangu Shrine, north of Nakanoshima Park. The shrine
was founded in 949 in honor of Michizane Sugawara, the patron
saint of learning. The festival of the shrine, the Tenjin Matsuri,
held here every July, is one of the most exciting events in Osaka.
On the evening of July 25, a sacred palanquin is carried from the
shrine to the river and placed on a decorated boat that then sails
upstream, accompanied by a flotilla of 130 elaborately adorned
craft. Songs and dances are performed on the boats, which are lit
by lanterns.

Other Attractions. Ikutama Shrine. Dedicated to the Shinto
gods Ikushima and Tarushima. The current building, reconstructed
after World War II, is on a hill and commands a beautiful view of
the city and its surroundings.

Imamiya Ebisu Shrine. Dedicated to the Sun Goddess and
other deities of good fortune. Every January there is a festival that
attracts numerous worshipers seeking good luck.

Kozugu Shrine. A Shinto shrine dedicated to the 16th-century
Emperor Nintoku, who held his court in Osaka. Nearby is Kozu
Park and a historical stone lantern.

Tomb of Monzaemon Chikamatsu. Located in the northern
part of the city, this is the burial site of the Osaka-born playwright
Monzaemon Chikamatsu (1653 to 1724), often referred to as the
Japanese Shakespeare. Many of his works are still performed in the
Kabuki theater and in Bunraku puppet plays.

MUSEUMS. Fujita Art Museum. The former residence of
Japanese millionaire Baron Fujita. Contains Fujita's art collection,
tea ceremony utensils and a garden. Open 10 A.M.–4 P.M., except
Mon.

Japan Handicraft Museum, about a 10-minute walk from
Namba Station. Houses an excellent collection of Japanese folk art
and crafts. Open 10 A.M.–5 P.M., except Mon.

Museum of Japanese Farmhouses, at Hattori Ryokuchi in

Toyonaka, a suburb of Osaka. Replicas of farmhouses from 12 regions of Japan. Open 9:30 A.M.–4:30 P.M., except Mon.

Osaka Municipal Art Museum. Both ancient and modern art are displayed here. Open 9:30 A.M.–5 P.M., except Mon.

Osaka Municipal Museum (see "Osaka Castle"), on the grounds of Osaka Castle. An extensive collection of exhibits that depict the history and culture of Osaka. Open 9:15 A.M.–4:45 P.M., except the second and fourth Mon. of every month.

SIGHTSEEING TOURS. Japan Travel Bureau has locations in
Osaka Station, tel: (06) 361–5471, and in the Hotel New Osaka, tel: (06) 441–4801, both open 9 A.M.–6 P.M. daily; and in the Hotel Osaka Grand, tel: (06) 201–1212, and Asahi Building, tel: (06) 203–1921, both open 9 A.M.–5 P.M., except Sun. and holidays.

Industrial Tours. In addition to regular sightseeing tours, JTB offers a variety of industrial tours that include factory visits and other excursions. The Osaka Mint, a dairy factory, the Port of Osaka, a brewery, an automobile factory, and a broadcasting center are among the places featured in JTB's industrial tours.

Information on industrial tours is also available from the Osaka Tourist Association's Trade & Tourist Dept. (See address below under "Home Visit System.")

Home Visit System. Osaka is one of the Japanese cities offering home visit programs. To apply, contact the *Osaka Tourist Association,* c/o Trade & Tourist Dept., Osaka Municipal Office, Semba Center Bldg. No. 2, 1-4 Semba-chuo, Higahsi-ku, Osaka; Tel. (06) 261–3948. Or contact the *Osaka Tourist Information Office,* Higashiguchi, JR Osaka Station, 3-1-1, Umeda, Kita-ku, Osaka; Tel. (06) 345–2189.

SHOPPING. Like Tokyo, Osaka is a world-class shopping city
where you can buy virtually anything from *shoji* screens and *Mikimoto* pearls to *Comme des Garçons* dresses and high-tech equipment. As in most cosmopolitan cities, there are neighborhoods that specialize in bargain prices in a particular category of merchandise.

If you're in the market for low-cost clothing, for instance, head for the Dobuike district. Bargains in electrical appliances can be found in the Nipponbashi underground mall. Another good area for budget shopping is the Jan-Jan Yokocho (Jan-Jan Lane). Osaka's underground shopping centers, in general, offer a wide selection of shopping items in all price ranges, including budget.

There are 10 department stores in Osaka, listed below. Store hours are 10 A.M.–6 P.M. Department stores close one day a week, either Wednesday or Thursday.

Daimaru, in Minami. Closed Wed.

Hankyu, near Osaka Station. A long-established department store that has an English-language video to help foreigners find their way around the store. Closed Thurs.

Hanshin, in Umeda. Closed Wed.

Kintetsu, at Tennoji. Closed Thurs.

Kintetsu, at Ueroku. Also closed Thurs.

Matsuzakaya, at Tenmabashi. Closed Wed.

Mitsukoshi. Closed Mon.

Sennichi. Closed Wed.

Sogo, in Minami. Closed Thurs.

Takashimaya, in Minami. A branch of the famous chain. Closed Wed.

SPORTS. Osaka hosts one of six **sumo** wrestling tournaments held every year in Japan. The 15-day event is usually scheduled for Osaka in March.

Osakans are as **baseball**-crazed as most Japanese. They also have four top teams that can be seen—when they're home—at their respective stadiums, from April through September.

Entertainment and Nightlife

As a free-spending port city, Osaka offers everything from astronomically expensive girlie shows and sleazy sailors' bars to distinguished Kabuki theater and Bunraku puppet plays.

Moderately priced pubs and other drinking places can be found in the Dotonbori and Shinsaibashi districts. At the **Tokuoka Wine Bar** near Shinsaibashi, you can enjoy a bottle of wine, bread, and cheese for ¥1,200 per person. **The Love Machine Disco** in Kita-ku has special laser effects and moderate prices. **The Samboa Bar,** reputed to be the city's oldest Western-style bar, is designed to resemble an English pub.

THEATER. Bunraku. Awaji Spa was the birthplace of Japan's ancient puppet drama, Bunraku, but it flourished in Osaka. Plays are performed six times a year for two or three consecutive weeks, at the *Kokuritsu Bunraku Gekijo* (National Puppet Theater) in Minami.

Kabuki. Japan's top Kabuki actors appear at *Shin-Kabuzi-za* in Minami for a series of special gala performances running most of the month of May.

S P L U R G E S

The New Otani, 1-4-1 Shiromi, Higashi-ku; Tel. (06) 941–1111. This hotel is known not just for its deluxe accommodations but also for the excellent cuisine served in its French, Continental, Japanese, and Chinese restaurants. Beautifully decorated rooms offer views of Osaka Castle. There is a large shopping arcade with famous designer boutiques, a tennis court, an extensive health club, and an indoor swimming pool. Singles, ¥13,000–¥16,500; twins, ¥22,000–¥40,000; doubles, ¥23,000–¥27,000.

Tsuruya, 5-9 Imabashi, Higashi-ku; Tel. (06) 231–0456. The international business executives and government officials who dine here regularly consider it Osaka's best restaurant. Tsuruya is best known for its superb, authentic kaiseki dishes. The menu is changed every day. The kaiseki dinner will cost you about ¥25,000. A Shokado bento lunch is ¥10,000. No credit cards. Open daily 11:30 A.M.–10 P.M., except Sun. and national holidays. Reservations are required.

WESTERN JAPAN

By Helen Brower

◆

The Western part of Japan's Honshu Island runs roughly from Yamaguchi in the west to the port city of Kobe in the southeastern corner, and from the castle town of Matsue in the north to Hiroshima in the south.

Throughout the centuries this region of Japan has been a magnet for foreigners. Today, about 35,000 people from other countries make their home in Kobe. It is the seventh-largest city in Japan and its busiest port. Just as Yokohama is the gateway to Tokyo and the cities of eastern Japan, Kobe is the entry port for Osaka and Kyoto in the west.

It was from Yamaguchi, in the 16th century, that St. Francis Xavier introduced Christianity to Japan.

Matsue's best-known foreigner was Lafcadio Hearn, who came to Japan in 1890 to teach English and decided to remain, eventually changing his name to Yakumo Koizumi. Hiroshima, where the first atomic bomb was dropped, is visited by thousands of international tourists every year, and has become a worldwide symbol of humanity's aspirations for peace.

Other noteworthy places in the region are the castle town of Himeji, about a half-hour west of Kobe; Kurashiki, where one of Japan's finest museums is located; Miyajima, the "floating" island on Japan's Inland Sea; Takarazuka Spa,

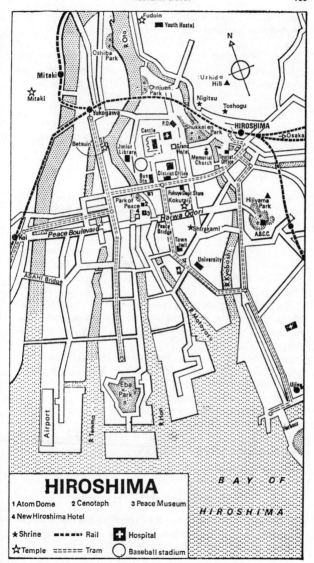

HIROSHIMA

1 Atom Dome 2 Cenotaph 3 Peace Museum
4 New Hiroshima Hotel

★ Shrine   ■■■■ Rail   ✚ Hospital
☆ Temple   ====== Tram   ○ Baseball stadium

near Kobe; Tsuwano, a charming old samurai town, and Akiyoshidai National Park, famous for its limestone grottoes.

Costs of accommodations, meals, and other typical tourist expenses are lower here than they are in the major cities and resorts, and yet there is no lack of historical and scenic attractions.

PRACTICAL INFORMATION FOR WESTERN JAPAN

How to Get There

Japan Railways offers frequent service throughout the day from Osaka and Tokyo to key cities in Western Japan. From Osaka to Kobe, the Rapid Train takes about 30 minutes (¥570). To Okayama (¥5,200), the trip takes about an hour by superexpress; to Hiroshima (¥9,100), about one hour 45 minutes by superexpress, and to Matsue (¥9,200), a little over four hours by Super Express and limited express, via Okayama.

There is also regular bus service between Osaka and Kobe that takes under an hour, and airport limousine service between Osaka Airport and JR's Sannomiya Station in Kobe that takes 40 minutes.

From Tokyo to Okayama, superexpress JR trains take a little over four hours (¥15,100). To Hiroshima (¥16,600), it takes 5 hours, and to Matsue (¥17,600), 7 hours 15 minutes by superexpress and limited express, via Okayama.

All Nippon Airways offers flights from Tokyo to Hiroshima seven times daily. The trip takes about one hour 30 minutes. ANA also offers twice-daily service from Tokyo to Okayama—the trip is just under two hours. *Royal Viking Line* cruise ships also call at Kobe.

Facts and Figures

POPULATION. Kobe has a population of about 1,400,000 people. Hiroshima, 870,000; Okayama, 550,000.; Kurashiki, 390,000; Matsue, 130,000; and Yamaguchi, 110,000.

Useful Addresses and Information

Kobe

Tourist Information. *Tourist Information Center,* 2d floor, Kobe Kotsu Center Bldg., west side of JR Sannomiya Station; Tel. (078) 392–0020. Also, try Japan Travel-Phone at (0120) 444–800. (For addresses of travel agencies, see "Sightseeing Tours.")

Consulates. The Kobe office of the U.S. Consulate recently closed. The closest consulate is in Osaka.

Medical Services. The *Kaisei Hospital,* at 3-11-15, Shinohara Kita-machi, Nada-ku; Tel. (078) 871–5201, is operated by the Franciscans.

Emergencies. Dial 110 for the police; 119 for fire or ambulance service. (These emergency numbers apply throughout Japan.)

Ship Information. A special phone number, (078) 331–8181, has been set up for those who need to call their ship in Kobe. Just dial the number and give the operator the name of your ship. To locate any ship at berth, call the Harbor Master at the same number.

Outside of Kobe

Kurashiki: *Railway Station Information Office,* 1-chome Achi; Tel. (0864) 26–8681.

Okayama: *Prefectural Government Tourist Section,* Uchisange; Tel. (0862) 24–2111.

Getting Around

By Taxi. For north- or southbound trips within Kobe, take a taxi, as fares are lower here than in the major cities.

By Train. For traveling east or west within Kobe, use *Japan Railways* or a private rail line.

To visit Portopia, the artificial port island built near Kobe in 1981, take the computerized transit system, the *Portliner*. Kobe's first publicly run subway network connects Myodani in Suma New Town with Shinnagata in the western business district.

There is excellent service offered by private interurban rail lines linking Kobe and nearby cities. Japan Railways' Main Line west of Osaka passes through Kobe, Himeji, Okayama, and Hiroshima.

On Foot. Kobe is a good city to see on foot. Walking provides the opportunity to explore Kobe's booming shipping industry and to look at how Kobe has acted as a conduit for the influences of the Western world on Japan.

By Boat. An attractive alternative to trains and buses is to take one of the moderately priced boat trips serving the area. The *Seitonaikai Kisen Co.*, for instance, operates daily hydrofoil cruises (¥6,500) from March through November. The cruises go from Miyajima to Hiroshima to Omishima, where a one-hour-15-minute stop is made before continuing to Ikuchi Island. The Tokyo-based cruise line has a Hiroshima office, tel. (082) 255–3344. This same company offers a Hiroshima Bay Cruise (¥11,500, including lunch) every Sun., Mon., Fri. and Sat. from Mar. through Nov. The trip leaves at 9:30 A.M. and returns at 3:10 P.M. The route includes Etajima, where a one-hour-45-minute stop is made, Miyajima and Enoshima. As there is no English-speaking guide on board, be sure to pick up a descriptive brochure of the area from the TIC office in Kobe in advance.

Where to Stay

With few exceptions, hotels in the major cities of Western Japan, as well as secondary cities, tend to be small- to medium-sized. Most are modern and Western-style though they usually have some Japanese-style rooms and a Japanese restaurant. Many hotels and inns have been built to take advantage of the spectacular scenery this part of Japan offers.

HOTELS. The price categories are based on the following rates: *Moderate* ¥6,500–¥9,000 for singles, ¥10,500–¥14,000 for doubles/twins; *Inexpensive* ¥5,000 for singles, ¥7,000 for doubles/twins, and *Low Budget* ¥4,000 for singles, ¥6,000 for doubles/twins. These prices do not include meals. ● = Highly Recommended.

Kobe

New Port Hotel (215 rooms), 6-3-13 Hamebedori, Chuo-ku; Tel. (078) 231–4171. An older hotel, recently refurbished and close to downtown. Singles from ¥7,500. Twins from ¥12,500. Doubles from ¥13,500.

Rokkosan (78 rooms), 1034 Minamirokko, Rokkosan-cho, Nada-ku; Tel. (078) 891–0301. A resort setting, located on Mt. Rokko. Singles ¥7,000. Twins, ¥10,500–¥14,000. Doubles, ¥14,000.

⬤**Sannomiya Terminal** (190 rooms), 8-1-2 Kumoidori, Chuo-ku; Tel. (078) 291–0001. Above Sannomiya Station, convenient location for shopping and sightseeing. Singles, ¥6,500–¥8,900. Twins, ¥12,800–¥14,000. Doubles, ¥12,000.

Inexpensive

Kobe Union (167 rooms), 2-1-9 Nunobikicho, Chuo-ku; Tel. (078) 222–6500. A 10-minute walk from Shin-Kobe Station on JR's Sanyo-Shinkansen Line.

Low Budget

Kobe Gajoen (74 rooms), 8-4-23 Shimo-Yamate-dori, Chuo-ku; Tel. (078) 341–0301. A three-minute walk from Hanakuma Station on Hankyu-Kobe Line.

Outside Kobe

Moderate

Hiroshima: **Hiroshima Century City** (76 rooms) 1-1-25 Matoba-cho, Minami-ku; Tel. (082) 263–3111. Close to Hiroshima Station.

Hiroshima: **Hiroshima City** (170 rooms) 1-4 Kyobashi-machi, Minami-ku; Tel. (082) 263–5111. A three-minute walk from Hiroshima Station.

⬤*Hiroshima:* **New Hiroden** (353 rooms) 14-9 Osuga-cho, Minami-ku; Tel. (082) 263–3456. Two minutes from Hiroshima Station. Spacious rooms.

⬤*Kurashiki:* **Kurashiki Kokusai** (70 rooms) 1-1-44 Chuo. Good location, next to the Ohara Museum of Art.

⬤*Okayama:* **Okayama Kokusai** (194 rooms), 4-1-16 Kodota Honmachi; Tel. (0862) 73–7311. Set on top of Mt. Soyo-Nanzan, offering spectacular city views. Outdoor pool, garden.

⬤*Tottori:* **New Otani Tottori** (143 rooms), 2-153 Imamachi; Tel. (0857) 23–1111. A member of the New Otani Hotels group. In front of Tottori Station. Good facilities.

⬤*Yamaguchi:* **New Tanaka** (198 rooms), 2 Yuda Onsen; Tel. (0839) 23–1313. Modern, attractive hotel in the center of Yuda Hot Spring Spa.

Inexpensive

Hiroshima: **Hiroshima River-side** (92 rooms), 7-14 Kaminobori-cho, Nak-ku; Tel. (082) 227–1111. In a quiet area, near the Otagawa River.

Okayama: **Okayama Grand** (31 rooms), 2-10 Funabashi-cho;

Tel. (0862) 33–7777. Near the Asahikawa River. Boating and other recreational facilities.

JAPANESE-STYLE ACCOMMODATIONS. The price categories are based on the following rates: *Moderate* ¥5,000–¥6,000/single; *Inexpensive* ¥4,000–¥5,000/single; *Low Budget* ¥5,000 per person, including two meals.

Kobe

Moderate

Ryokan Takayama-so (22 rooms), 400-1 Arima-cho, Kita-ku; Tel. (078) 904–0744. Located in Arima Onsen Spa, this ryokan features hot springs and a ¥5,000 Kobe beef dinner.

Inexpensive

TOR Ryokan, 3-12-11 Kitanagasa-Dori, Chuo-ku; Tel. (078) 331–3590. A two-minute walk from Sannomiyo Station, in the city center.

Outside Kobe

Moderate

Hiroshima: **New Matsuo** (24 rooms), 14-9 Kami-Osugacho, Higashi-ku; Tel. (082) 262–3141. A three-minute walk from Hiroshima Station.

Inexpensive

Hiroshima: **Mikawa Ryokan** (13 rooms), 9-6 Kyobashi-cho, Minami; Tel. (082) 261–2719. Convenient for sightseeing.

● *Hiroshima:* **Minshuku Ikedaya** (16 rooms), 6-36 Dobashi-cho, Nak-ku; Tel. (082) 231–3329. Near Hiroshima Peace Memorial Park.

Yamaguchi Pref.: **Bizenya Ryokan** (13 rooms), 3-11-7 Kamitanaka-machi, Shimonoseki City; Tel. (0832) 22–6228. Located in the major port city for ferries to Korea, connected to Japan's Kyushu Island by undersea tunnel and Great Kanmon Bridge over Kanmon Strait.

Low Budget

● *Hiroshima:* **Ikedaya** (16 rooms), 6-36 Dobashicho, Nak-ku; Tel. (082) 231–3329. Conveniently located within walking distance of Peace Park and other attractions.

Kurashiki: **Kurashiki Tokusankan** (Minshuku) (14 rooms), 8-33 Honcho; Tel. (0864) 25–3056.

Yamaguchi Pref.: **Higashi Hagi** (11 rooms), 3064-1 Shinkawa Minami, Hagi; Tel. (08382) 2–7884.

YOUTH HOSTELS. The rates are ¥2,000 for guests 19 and over; ¥1,700 for guests 12–18; ¥1,300 for children 4–11.

⬤*Hiroshima:* **Hiroshima** (104 beds), Higashi-ku; Tel. (082) 221–5343.

Kurashiki: **Kurashiki** (80 beds), Mukaiyama; Tel. (0864) 22–7355.

Okayama: **Okayama Ken Seinen-Kaikan** (65 beds), Tsukura; Tel. (0862) 52–0651.

Yamaguchi: **Yamaguchi** (25 beds), Miyanokami; Tel. (0839) 28–0057.

Yamaguchi Pref.: **Hagi Shizuki** (100 beds), Jonai, Hagi; Tel. (08382) 2–0733.

Where to Eat

The Western region features a wide array of international and regional foods. Kobe offers not only its famous beer-fed beefsteak but also American, Continental, Indian, and Chinese cuisines. If you're hankering for Western food, head for Kitanocho, where you'll find French, German, Italian, and Moroccan—as well as a branch of the famous Gaylord's Indian restaurant. Throughout Western Japan, there are plenty of moderately priced restaurants specializing in seafood delicacies. Try sea bream in Okayama, oysters in Hiroshima and blowfish in Shomoseki. Watch out for the last—it's poisonous when in an unprepared state.

RESTAURANTS. Low- and medium-priced rates average ¥1,000–¥2,000 for lunch, ¥4,000–¥5,000 for dinner. ⬤ = Highly Recommended.

Japanese
Hiroshima

Hanbei, 8-12 Honura-cho; Tel. (082) 282–7121. Good traditional Japanese food at low prices. American Express, Diners Club, Mastercard, Visa.

⬤**Suehiro** 1-21 Tatemachi; Tel. (082) 247–7175. Good steaks and sukiyaki. No credit cards.

Kobe

⬤**Blanc de Blancs,** 7th floor, Shinyei Bldg., 77-1 Kyomachi, Chuo-ku; Tel. (078) 321–1455. Good tempura, sukiyaki, as well as French dishes. American Express, Diners Club, Mastercard, Visa.

Ohnishi, 3d fl., You Bell Bldg., 1-4-6 Nakayamate-dori, Chuo-ku; Tel. (078) 332–4029. Specializes in teppan-yaki. Open 5:30 P.M.–2 A.M., except Wed. No credit cards.

Okayama

●**Miyoshino Kaikan,** 1-3-1 Edimae-cho; Tel. (0862) 25–2255. Very good Japanese, as well as Western dishes, at reasonable prices. American Express, Diners Club, Mastercard, Visa.

Western
Kobe

Attic, Ijinkan Club Bldg., 4-30-2 Kitano-cho; Tel. (078) 222–1586. Good Kobe beef, served with Australian wine, at reasonable prices. No credit cards.

●**Coco a coco,** 4-7-11 Kano-cho, Chuo-ku; Tel. (078) 392–4031. Claims to offer 89 varieties of sandwiches. Good for lunch, and very reasonable. No credit cards.

Restaurant Hook 2-9-11 Sazkaemachi-dori, Chuo-ku; Tel. (078) 332–4129. The specialty is charcoal-grilled steak. American Express, Diners Club, Mastercard, Visa.

Other
Kobe

●**Maya,** I.T.C. Bldg., 4-1-8 Isobe-dori, Chuo-ku; Tel. (078) 231–0703. Very attractive restaurant, serving excellent, reasonably priced Indian cuisine. American Express, Diners Club, Mastercard, Visa.

BARS/CAFES. *Kobe:* **Cosmopolitan,** 1-3-16 Sannomiya-cho, Chuo-ku; Tel. (078) 331–1217. Good for brunch and sweets. American Express, Diners Club, MasterCard, Visa.

What to See and Do

MAJOR ATTRACTIONS. *Hiroshima:* **Hiroshima Castle.** Built in 1589 by a feudal lord, Terumoto Mori, the castle was totally destroyed in 1945, and rebuilt in 1958. Inside are historical displays and memorabilia.

Kobe: **Foreigners' Houses,** near Kitznozaka. A historic district where some of the homes of foreigners *(ijinkan)* have been preserved, transformed into museums and given the names of the nationalities they represent—e.g., "American," "English," etc.

Himeji Castle, about a half-hour west of Kobe by "bullet" train. Considered by many architectural scholars to be the finest Japanese castle still standing. Built in the 14th century, it originally served as a fort. Because of its white-plastered walls and gray tiles, it is referred to by the Japanese as *Hakurojo* (Egret Castle). The castle was restored in 1964 and is essentially the same as it was under the Tokugawa Shogunate in the 17th century.

Matsue: **Matsue Castle,** a 10-minute ride from Matsue Station. Built as a castle-fortress, offering fine views of Lake Shinji and Mt. Daisen.

Yakumo Memorial Hall, near the Castle. This hall is dedicated to Lafcadio Hearn, who spent 15 months here in 1890 as an English teacher at Matsue Middle School. Many of his manuscripts are kept here, as well as other valuable articles. The house where he lived is located next door.

Miyajima Island: **Itsukushima Shrine,** believed to have been built by the Empress Suiko in the 6th or 7th century and later enlarged, consists of a series of interconnected buildings. Both sides of the shrine stretch out over the sea and during high tide, the building appears to be floating on the water. The O-torii, a 52-foot-high red-painted camphor wood gate that rises out of the sea, is the shrine's most important treasure.

Okayama: **Okayama Castle.** Built in the 16th century, the present donjon was reconstructed in 1966. Features displays on local history.

Yamaguchi: **Xavier Memorial Cathedral,** a five-minute ride from Yamaguchi Station. This Romanesque Catholic church was constructed in 1952 in memory of St. Francis Xavier, the Spanish Jesuit missionary who introduced Christianity to Japan in the 16th century.

MUSEUMS. *Hiroshima:* **Peace Memorial Museum and Park,** about a 10-minute bus ride from Hiroshima Station. The museum contains objects showing the devastation that resulted from the atomic bomb in 1945. You can read the names of known A-bomb victims at the Peace Memorial Hall and the Memorial Cenotaph, also located in the park. Open 9 A.M.–4:30 P.M. Admission ¥50.

Kobe: **Kobe City Museum,** near the Kaigan-dori. The museum has an excellent collection of exhibitions depicting the Western influence on Japan, and is well known for its fine collection of works by Japanese artists, featuring foreigners and missionaries who have come here since the 16th century. Open 10 A.M.–5 P.M. (last admission at 4:30 P.M.), except Mon.

Kurashiki: **Kurashiki Folkcraft Museum,** about 10 minutes on foot from Kurashiki Station. The building consists of four two-story wooden rice granaries with walls covered in white plaster and roofs made of black tiles, following the style of the Edo period (from 1602 to 1867). Inside is an interesting collection of ceramics, rugs, mats, wooden objects, and other handicrafts. Open 9 A.M.–4 P.M., except Mon. and Dec. 29–Jan. 1. Admission ¥400.

Ohara Art Gallery, near the Folkcraft Museum. The gallery contains a priceless collection of works by Western artists, including El Greco, Corot, Rodin, Gauguin, and Picasso. With the addition of a new wing in 1961, works by Japanese painters, as well as artists from other parts of the world, were added. Open 9 A.M.–4:30 P.M., except Mon. and from Dec. 28–Jan. 1. Admission ¥500.

SIGHTSEEING TOURS. City sightseeing and excursions are offered by *Japan Travel Bureau,* Sannomiya Station, Kobe; Tel. (078) 231–4701. JTB also has an office in Hiroshima at Kamiya-cho; Tel. (082) 261–4131. JTB's *Sunrise Holidays'* division offers package tours from Tokyo, Kyoto, and Osaka that include western Japan.

Home Visit System: If you'd like to visit with a Japanese family, contact the *Kobe International Tourist Association,* Kobe International Conference Center; Tel. (078) 303–1010. Make your request at least one or two days in advance.

SHOPPING. There are good buys throughout the region. In Kobe, kimonos, silks, curios, articles made of bamboo, and tortoise-shell items can be purchased at good value. In Hiroshima, check out the Japanese clogs, writing brushes, and musical instruments. Kurashiki's specialties are pottery, papier-mâché toys, table mats, dolls, and woven handbags. In Okayama, look for Bizenyake stoneware, which can be purchased directly from the *Bizen Ware Center* workshop at 974 Bizen City; Tel. (0862) 4–2453. For paper products and woodcrafts, try Tottori.

Kobe's best shopping streets are Sannomiya and Motomachi. The three large department stores here are *Sogo* (8-1-8 Onoe-dori, Chuo-ku), closed Thurs.; *Daimaru* (40 Akashi-cho, Chuo-ku), closed Wed., and *Hankyu* (4-2-1 Kano-cho, Chuo-ku), closed Tues.

SPORTS. There are good **beaches** throughout the area, including *Shioya* in Kobe, and *Awaji,* an island just off the southern tip of Kobe, which is frequented by many foreign residents. Ohama Island is popular for swimming, as are some of the beautiful villages on the Japan Sea Coast, such as Amanohashidate. Simple but comfortable lodges are located near many of the area beaches for those who want to spend a weekend in the sun.

Both Kobe and Hiroshima have major-league **baseball** teams that play regularly between Apr. and Oct. For a schedule, get a copy of *Play Guide* from your hotel or the TIC office.

Mt. Kannabe is a popular **ski** resort. During the season, special trains run from Osaka to the resort, which is in Hyogo Prefecture, in the eastern part of the region. Mt. Daisen is also good for skiing and winter sports, and is accessible by bus from Yonago Station in about one hour.

Nightlife and Entertainment

Bars, nightclubs, and other evening entertainment spots abound in Kobe, particularly in the area north of Sannomiya Station. The bars and cafes in the underground district known as *Santica Town* are cozy and friendly.

The Takarazuka all-female musical troupe presents light opera in the local opera house. Westerners were introduced to this unusual musical group through James Michener's famous novel *Sayonara.* The town is also famous for its hot springs and its amusement park called *Takarazuka Familyland.* The park consists of a zoo, botanical gardens, a science hall, and the 4,000-seat theater where the musical troupe performs. Takarazuka is about a 35-minute express train ride from Kobe on the Hankyu Railway Line from Hankyu Umeda Station.

◆

S P L U R G E S

Ryokan Iwaso, 345 Miyajimacho, Hiroshima, Pref.; Tel. (0829) 44–2233. A tranquil, wooded setting, near the Inland Sea National Park on Miyajima Island, where tame deer roam. There are 45 rooms beautifully decorated in traditional Japanese style. Rates range from ¥18,000–¥45,000 per person in a share-twin, and includes breakfast and dinner.

Escargot Restaurant, 1-22 Sannomiya-cho, chuo-ku, Kobe; Tel. (078) 331–5034. Excellent French cuisine and an equally fine selection of vintage wines, in a handsome setting. Dinner, with wine, will cost about ¥10,000–¥15,000. Accepts Visa.

◆

INLAND SEA AND SHIKOKU

By Helen Brower

Japan's mild and beautiful Inland Sea region boasts about 600 islands that stretch from Osaka in the east clear across to Beppu Spa on Kyushu Island in the west.

The Inland Sea itself is relatively shallow. In the Naruto Strait, between Awaji and Shikoku islands, opposing currents create powerful whirlpools, and the Hoyo and Kammon Straits also have very strong tidal currents. Crossing these waters was once regarded as a challenge. In the 7th century B.C., the first emperor, Jimmu, made a point of traversing the Inland Sea on his way to settle in what is now Nara Prefecture. The sea has also been the scene of tragedies that have become part of Japanese lore. In the 12th century, after a battle for power between two rival clans, the child-emperor Antoku was drowned here. Nowadays, the Inland Sea has more romantic associations. Honeymooners and other young couples cross it on day ferries or on four-day Japanese-style love boats.

The northern shores of Shikoku Island border the Inland Sea. The island is divided into four prefectures: Tokushima, Kagawa, Ehime, and Kochi. Several mountain ranges extend through the central part of Shikoku, the highest of which are Mt. Ishizuchi and Mt. Tsurugi, each about 6,000 feet.

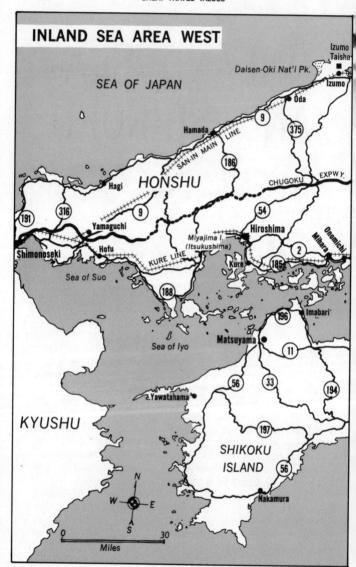

INLAND SEA AREA WEST

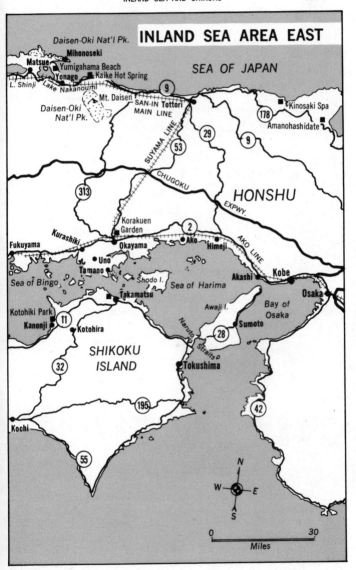

INLAND SEA AREA EAST

Daisen-Oki Nat'l Pk.

Mihonoseki

Matsue

SEA OF JAPAN

Yumigahama Beach
Yonago Kaike Hot Spring

L. Shinji Lake Nakanoumi

Daisen-Oki Nat'l Pk.

Mt. Daisen SAN-IN
MAIN LINE **Tottori**

⑨

■ Kinosaki Spa

178

Amanohashidate

㉙

⑨

53

SUYAMA LINE

313

CHUGOKU

HONSHU

Korakuen
Garden ②

EXPWY.

AKO
LINE

Kurashiki

Fukuyama

Okayama Ako **Himeji**

● Uno

Tamano

Shodo I. Sea of Harima

Akashi **Kobe**

Osaka

Sea of Bingo

Takamatsu

Awaji I.

Bay of
Osaka

Kotohiki Park

11

Kanonji ● Kotohira

28

Sumoto

32

SHIKOKU
ISLAND

Naruto
Straits

●**Tokushima**

42

195

● **Kochi**

55

N

W   E

S

0 _____ 30

Miles

The island has developed many distinctive customs. In the spring, visitors can see Buddhist pilgrims garbed in white kimono, white gloves and trousers, traveling to one of 88 shrines dedicated to the Buddhist priest Kukai who was credited with developing Japan's hiragana alphabet and introducing a Chinese sect of Buddhism.

Travelers to the Inland Sea and Shikoku are likely to enjoy mild weather any time of the year, except during typhoon season in September and October.

PRACTICAL INFORMATION FOR THE INLAND SEA AND SHIKOKU
How to Get There

By Boat. Daily commuter ferries connect Honshu and Shikoku Islands' main port cities—Osaka, Kobe, Akashi, Okayama, Uno, Fukuyama, Onomichi, Mihara, Kure, and Hiroshima on Honshu; Takamatsu, Marugame, Niihama, Imabari, and Matsuyama on Shikoku.

The hovercraft from Uno to Takamatsu takes 23 minutes and costs ¥1,600; by ferry, the trip is 55 minutes and costs ¥500. From Hiroshima to Matsuyama is a little over an hour by ferry and costs ¥1,800–¥3,600; from Kure to Matsuyama is 50 minutes and costs from ¥1,450–¥3,800.

There is also ferry service from Tokyo that operates every other day and takes 19 hours 40 minutes to Tokushima (¥8,200), and 21 hours 20 minutes to Kochi (¥13,500). There are three ferries a day from Osaka-Nanko to Tokushima (¥1,920). It takes about 3½ hours. From Osaka-Nanko to Kochi takes nine hours 50 minutes (¥4,400).

By Air. From Tokyo, *All Nippon Airways* (ANA) offers service six times a week to Matsuyama. Flight time is one hour 25 minutes. Eight flights a week are operated by ANA and *Toa Domestic Airlines* (TDA) from Tokyo to Takamatsu.

By Rail. *Japan Railways* has frequent service from both Tokyo and Osaka. *From Tokyo:* An express train and ferry combination to Takamatsu, via Okayama and Uno, takes six hours 12 minutes (¥16,480 in ordinary class, including surcharges); a combination of train and hovercraft takes five hours 36 minutes (¥17,580). From Tokyo to Kochi, by express train and ferry, the trip is nine hours 21 minutes (¥19,750); and to Matsuyama, by the same combination, nine hours 19 minutes (¥19,050).

From Osaka: Express train and ferry to Takamatsu (¥6,780) takes two hours 56 minutes; by train and hovercraft (¥7,800), two hours 48 minutes. To Kochi, by express train and ferry (¥10,350) takes six hours 22 minutes, and to Matsuyama, also by train and ferry (¥10,850), the trip is six hours nine minutes.

Facts and Figures

POPULATION AND AREA CODES. The population of Matsuyama is about 395,000; Takamatsu, about 315,000; Kochi, approximately 295,000, and Tokushima, about 250,000. Awaji Island is the largest island in the Inland Sea. It is also the birthplace of Japan's famous Bunraku puppet theater.

The area codes are: Kochi (0888); Matsuyama (0899); Takamatsu (0878); Tokushima (0886).

USEFUL ADDRESSES. Matsuyama: *Matsuyama City Office,* Tourist Section, 7-2 Niban-cho, 4-chome; Tel. (0899) 48–6557.

Takamatsu: *Kagawa Prefectural Government Tourist Section,* 4-1-10 Bancho; Tel. (0878) 31–111.

The closest JNTO Tourist Information Center is in Kyoto.

Getting Around

Japan Railways provides frequent intercity train service on Shikoku between the main cities. From Takamatsu, the trip takes one hour 30 minutes to Tokushima, three hours to Kochi and three hours to Matsuyama.

Where to Stay

HOTELS. The Inland Sea is a popular vacation spot with Japanese travelers and offers more opportunities for staying in typical Japanese-style lodgings. Even the more modern hotels combine many Japanese touches—like a Japanese Garden and several Japanese restaurants—with Western-style amenities. The hotels below are priced moderately and inexpensively. ● = Highly Recommended.

Kochi

Kochi Dai-ichi (118 rooms), 2-2-12 Kitahon-cho; Tel. (0888) 83–1441. Located in front of Kochi Station. Good, functional hotel. Singles, ¥5,200–¥5,800. Twins, ¥10,600–¥13,800. Doubles, ¥9,000–¥10,600.

Matsuyama

● **ANA Hotel Matsuyama** (246 rooms), 3-2-1 Ichiban-cho; Tel. (0899) 33–5511. Attractive modern hotel, with a large shopping arcade, near two major shopping districts. Singles, ¥7,800–¥12,500. Twins, ¥15,000–¥20,000. Doubles, ¥15,000.

● **Okudogo** (305 Western- and Japanese-style rooms), 267-1 Sue-machi; Tel. (0899) 77–1111. Next to Glen Ishitegawa, in a beautiful garden setting. Combines traditional Japanese and modern Western design. Singles, ¥3,500–¥7,000. Twins, ¥7,000–¥25,000. Japanese-style rooms, ¥13,000–¥15,000. (Deluxe Japanese- and Western-style rooms start at ¥15,000.)

Takamatsu

● **Keio Plaza Hotel Takamatsu** (180 rooms), 11-5 Chuo-cho; Tel. (0878) 34–5511. In the city center, near Ritsurin Park. Singles, ¥6,000. Twins, ¥11,000–¥13,000. Doubles, ¥12,000–¥17,000.

Rich Takamatsu (126 rooms), 9-1 Furujinmachi; Tel. (0878) 22–3555. Faces the city's main street, near Takamatsu Station. Singles from ¥5,500. Twins/Doubles from ¥11,000.

Takamatsu Grand (136 rooms), 1-5-10 Kotobuki-cho; Tel. (0878) 51–5757. Across from Takamatsu Station and close to ship berths. Offers views of the Inland Sea. Singles, ¥5,900–¥6,100. Twins, ¥10,000–¥18,000. Doubles, ¥11,500.

Takamatsu International (105 rooms), 2191-1 Kita-cho; Tel. (0878) 31–1511. On a beach, facing the Inland Sea and Yashima. Ice-skating rink, indoor and outdoor pools, nearby golf course. Singles, ¥5,300–¥8,500. Twins, ¥17,500. Doubles, ¥17,500–¥19,000.

Tokushima

Astoria (25 rooms), 2-26 Ichiban-cho; Tel. (0886) 53–6151. Near Tokushima Station. Singles, ¥5,500. Twins/doubles, ¥10,000. Japanese-style rooms, ¥12,000.

● **Awa Kanko** (35 rooms), 3-16 Ichiban-cho; Tel. (0886) 22–5161. Near Tokushima Station. Has mostly Western-style rooms that are attractively furnished and soundproofed. Swimming pool and tennis courts. Singles, ¥5,600. Twins/doubles, ¥10,000. Japanese-style rooms, ¥10,000.

Tokushima Park (81 rooms), 2-32-1 Tokushima-cho; Tel. (0886) 25–3311. In front of Tokushima Park. Singles, ¥5,200–¥8,200. Twins/Doubles, ¥10,000. Japanese-style rooms, ¥10,000.

BUSINESS HOTELS. *Matsuyama:* **Business Hotel King** (16 Japanese- and 30 Western-style rooms), 7-14 Konnohanacho; Tel. (0899) 46–2511. Five-minute ride to Matsuyama Station.

JAPANESE-STYLE ACCOMMODATIONS. The price categories below are based on the following: *Moderate* ¥5,000/single, not including meals; *Inexpensive* below ¥5,000/single, not including meals, or ¥5,000–¥6,000 per person, including two meals.

Moderate

Kagawa Pref., (Takamatsu area): **Kankakei-so** (65 Japanese, 7 Western/Japanese-style rooms), Sakate, Uchinomicho, Shozu-gun; Tel. (0879) 82–2255.

Ryokan Kabagawa-so (16 rooms), 1394-1 Shionoecho, Kagawa-gur; Tel. (0878) 93–0106.

Matsuyama: **Dogo International** (77 Japanese, 11 Western and 9 Western/Japanese-style rooms), 20-8 Dogo-Yunomachi; Tel. (0899) 41–1137. Short walk from Dogo-Onsen Station on the Dogo Line.

Inexpensive

Kagawa Pref. (Takamatsu area): **Maruse Minshuku** (6 rooms), Ko-5978, Tonoschocho, Shozu-gun; Tel. (0879) 62–2572.

●*Kochi:* **Yasuoka Minshuku** (15 rooms), 653 Urado; Tel. (0888) 41–3898.

Matsuyama: **Matsuyama Minshuku** (10 rooms), 414 Yamagoemachi; Tel. (0899) 24–8386.

YOUTH HOSTELS. The following rates are: ¥2,000 for guests 19 and over, ¥1,700 for guests 12–18, and ¥1,300 for children 4–11.

●*Ehime Pref.;* **Uwajima** (80 beds), Atagokoen, Uwajima; Tel. (0895) 22–7177.

Mannen-so (120 beds), Matsuno-cho, Kitauwa-gun; Tel. (08954) 3–0205.

Kochi: **Kochi-Ekimae** (104 beds), Kitahon-cho; Tel. (0888) 83–5086.

Tokushima: **Tokushima** (80 beds), Ohara; Tel. (0886) 63–1506.

Where to Eat

It should come as no surprise that the Inland Sea region and the island of Shikoku are known for their seafood specialties. However, llke Kobe and some of the other neighboring cities in Western Honshu, there are some excellent beefsteak restaurants and dining spots specializing in *shabu-shabu*–beef and vegetables dipped in a savory, boiling stew and eaten with noodles.

Kochi: **Kochi Dai-Ichi Hotel** (see above); Tel. (0888) 83–1441. Has a well-regarded Continental restaurant. Lunch is about ¥3,000, and dinner ¥5,000–¥7,000.

Matsuyama: **Komadori,** near Matsuyama Castle, 1-2-4 Ohkaido; Tel. (0899) 21–0046. Serves good, reasonably priced steak dishes. Also Indian curry. No credit cards.

Takamatsu: **Takamatsu Grand Hotel** (see above); Tel. (0878) 51–5757. Has a good, moderately priced Chinese restaurant. Lunch is about ¥2,500; dinner ¥3,500–¥5,000.

Tokushima: **New Tokushima,** Keizai Center Bldg., Nishi Shinmachi, Tel. (0886) 23–6333. A very good grill room. American Express, Diners Club, Mastercard, Visa.

What to See And Do

Major Attractions
Kochi

Godaisan Park. A 20-minute bus ride from the Harimayu Bridge. The Chikurinji Temple, one of Shikoku's 88 sacred places, is the best known monument in the park. Founded in 724, the temple is believed to be the oldest in the prefecture, and contains several Buddhist statues that are Important Cultural Properties.

Kochi Castle, about a 20-minute walk from the station. Formerly the home of the Yamanouchi family, a feudal clan who ruled the area, this five-story donjon dates from 1753 and is an Important Cultural Property.

Ryugado Stalactite Cave. A limestone grotto with limestone pillars and stalagmites. Several clay dishes, presumed to have been used by prehistoric people, have been found here.

Matsuyama

Matsuyama Castle, on the top of Katsuyama Hill. Originally built in 1603, this is considered one of Japan's best preserved castles. The museum inside features exhibits of old palanquins, armor, and swords. The castle is surrounded by Matsuyama Park.

Takamatsu and Environs

Ritsurin Park. The park consists of two gardens, the Northern and the Southern, and originally served as both villa and park for a 17th-century feudal family, the Matsudairas. Today the park encompasses a zoo, a folk art gallery, and a museum.

Yashima, about a half hour by bus from Takamatsu. Yashima was once an island but is now connected to the mainland. A cable car takes visitors to the top for a breathtaking view and a stop at the Buddhist temple, Yashimaji.

Kotohiragu Shrine, at Kotohira, about 45 minutes by bus from Takamatsu. One of the most important Shinto shrines in Japan, the Kotohiragu is associated with the deity who protects sailors. The main shrine is located more than 800 feet up Mt. Zozusan and is approached by a flight of granite stairs. From the top, there are beautiful views of the Sanuki Plain.

Shodo Island, about 35 minutes by high speed boat from Takamatsu. This resort island, the second-largest in the region (next to Awaji Island in the Inland Sea), is admired for its scenic beauty. Attractions here include Kankakei Gorge and Utsukushinohara Heights.

Tokushima

Naruto Straits, about a 45-minute rail trip from Tokushima. Known for their giant whirlpools; an observatory platform in Naruto Park provides good views of the straits.

Uwajima

Ashizuri-Uwakai National Park. This large park extends almost 50 miles over the southwestern coast of Shikoku's Kochi and Ehime Prefectures. Interesting limestone caves with oddly shaped stalactites can be seen at Cape Ashizuri.

SIGHTSEEING TOURS. Japan Travel Bureau offers two- and three-day *Sunrise Inland Sea Tours* from Osaka and Kyoto on Sun., Tues., and Thurs., from early Mar. through late Nov. These deluxe cruises visit several ports on Honshu and Shikoku and include English-speaking guides. The cost of the two-day tour is ¥82,000 including one lunch; for the three-day, ¥120,000, including one breakfast, two lunches and one dinner.

The nearest Japan Travel Bureau offices are in Hiroshima and Okayama. (See "Western Japan.")

SHOPPING. Kochi's best buys are ornamental hairpins and combs, and articles made of coral. Ino, near Kochi, is known for its fine handmade paper, Matsuyama for hand-dyed towels with traditional Japanese designs. Fans, lacquerware, paper products, patterned parasols, and items made of cotton can be found at Takamatsu. Tokushima is famous for its folk art, especially its wooden dolls, as well as bamboo products. You might wish to try some of the following recommended shops.

Kochi: **Nihon Sango,** at 2552–21 Niida; Tel. (0888) 47–3535. Coral shop. **Masaki Sango,** 2254-9 Fukui-cho, Tel. (0888) 24–8338. Folk crafts shop.

Matsuyama: **Tobe Yaki Baizen,** in the Matsuyama ANA Hotel; Tel. (0899) 33–6388. Sells Tobe pottery. **Iyo Kasuri Kaikan,** 1165 Kumanodai; Tel. (0899) 22–0405. Sells Iyo Kasuri cloth.

Takamatsu: **Kagawaken Bussan Kyokai,** in Ritsurin Park; Tel. (0878) 33–7411. Local crafts.

Tokushima: **Aigura,** Nishi-Shinmachi, 1; Tel. (0886) 54–3864. Folk art and crafts.

SPORTS. You may not believe it until you see it, but there is actually a Municipal Bull Ring in Uwajima where bullfights take place.

Index

INDEX

FODOR'S TRAVEL GUIDES

Here is a complete list of Fodor's Travel Guides, available in current editions; most are also available in a British edition published by Hodder & Stoughton.

U.S. GUIDES

Alaska
American Cities (Great Travel Values)
Arizona including the Grand Canyon
Atlantic City & the New Jersey Shore
Boston
California
Cape Cod & the Islands of Martha's Vineyard & Nantucket
Carolinas & the Georgia Coast
Chesapeake
Chicago
Colorado
Dallas/Fort Worth
Disney World & the Orlando Area (Fun in)
Far West
Florida
Fort Worth (see Dallas)
Galveston (see Houston)
Georgia (see Carolinas)
Grand Canyon (see Arizona)
Greater Miami & the Gold Coast
Hawaii
Hawaii (Great Travel Values)
Houston & Galveston
I-10: California to Florida
I-55: Chicago to New Orleans
I-75: Michigan to Florida
I-80: San Francisco to New York
I-95: Maine to Miami
Jamestown (see Williamsburg)
Las Vegas including Reno & Lake Tahoe (Fun in)
Los Angeles & Nearby Attractions
Martha's Vineyard (see Cape Cod)
Maui (Fun in)
Nantucket (see Cape Cod)
New England
New Jersey (see Atlantic City)
New Mexico
New Orleans
New Orleans (Fun in)
New York City
New York City (Fun in)
New York State
Orlando (see Disney World)
Pacific North Coast
Philadelphia
Reno (see Las Vegas)
Rockies
San Diego & Nearby Attractions
San Francisco (Fun in)
San Francisco plus Marin County & the Wine Country
The South
Texas
U.S.A.
Virgin Islands (U.S. & British)

Virginia
Waikiki (Fun in)
Washington, D.C.
Williamsburg, Jamestown & Yorktown

FOREIGN GUIDES

Acapulco (see Mexico City)
Acapulco (Fun in)
Amsterdam
Australia, New Zealand & the South Pacific
Austria
The Bahamas
The Bahamas (Fun in)
Barbados (Fun in)
Beijing, Guangzhou & Shanghai
Belgium & Luxembourg
Bermuda
Brazil
Britain (Great Travel Values)
Canada
Canada (Great Travel Values)
Canada's Maritime Provinces plus Newfoundland & Labrador
Cancún, Cozumel, Mérida & the Yucatán
Caribbean
Caribbean (Great Travel Values)
Central America
Copenhagen (see Stockholm)
Cozumel (see Cancún)
Eastern Europe
Egypt
Europe
Europe (Budget)
France
France (Great Travel Values)
Germany: East & West
Germany (Great Travel Values)
Great Britain
Greece
Guangzhou (see Beijing)
Helsinki (see Stockholm)
Holland
Hong Kong & Macau
Hungary
India, Nepal & Sri Lanka
Ireland
Israel
Italy
Italy (Great Travel Values)
Jamaica (Fun in)
Japan
Japan (Great Travel Values)
Jordan & the Holy Land
Kenya
Korea
Labrador (see Canada's Maritime Provinces)
Lisbon
Loire Valley
London

London (Fun in)
London (Great Travel Values)
Luxembourg (see Belgium)
Macau (see Hong Kong)
Madrid
Mazatlan (see Mexico's Baja)
Mexico
Mexico (Great Travel Values)
Mexico City & Acapulco
Mexico's Baja & Puerto Vallarta, Mazatlan, Manzanillo, Copper Canyon
Montreal (Fun in)
Munich
Nepal (see India)
New Zealand
Newfoundland (see Canada's Maritime Provinces)
1936 . . . on the Continent
North Africa
Oslo (see Stockholm)
Paris
Paris (Fun in)
People's Republic of China
Portugal
Province of Quebec
Puerto Vallarta (see Mexico's Baja)
Reykjavik (see Stockholm)
Rio (Fun in)
The Riviera (Fun on)
Rome
St. Martin/St. Maarten (Fun in)
Scandinavia
Scotland
Shanghai (see Beijing)
Singapore
South America
South Pacific
Southeast Asia
Soviet Union
Spain
Spain (Great Travel Values)
Sri Lanka (see India)
Stockholm, Copenhagen, Oslo, Helsinki & Reykjavik
Sweden
Switzerland
Sydney
Tokyo
Toronto
Turkey
Vienna
Yucatán (see Cancún)
Yugoslavia

SPECIAL-INTEREST GUIDES

Bed & Breakfast Guide: North America
Royalty Watching
Selected Hotels of Europe
Selected Resorts and Hotels of the U.S.
Ski Resorts of North America
Views to Dine by around the World

AVAILABLE AT YOUR LOCAL BOOKSTORE OR WRITE TO FODOR'S TRAVEL PUBLICATIONS, INC., 201 EAST 50th STREET, NEW YORK, NY 10022.